GROWTH POLE THEORY
AND ECONOMIC DEVELOPMENT

Growth Pole Theory and Economic Development

Professor FRIEDRICH BUTTLER
Gesamthochschule Paderborn

Translated from the German by
JOHN CUTHBERT-BROWN

Published by
SAXON HOUSE, D. C. Heath Ltd.
Westmead, Farnborough, Hants, England

Jointly with
LEXINGTON BOOKS, D. C. Heath & Co.
Lexington, Mass. U.S.A.

cc

ISBN 0 347 01068 7
Printed in Great Britain by Eyre & Spottiswoode Ltd, at Grosvenor Press, Portsmouth

Contents

List of tables

Introduction

Theories about polarised economic growth are no more novel than the attempt to adopt them in order to establish measures of regional policy. On this score one must certainly agree with those authors who, in the past, have sometimes levelled powerful criticisms at the theoretical content and strategic realisability of the current polarisation hypotheses. The reasons for setting about the examination of polarisation theory and growth policy again here are manifold. In the first place, there is a case for refurbishing a large number of theoretical contributions to the subject which have been made in the last few years. Secondly, preoccupation with considerations of polarisation theory seems to appeal increasingly to authors who regard the neo-classical growth theory with scepticism. Many of them are agreed that attempts to transpose calculations of economic equilibrium with the object of clarifying dynamic allocation and distribution processes are far removed from reality. Some of them, among whom the present author may be numbered, go so far as to detect a close connection between the economic key expositions of polarisation theories on the one hand and theories of imperialism on the other. In the third place, when in receipt of a grant from the Deutsche Forschungsgemeinschaft in 1969-71 the present author had an opportunity to prepare a programme for the evaluation of the results of the Spanish growth poles inaugurated since 1964, and to test it in a pilot study for the Andalusian poles of Huelva and Seville. The Spanish Planning Commission of the day helped me in my research by extending the most comprehensive facilities for enquiry and every form of assistance that could be wished. The evaluation scheme, which is constantly being improved with friends in the Planning Commission, is today a standard instrument of planning control for the current regional programme.

The following text represents a revised version of the author's book 'Entwicklungspole und räumliches Wirtschaftswachstum' published in 1973. In view of this and of the Spanish publication of the individual results ('study for the evaluation of development poles', Vol. I, Madrid 1972, and 'studies of the institute of economic development', Vol. II, Madrid 1973, Alcalá de Henares), a large part of the empirical material has not had to be reproduced here.

As was shown by, *inter alia,* the negotiations conducted at the end of 1973 on the European Regional Fund, regional policy is no longer merely a side-effect of growth-orientated structural policy. No longer is its object to be perceived solely as the reduction of inter-regional distributive inequalities arising from growth-conditioned structural changes, but also as promoting the best possible contribution to economic development by the regions. There are various grounds for saying that the economy's distribution and allocation function should not be left to the market mechanism alone, hence the necessity for planning intervention. Since at least two objects must be considered in this connection, namely overall economic allocation efficiency and interregional equality of distribution, it follows that in simultaneous regional and overall economic planning a problem of consistency must arise as a general rule.

Consequently the object of the enquiry will be to clarify the relationship between overall economic and regional development planning. For this it will be necessary to consider the spatial economic effects of general economic planning on the one hand and the effects of regional planning on general economic growth on the other. Ideally, the consequent aim would be for an integrated global, sectoral and regional planning. In concrete plans, on the other hand, regional programmes are often completely unrelated to the general economic sector programming, whose locational dimension is unknown. Mennes, Tinbergen and Waardenburg (69) have made an attempt to develop planning models incorporating the space dimension. Their applicability is extremely questionable, however, because in the first place, despite certain formal subtleties, they had to remain theoretically simple; secondly they do not reflect the question of controllability of strategically decisive variables by means of plans incorporated in an indicative control system, and thirdly it is to be assumed that neither a refinement of the theoretical assessment adopted nor the inclusion of the mechanisms of the political process in its strategic instrumentalisation will prove fruitful, because it has not yet been possible to include polarising factors in the patterns direct.

One would be doing the above-mentioned authors an injustice, however, if one did not admit that so far it has only been possible to prove to a limited extent the effects of polarising factors regarding the spatial dimension of the overall economic development process in accordance with the strict rules of empirical science. In what follows, only the three first steps have been taken in this direction, and the book has been divided into Parts I – III accordingly. The first of them contains a statement of the plausibility of the polarisation argument and sets out the prospects for empirical statements of the problem. The second is concerned with the attempted instrumentalisation of the polarisation theory, and, in relation to the traditional theory of economic policy, considers the aims, makers and means of polarisation-orientated regional policy from the example of the Spanish development plans since 1964. The third stage represents an attempt at planning control. Within its modest limits it often displays a generalisable lack of the Spanish regional policy under consideration. To draw conclusions from this as to the limited feasibility of the polarisation theories would be precipitate, however, for deficiencies in such theories do not necessarily amount to simultaneous confirmation of the competing theories evolved so far.

As a starting point for further development three hypotheses can be adopted:

H_1: '... the field of growth poles and growth centers ... (provides) the most tangible link between *national and regional policies and plans*' (Kuklinski, 70, 276, the italics being mine). It is also claimed here that the development pole concept has a particularly integrational function in relation to the present statement of the problem. In the sense of the theoretical explanatory statement (polarisation theory) it must in accordance with the above include a sustainable hypothesis regarding the connection between general economic growth and regional development. This runs:

H_2: 'Growth takes place in successive spurts in sectoral-geographical clusters from which it spreads to the rest of the system' (Lasuen, 71, 5). Formulated as a positive hypothesis, the connection can be expressed in the words that general economic growth can be polarised not only from a sectoral but also from a regional point of view. In this way the significance of the space dimension is first postulated for the growth theory, and in the second place a statement is implied regarding the connection with the localisation theory, namely $H_{2\,1}$: 'whereas transport costs in the strict sense of the term are becoming less important in explaining the dispersion of activities over space, communication costs (including transport costs) — given the increasing complexity of production processes — are becoming more important', and $H_{2\,2}$: 'Communication costs prevent economic activities from spreading arbitrarily over a given space' (van Wickeren, 71, 3). Having regard to $H_{2\,1}$ and $H_{2\,2}$,

$H_{2\,3}$ seems meaningful: 'The focus on specific geographical centers (i.e. growth poles, F.B.) at the sub-regional level has helped to bridge the gap between locational analysis and regional economics' (Richardson, 69, 415; 'regional economics' can be interpreted by Richardson in the present connection in the sense of regional economic theory). To sum up, it can be said that *a priori* considerations support the feasibility of the polarisation theory as a basis for the connection between general economic growth and regional growth.

The integrational function of the development concept is now to be developed in connection with the instrumentalisation notion (growth pole policy) associated with it. Not only is it unnecessary to refer to specific growth pole strategies, but it is also undesirable, because these can lead, as will be demonstrated, to considerable narrowing of the underlying theoretical concept. The important hypothesis in respect of the development pole concept, for the formulation of the claim that an optimum growth policy is only possible through regional policy (Gerfin, 64, 575), is re-formulated in H_3 and runs:

H_3: Sectoral polarisations are more efficient when they are polarised regionally than when they are regionally dispersed. Furthermore, the positive assertion that general economic growth is apt to be regionally polarised has become a strategic concept, while it is further claimed that such regionally polarised growth is 'better'. That is not to say that the market economy development process alone produces optimum polarisation. This means that for planning purposes one of the tasks can actually consist in the instrumentalisation of the growth theory concept of the polarisation theory by growth policy. This can also mean: H_{31}: that by pursuing locationally-based welfare objects the growth pole concept is superior to others, and H_{32}: that having regard to general economic efficiency it may be right on account of the partial failure of the market mechanism to give preferential treatment to depressed areas and so serve the interests of growth pole policy.

This is a task of development planning, and the purpose of development planning is the formulation, implementation and control of a conception of economic policy. This can further be defined as an example representing a rational aggregation of aims, principles and methods of economic policy (Pütz, 60, 11). The postulate of a rational aggregation calls for theoretically based statements regarding the aims and means relationship. After the above-mentioned simplified representation of the planning task come the priority aims, which are out of sight of the central planners, of the maximisation of the social product and inter-regional equality of distribution. The welfare implications of these aims will not be discussed in detail here. That they should be considered carefully in the discussion of distribution targets is shown by the following quotation: 'Paradoxically, the result of policies adopted to raise incomes in depressed areas may be to benefit the rich in the poor regions at the expense of the poor living in rich ones' (Richardson, 69, 366).

What does the polarisation hypothesis do to clarify the relationship between locational and general economic growth and the corresponding objects?

PART I

Assumptions Regarding Sectoral and Regional Polarisation

A conclusive polarisation theory does not yet exist. Assessments claimed to be aimed at its formulation are to be found in John Friedmann (72) and José R. Lasuen (71, in mimeograph). In order to bring out the hypothetical character of previous assessments, it may be appropriate to refer to a number of inter-connected, empirically relatively untested theories. All the authors who have had critical exchanges with one another on polarisation theories are united in stressing the multiplicity, partial contradiction and complete inaccuracy of their assertions (Blaug, 64; Körner, 67; Darwent, 69; Hermansen, 70, for example). Strongest of all is the criticism which calls in question the theoretical content of the polarisation hypothesis itself: 'It is simply a slogan masquerading as a theory' (Blaug, 64, 560).

The empirical content of the polarisation theory can best be determined by asking whether and to what extent it has proved successful as used in connection with regional planning. The example of the growth pole policy followed in Spain since 1964 is calculated to contribute to the determination of the reality content of that part of the polarisation hypotheses for which operational criteria are to be found in the literature. Without any doubt, the most striking of these criteria hitherto has been (under the influence of the 'French school' in succession to Perroux) the input-output criterion. Consequently a substantial portion of the following theoretical and empirical analysis is devoted to its consideration.

In view of the fact that a spatial economic planning theory and practice orientated towards a national welfare function is still in its infancy, it also seems legitimate to ask whether competing clarification and planning patterns turn out to be more suitable than polarisation-orientated ones when they are examined by the same standards. For it could simply be a case of falling out of the frying-pan into the fire to turn away from polarisation-orientated patterns on grounds of justified criticism, in an attempt to find salvation in alternative, similarly unproved models.

Such a competing pattern is that proposed by Mennes, Tinbergen and Waardenburg (69) and that first tested by Carrillo-Arronte (70) for Mexico. A serious attempt was made in this case to incorporate the space element in the general economic planning. Its representation makes it possible to accentuate the objections of a polarisation theoretical character and to confirm their plausibility. In his approach the writer finds himself in agreement with the authors named to the extent that it is obviously to be admitted that the pattern is in need of improvement, first as regards the formal technique, and secondly on the question of obtaining and including additional information. In contrast with them, however, he regards the basic assessment as being equally at fault. This latter criticism will be elaborated below, and for this purpose the Mennes,

Tinbergen and Waardenburg model will first be set out. Then follows a critique from the polarisation-theory point of view, and thereafter an attempt will be made to assemble existing polarisation-theory considerations in a systematic relationship and to establish their plausibility.

The following steps will therefore be taken: it will first be shown to what theoretical basis the regional polarisation argument can be reduced. Secondly, it will be represented that the French school has in substance done no more than to clarify sectoral polarisation, which was done by Hirschman (67) and Schumpeter (12) independently and possibly more clearly. Thirdly it will be considered under what conditions sectoral polarisation may lead to regional agglomerations. Attraction-theory considerations will thus be of great importance. Fourthly, it will be asked to what extent regional concentrations of economic activity are independent of sectoral polarisations. Reference will thus be made here to the recent discussion on growth poles and growth centres. Fifthly and finally an attempt will be made to establish a relationship between the present considerations and the above-mentioned attempts regarding a general polarisation theory. Authority-dependency relationships between peripheral and central regions and communication costs will be shown to be significant for regionally polarised production, income and settlement structures.

1 Integrated Sectoral and Regional Planning on General Economic Planes - Discussion of a Model

1.1 Setting the problem

General economic planning is at once dependent on space and significant for space. While this assertion will probably be accepted by all regional planners, and while to many people the concept of an integrated global/sectoral/regional planning appeals as an ideal, true planning solutions have not yet been formulated. A first assessment is to be discussed here. It was selected because its applicability is not dependent on whether plainly exacting statistical material is available for the individual sub-districts of an economy and its appendages − e.g. regional input-output tables, regional balances of payments, inter-regional flow-of-funds analyses, for which reason it seems at first sight to apply particularly to development countries.

In order to classify the model to be discussed, the reader should imagine that the national planning authority has managed to develop a general economic sector programming pattern. In its simplest form − in particular ignoring foreign trade relations − the pattern could be gradually established on the following lines: first, general economic target values would be set for income, consumption and employment. An assumption would be made regarding personal income distribution. Then, by means of estimated income elasticities for demand, the structure of the necessary supply of consumer goods would be determined. Furthermore, with the help of a national input-output pattern, the demand would be established for work previously performed for consumer goods production. From this, after various iteration steps for which the general economic target values are the subject of examination, target values are established for production in the various sectors, for which the total amount of net worth creation (gross output value less depreciation less previous work) in the sectors must equal the target value for the net social product at market prices. It can at once be established that we are dealing with an exclusively demand-orientated planning pattern; there is a further simplification here,

5

but one which does not substantially change the considerations at this point.

The object of the plans concerned with the integrated sectoral and regional programming is now to 'regionalise' the results of this pattern. In the Spanish Planning Commission sitting in 1971/72 to consider the preparation of the Third Plan (1972-75), the following regional pattern was discussed and finally rejected. It will be worth while outlining briefly the lessons we learned at the time.

The planning for sectoral development within the framework of the Spanish Development Plan was arranged in the First and Second Plans in such a way that an investment programme was drawn up for important sectors. Only for the Third Plan was a general economic sectoral programming pattern made available. With the help of this the co-ordination of the sectoral investment programmes should be provided and an optimum determination of the investment volume in each case achieved (Planning Commission, Project . . . , 70). No attempt is made to determine the spatial allocation of the sectors in this pattern. For co-ordination of regional planning with sectoral planning it therefore seemed desirable to discuss alternative possibilities for the spatial allocation of the new activities. In this connection, two questions stood out: first, how the spatial dimension of the sector programming pattern would look in the absence of corrective adjustments of regional policy if the allocation conditions observed in the past continued to apply; and secondly, how pre-setting the target values for incomes in peripheral regions and corresponding sectoral investment programmes in these would change the results of the sector programming patterns, and what consequences for the achievement of general economic rates of growth in the social product would follow. The first question relates to the space effectiveness of sectoral planning, and the second depends on the space-dependency of the results of sectoral planning. Attempts to answer both questions were made with the project for an additional pattern to the sector programming pattern (Planning Commission, Specification . . . , 71). They represent a first step in the direction of the integration of sectoral and regional planning.

Two versions of the pattern which was developed to settle the above-mentioned questions are set out briefly below. It is also shown that both versions are essentially unsuitable for clarifying the reality, when the polarisation theory can claim empirical evidence for itself. It is then considered whether integrated sectoral-regional planning in an indicative plan is at all meaningful. As regards the regional political strategy in the Third Plan, the following thesis is here presented: the sectoral-regional integrated planning process is orientated towards the patterns of Tin-

6

bergen and his followers (Mennes, Tinbergen, Waardenburg, 69). For this, the sectoral planning is given priority over regional planning ('sector first – region second', Richardson, 72, 4). This orientation contradicts the doctrine of a polarisation-orientated regional policy, its results not being suitable for the formation of a strategy for regional policy.

1.2 Two versions for a regional pattern

The project for a regional pattern is based on Carrillo-Arronte's (70) work on Mexico, which is regarded as an empirical test of the patterns proposed by Mennes, Tinbergen and Waardenburg. The form the problem takes can be indicated briefly:

The spatial distribution of directly productive activities already existing and those to be created by new investments can be presented in a matrix for n sectors s and m and regions i.

Sectors / Regions	1	2	...	l	...	n	Regional totals
1	W_{11}	W_{21}	...	W_{l1}	...	W_{n1}	W_{s1}
2	W_{12}	W_{22}	...	W_{l2}	...	W_{n2}	W_{s2}
⋮							
j	W_{1j}	W_{2j}	...	W_{lj}	...	W_{nj}	W_{sj}
⋮							
m	W_{1m}	W_{2m}	...	W_{lm}	...	W_{nm}	W_{sm}
Sectoral totals	W_{1i}	W_{2i}	...	W_{li}	...	W_{ni}	W_{si}

In the matrix the W can be shown as the target value for the net value creation at factor cost (and thus the amount for the national income) of the sectors in the regions. The column totals give the sectoral target values, which are identical with those of the sector programmes. The line totals give the total income for the regions (domestic income). ΣW_{si} is the target value for the national income.

From the previous period it can be determined how high the values for all the W_{si} were individually. If it can be expected that the sectors producing in the regions in the previous period can maintain their production at constant prices at precisely the same value, only new or expanded activities need to be included in the programming. If the matrix

7

is interpreted accordingly ΣW_{si} will give the real planned growth in the net social product for the planning period or for each planning year t ($t = 1, \ldots, 4$).

If it can be assumed that capital is the strategically decisive scarce factor $\tilde{c}_{si}$ can be inserted for the W_{si} of the new activities. $\tilde{c}_{si}$ is the quotient of net investment and value creation in sector s in region i, the investment/net worth creation relationship. Stock changes are not considered in determining net investment. If it can be further assumed that none of the $\tilde{c}_{si}$ is changed by the development of new activities, the investment requirement for the sectors in the regions can be arrived at from the target values for the W_{si}, as is requisite for the realisation of these income target values. It is important to recognise that it is a question of regional domestic income values, not of residents' income values.

If the $\tilde{c}_{si}$ is given and is independent of the planning decisions, and it is further assumed that $\tilde{c}_s$ is different for all the regions i, then for the plans the question arises for which regional distribution of the sectors the target value ΣW_{si} can be precisely achieved or even exceeded, if a particular net investment is appointed for each sector. If in addition the target values are laid down for regional income, that is to say ΣW_s ($s = 1, \ldots n$) is laid down for each of the regions i ($i = 1, \ldots, m$), then the planning task will be to determine the distribution of the sectors among the regions in such a way that for each of the individual sectors and also for each region the target values can be achieved at a minimum investment outlay. In that case the general economic investment volume will be the dependent variable.

According to the assumption adopted, two variations of the regional pattern must be considered.

1   The first version should provide an answer to the question as to which regional dimension the sectoral programming pattern has, on the assumption that the spatial allocation conditions observed in the past still obtain. The framing of this question is only identical with the planning task of establishing the spatial distribution of the sectors which makes it possible to achieve all the sectoral target values, if it can be assumed that the appointed $\tilde{c}_{si}$ is constant in the diagnosis-prognosis-period adopted and is correctly reflected in the general economic input-output data underlying the sectoral planning. In the case of $\tilde{c}_s$ which is different for all regions, this means that the net value creation coefficient of a sector shown in the national input-output tables represents the weighted arithmetic mean of the regional value creation coefficient for the sector.

This version of the pattern is described by analogy with Carrillo's presentation as the 'historical pattern', the second version as the 'income redistributive pattern'. The object of the 'historical' variation is to obtain an idea of the space dimension of the investment process not specifically evaluated in the sector planning. This could provide an important source of information and an aid to decision on regional policy, for these may not only relate, in the formation of their measures, to the diagnosis of the situation from a planning point of view: they must also recognise the development tendencies to be reckoned with in the absence of a new regional policy programme. Without a knowledge of the spatial implications of sector programming it is more sensible to pay as little attention to a proper spread of funds employed as to the co-ordination of regional policy with the other measures of development policy. A clear discussion of the so-called historical patterns should serve to show to what extent the aim pursued by means of the simple approach discussed in the Planning Commission might be achieved.

(a) The starting point for the discussions will be the additional contributions of the sectors to the national income which is assumed to come from sector programming. The regional make-up of these contributions should be clarified, and for this purpose the following assumptions are made:

— All the production processes can be described in linear input-output terms.
— Three categories of goods can be distinguished: regional goods are only produced in the region in which they are also consumed, and inter-regional communication costs are prohibitively high; national goods have no communication costs within the national economy, and international communication costs are prohibitively high. All non-regional and non-national sectors are international sectors, and for them all communication costs are nil.
— The production of national sectors is a function of the national income, that of the regional sectors a function of the regional income; and the general economic output of all sectors, whether regional, national or international, is set out in the sector programming pattern.
— Only capital is regarded as a scarce factor, the sectoral-regional relationships investment/net worth creation are in their differences representative of sectoral-regional average cost differences.
— The prices of all goods and factors are constant.
— Investment and production starts coincide, the duration of the investment period is nil.
— All activities go ahead from the start of production onwards with a normal utilisation of capacity.

(b) In these simple patterns there are basically two problems which, apart from the emergence of appropriate sectoral and regional limits, have to be solved.

(i) For national and international sectors the term

$$W_{si} = \beta W_s \text{ applies}$$

where W_{si} signifies the value creation of any sector in any region, and W_s the value creation of the sector in the total national economy. The parameter β, that is the portion which the sector in the region i has of the value creation of the sector in the national economy, has also to be defined.

As regards the past, the β values are known or can be determined by the appropriate treatment of the available material, which was also used for preparing the total accounts of the regions. For the planning period to be considered these depend on the regional distribution of investment in the sectors. For forecasting the regional distribution of investment, the total amount of which for each sector is given in the sector pattern, an extrapolation can be made from the development tendencies established in the past from time series of adequate length. However, this brings us to a serious difficulty regarding the calculation of this extremely simple pattern: first because sufficiently accurate and detailed past figures for the volume of investment in the sectors in the regions are very hard to come by, and secondly for a large number of sectors and regions it cannot be assumed that an appraisal of past values will disclose clear-cut development tendencies. For the national and international sectors an adequate result is thus only to be obtained with the historical pattern if it is possible, for the bigger sector demarcations at least, to appraise regional investment functions from the past. The draft pattern submitted to the Planning Commission provides for the appraisal of such investment functions.

(ii) The second problem arises in connection with the fact that the development of the 'regional sectors' depends on the development of regional incomes, which in turn depends on the results of growth in the national, international and regional sectors in each region. In respect of each region, therefore, it is necessary to assess from past values how the social product contribution of the regional sectors stands in relation to the social product contribution of the other sectors. On the assumption that this relationship is quite inelastic as compared with income, it can be applied as an export basis multiplier to the results of the distribution of the other sectors to the regions.

It is not to be assumed, however, that the relationship on which the export basis multiplier depends remains constant in the development process. For a higher regional income level will bring about a shift in the demand structure in favour of higher value and more differentiated goods, which are to a large extent national and international. From this it can be assumed that other things being equal, the income elasticity of demand in comparable circumstances in other respects is lower for regional than for national and international goods. This means that the constancy of the above-mentioned relationship will only serve as a working approximation in the short term. It is also to be noted that the accuracy of the statements regarding the development of the regional sectors as a result of the export basis multiplier, depends on the correctness of the statements regarding the development of the national and international sectors in each region.

(c) From the investment/value creation relationship of the regional sectors, the investment requirement for these sectors in the regions can be established by inference. The consistency requirement, with regard to the investment planning underlying the general economic sector programming pattern, can again be summed up by saying that the sum of investments in regional, national and international sectors must be equal for all regions to the investment volume assumed in the sector programming. The consistency requirement with regard to the general economic growth rate of domestic income is satisfied when, for all regions, the sum of the net domestic product contributions of the sectors is equal to the sectoral target values of the sector programming pattern. The sum of the regional domestic income growth will then also be equal to the national income growth assumed in the sector programming. The distribution of the new activities which satisfies these requirements leads to a regional income distribution which represents the space dimension implied by the sector programming pattern.

2   In the second version the regional income target values are regarded as assumed. They must satisfy the requirement that their sum is equal to the target value for the national income. The determination of the regional income target values is subject as before to the restriction that only the income to be created in the planning period in addition can be distributed differently in its regional emergence. The planning task is to discover the distribution of new activities over the regions by which all the sectoral and regional target values can be achieved simultaneously with the least possible investment expenditure. The other assumptions underlying the historical pattern are thereby accepted; they correspond to those of the Carrillo-Arronte pattern (Carrillo-Arronte, 70, 9 et seq.). The minimisation function can be expressed as

$$Z = \sum_{i=1}^{n} \sum_{s=1}^{m} \tilde{c}_{si} \cdot w_{si} \longrightarrow \text{min!}$$

11

Here c_{si} again represents the sectoral-regional investment and value-creation coefficients, expressing the capital requirement demanded by the production of an additional value creation unit of a sector s in a region i.

The variables to be defined by the pattern are the additional value creation units W_{si} to be produced in each sector in each region. On the other hand the coefficients are given as in the historical pattern, as well as the additional value creation of each sector for the sum of all the regions and the additional value creation in each region for the sum of all the sectors producing in it. This means that

$$\sum_{i=1}^{n} W_{si} = W_s \quad \text{and} \quad \sum_{s=1}^{m} W_{si} = W_i.$$

In addition $W_{si} \geqslant 0$ should also hold good.

The solution takes the form of a linear programme. This process has only to be used, however, for the national and international sectors, for which in addition certain W_{si} values are put at practically nil, while because of the size structure of the undertaking, for instance, it may not be possible to install each sector in all the regions simultaneously.

For the regional sectors an investment requirement arises in each region immediately, as their additional value creation depends on the target values for regional incomes in each case assumed in this pattern. The relationship

$$W_{si} = \Upsilon_{si} \cdot W_i$$

applies in each case.

Here Υ expresses the portion of a regional sector detected in the past constituting the value creation of a particular region. If the W_{si} is established in this way the necessary capital required for additional regional production in each region is determined from $\tilde{c}_{si}$.

In conjunction with the capital requirement for the national and international sectors the total sectoral-regional investment programme will also be obtained. A comparison of the investment volume of the general economic sector programming pattern and of the income redistributive regional pattern will show the alternative costs of regional policy arising from the assumptions adopted.

1.3   Critique of the pattern

The critical evaluation of the pattern brings out two particular objections, first that the effect of the space dimension is treated as negligible, and

12

secondly that the pattern can only have strategically utilisable results when it is established that the polarisation theory cannot make use of any kind of empirical evidence. On the other hand it is not to be denied that the pattern is over-simplified. A prior requirement for this would be a presentation setting out more of the details. Mennes, Tinbergen and Waardenburg do not themselves dispute that their projection of the model is too simple, and, as regards the exceedingly restrictive assumptions, is geared to the existence of mathematically more exact solutions. The authors concerned will not agree, however, with a critique alleging that the assessment is basically unsatisfactory. This will be reasoned out below (cf. on this point Richardson 72, 2 et seq.).

1   Models of the type proposed by Mennes, Tinbergen and Waardenburg reduce the consideration of space-differentiating factors in economic growth to a minimum:

(a)   Transport costs only receive implicit attention in that an attempt is made in national, regional and international sectors to discriminate on the basis of the sensitivity to transport costs of the products concerned. Communication costs in a wider sense are substantially unaffected. The implied procedure for considering transport costs has decisive weaknesses, quite apart from the fact that it only represents a substitute solution. When it has also to be acknowledged − though in the case of concrete planning decisions it is a matter for consideration on each occasion − that transport costs have lost much of their significance as a space-differentiating factor, they are still not to be regarded as negligible.

(b)   The delimitation of the sectors must be very rough for the purposes of calculation in connection with the pattern, so that only some thirty to fifty sectors will be distinguished. This constitutes a further obstacle to the utilisation of the implicit transport cost calculation, for the lower the number of sectors, the more problematical will it be to classify the products simply into national, regional or other groups according to their sensitivity to transport costs. It is also to be noted that, the rougher the sector allocation, the less expressive of differences in spatial localisation requirements will be sector delimitation according to the ISIC classifications of activities.

(c)   Mennes, Tinbergen and Waardenburg only assume regionally differentiated investment/value creation relationships for regional activities. This seems consistent considering the assumptions that capital is the sole strategically important scarce factor and is regarded implicitly as completely mobile spatially; that the necessary manpower with the required qualifications is always available in sufficient quantities (through migration movements) at any place, without charge, and that the communication costs for national and international products are at a negligibly low level. On the other hand, in both versions of the pattern discussed in the Spanish Planning Commission the assumption was adopted that for the national and international sectors the investment/ value creation relationships are regionally different. If this proves correct, it must be concluded that the assumptions drawn from the assessments by Mennes, Tinbergen and Waardenburg are not valid.

A further obstacle to the utilisation of the model for forecasting and planning now arises from the fact that regionally differentiated investment and value-creation coefficients cannot be meaningfully estimated for even fifty sectors. This is because the results will reflect, in so far as they can be achieved at all, differences in the product-mix of the sectors by regions rather than regional productivity differences or comparative cost advantages. Moreover, even if regional productivity differences are established, nothing would be disclosed thereby regarding the degree to which they can be influenced. This point of view leads on to the following argument.

(d) The constancy of the investment/value creation relationships in the planning period under consideration is a simplification which seems to be justified by the fact that the consequences of regional policy which are reflected, inter alia, in changes in the sectoral capital productivity with suitable product composition, are not to be achieved at short term. A polarisation-orientated regional policy is designed to change these relationships. That this is not to be achieved in the short run cannot be regarded as sufficient grounds for implementing the investment linkage on the assumption of a constancy in the relationship. Under ideal conditions, the planning pattern will certainly give forecasting results that will be thoroughly valid at short term, but as regards the long-term orientation it can lead to false assumptions.

Overall, it is a question of a pattern in which space differentiating factors are eventually considered implicitly and to an unsatisfactory extent. For purposes of calculation, the sectoral and regional classification must be so rough that even if the results were to be regarded as valid they are still too general to permit strategic final conclusions.

2 Refinements of the pattern are possible. First of all, transport costs can be included direct (Saigal, 65), the problem here being to establish the data. On the other hand, Mennes, Tinbergen and Waardenburg themselves refer to attempts to take account of the existence of indivisibilities and rising scale profits in production, while connections are discerned between the hierarchy of settlements in the area and the distribution of industries (Mennes, Tinbergen, Waardenburg, 69, 211 et seq.). For Spain, Angelet Cladellas and Clusa Oriach (72, 467 et seq.) have worked out and

established correlations between the structure size of cities and under-takings: 'The size of cities seems ... to have statistically significant importance for the clarification of the differences observed in the size of undertakings of certain sectors' (op. cit. 470, translated by the author).

Basic objections are not removed thereby: (a) even if rising scale earnings are considered, the pattern assessment reduces the observable dynamic of the growth process to a plan period (Richardson, 72, 2); (b) spatial external effects are not considered; (c) the assumption of complete mobility for capital leaves the existence of authority-dependency relation-ships between centre and periphery unconsidered, which often permits only a 'selective' mobility of capital; (d) the assumption regarding the mobility of the labour force leaves the quality of the supply of manpower and the social opportunity costs of inter-regional migration movements out of account; (e) as no distinction is made between regional internal incomes and incomes of residents, the substantial flow effects of the polarisation theory are not ascertained — the calculation of the invest-ments necessary to achieve the income target values is therefore basically in need of correction; (f) the necessary complementary infrastructure investments are not determined by the pattern, neither will the regional effect on incomes stemming therefrom be taken into account; (g) the pattern is overloaded if social aims of regional policy, such as that of integration by social participation, are put into effect.

Altogether the economic system on which the pattern is based is too narrow to embrace the empirical facts that are relevant to the strategy of 'growth policy through polarisation-orientated regional policy'. It is also unsuitable for the valid clarification of connections in a sub-district, because this would assume that the sub-district presented itself as a relatively closed economic sub-system.

3   Integrated sectoral-regional planning is an ideal which, from the planning point of view, may seem attainable in the case of imperative planning, but in that of indicative planning calls for controlling powers in the form of action parameters on the part of the makers of economic policy which are not at their disposal. Imperative planning undoubtedly has to contend with the same difficulties as were set out in the preceding section. If, as in the Spanish case, a basic decision is taken in favour of indicative planning, however, implementation is still not assured in the cases where programming patterns also yield 'correct' results. Two important viewpoints will make this clear:

(a)   Planning practice in Spain has shown that even global principles in the former sector programme could not be put through. It is to be expected that the indications specified through regional disaggregation will prove still less effective, particularly if, as has been pointed out here, the basis for the instructions is on a weak footing.

(b)   The implementation of results of a programming pattern in the execution of the plan must take account of the domination and interest structure as between the planes of the planners and politicians on the one hand, and of the addressees of the planning indications on the other hand, also within the planes of both contracting parties (cf. also Cohen, 69, 28 et seq.).

Failure to consider these problems arises in the concrete case from an idea of solidarity glossing over the social conflict of interests. In judging the chances of carrying out integrated sectoral-regional planning, account must be taken of the fact that the solidarity postulated in this form just does not exist. The observation has also to be made in Spain, however, that other things being equal, the less differentiated are the structural inter-relationships on which a decision has to be taken, the easier it is to achieve a consensus. This observation at the same time places the ideological conflict between imperative and indicative planning in a perspective nearer to reality, in so far as it can be established that in the system of imperative planning too, the lower the degree of complexity of the interdependence relations concerned, the better are the chances of carrying through the programme results, as for example in the construction of integrated plant for the raw materials industry.

(c)   Integrated sectoral-regional planning should be an instrument of consistent planning. If it is desired to satisfy this claim by means of a programme pattern, account must also be taken of the fact that the consistency of the programme is perhaps only to be achieved because of the sensibility of the pattern if strict control and link-up of investment are maintained. Within the framework of the Spanish indicative planning there is thus also an obligation to obtain approval for particular key industries such as refineries, steel works and so on. Consideration could also be given to correcting the position by setting up state undertakings. The practice of the Instituto Nacional de Industria (INI) has shown in the past, however, that such a stopgap solution is viewed with disfavour. For the guidance of investment policy by the INI the line that was proposed by Richardson for private firms might be followed: 'I suspect that regional and local firms that follow the regional guidelines of the sector plan will probably make rather worse investment decisions than if they relied on their own unaided judgement' (Richardson, 72, 8).

To sum up it may be said that the necessary investment guidelines run counter to the basic idea of indicative planning, and that even if this basic idea is deliberatately not followed consistently, the chance of following through the programme results will be small. Finally it is doubtful whether following through the programme results is desirable in any case.

2 Polarisation and Regional Growth Theory

One possibility of bringing out the special character of statements of polarisation theories consists in contrasting them with competing theories. At this point therefore the Ohlin-Heckscher theorem and Myrdal's critique will be set out briefly (cf. for details Buttler, 73, 11 et seq.).

The general economic growth theory ignores the space dimension and treats national economics as space points (Gerfin, 64, 568; Siebert, 67, 1). The regional growth theory is often distinguished from the general economic growth theory only by the fact that it disaggregates the space point regionally from the general economy. Regions are again treated as space points whose interdependence with the instruments of the pure theory of international trade is explained.

The Ohlin-Heckscher theory is concerned *inter alia* with the conditions of international factor price equalisation. Regarding the mobility of goods and the immobility of factors in international trade, it explains under what conditions the factor price equalisation occurs. It is to be expected that the more mobile the factors are, the more readily factor price equalisation will come about. Only in borderline cases is there any doubt that inter-regional factor mobility will be greater than in the international case. As a rule the regions — the argument as to size can be ignored at present — are characterised by a much higher degree of openness[1] than are nations.

The Ohlin-Heckscher theory states that free trade results in factor price equalisation. This implies an international or regional approximation of income per head.[2] Myrdal, on the other hand, does not believe that trade liberalisation makes for a levelling out of *per capita* income differences. Free trade, he fears, makes rich nations or regions richer, and poorer ones poorer (Myrdal, 67, 51 et seq.). Myrdal's is a typical polarisation hypothesis based on the principle of circular causation (Myrdal, 57, 11 et seq.), which describes polarisation of the income level as the net result of centripetal (backwash) and centrifugal (spread) effects.

2.1 The principle of circular causation

For the polarisation theory the principle of circular causation is fundamental. Formally stated, it is a mutual connection between cause and effect applied to the principle of economic development: between growth and growth determinants. Spatially polarised growth comes about from the fact that individual growth determinants are completely or partially immobile. Where there is a general openness of regions in the market economy system, mobility limitations can arise from monopolistic rigidity and communication costs. Both concepts are at the outset very widely based: monopolistic rigidities include authority-dependency relationships (Friedmann, 72), and through them communication costs can be increased further or a communication can be obstructed. Communication costs include transport costs. Their emergence means that the production or profit function of any activity i in region j is influenced thereby, whether their direct and indirect inputs-outputs are offered/demanded in spatial proximity or not.

Our main argument thus runs: comparative development advantages of regions in relation to other regions do not lead by their mere existence to spatial differential processes. In addition, they themselves and/or their effects are spatially not transferable at all, or only to a limited extent, so that they are (partially) immobile or are kept (partially) immobile by 'monopolisation'.

1 Communication costs are the (partial) result of immobilisation by growth determinants (cf. Siebert, 66, 166 et seq.), and as has been said, they include transport costs. The transport cost argument does not suffice to establish polarisations by itself, however, unless the transport costs are prohibitively high. The Ohlin-Heckscher theory thus shows that transport costs certainly hold up factor price equalisation, but not the tendency thereto. The causes of cumulative linkages must therefore be sought in the effects of the immobility of additional growth determinants. Other factors affecting the situation are: (a) spatial external effects (agglomeration-advantages and disadvantages); (b) indivisibility in consumption and production and increasing returns to scale; (c) adjustment frictions in the market mechanism and monopolistic distortions.

According to Kaldor (70, 340) increasing returns to scale play the decisive role in the spatial differentiation process. This constitutes no contradiction to what has been said above, though perhaps a shift in the emphasis, for Kaldor subsumes under this head: 'not just the economies of large-scale production, commonly considered, but the cumulative advantages accruing from the growth of industry itself — the development of skill and know-how; the opportunities for easy communication of ideas and experience; the opportunity of ever increasing differentiation of processes and of specialisation in human activities' (ibid.).

18

Increasing returns to scale thus produce communication advantages. These are not automatically spatially transferable, that is to say they are partially immobile spatially. For suppliers in peripheral regions their appearance in industries in the centre constitutes a comparative disadvantage, communication costs.

It is arguable whether the conditions set out in (a), (b) and (c) relating to the immobility of growth determinants necessarily influence the level of communication costs, or whether they are partly attributable to an artificial change in communication costs by reason of authority-dependency relationships between centres and peripheries. In effect this is immaterial. To clarify the connection between the communication cost argument on the one hand, and the authority-dependency argument on the other hand, the following formula can be offered: authority-dependency relationships between centre and periphery have the effect that for the growth of the periphery strategical information, activities and institutions are controlled by the functions élite in the centre and are only passed on as innovations to the extent that it serves the interests of the élite. Authority-dependency relationships signify additional mobility limitations on growth determinants.

2 Mobility limitations are linked together circularly. First the linkage mechanisms will be considered, and then some considerations on the results of the process will be added.

(a) By analysing the mechanisms the arrangement of the above-mentioned determining causes can be observed. For this purpose a distinction must be made as to whether a determining cause will in any case suffice to touch off a dynamic feedback effect, and whether the feedback will only come about by the interaction of two determining causes.

(i) It was established that the transport cost argument alone represents insufficient condition for circular feedbacks. Transport costs have a strengthening effect on causative processes based elsewhere, that is to say that the effect produced by polarisation only arises in connection with the interaction with other limitations of mobility.

(ii) The externality argument taken by itself, on the other hand, is sufficient for the establishment of circular causation. For this purpose it is not necessary that two-sided externalities should exist, for: if by reason of the spatial attractive effect of a producer another has been developed in a neighbouring area, it will then be sufficient that owing to the remaining attractive effect of the former, the attractivity of the spatial position will be increased by external effects which the second could produce.

(iii) The indivisibility argument, or the argument of increasing returns to scale, is sufficient when taken by itself, for either (in the event that the goods are still being produced) still lower alternative costs will be produced by the preparation of additional production units, or (in the event that production could not yet be started) by starting production the degree of diversification and flexibility of the position concerned will be increased and its site quality (attractiveness) thereby improved. For this purpose it is basically irrelevant whether the new or increased supply represents a direct or indirect input for consequent activities. [3]

(iv)   The authority-dependency argument is also treated as sufficient on its own account: the control which the central élites exercise at the periphery strengthens the power of the centre also by the fact that use can be made of the scarce production factors necessary for the production of innovations available at the periphery. Friedmann mentions six principal feedback effects which contribute to the self-reinforcement of the domination of a centre over its periphery (Friedmann, 72, 94 et seq.).

It is really a question of a range of phenomena which by and large embrace the essential factors which, with the immobility of growth determinants, work in the direction of further differentiation. This is not pursued specifically here. However, in the author's view the clarifying value of such a juxtaposition of effects can only satisfy if each individual argument is seen in the light of the analysis of the communication cost argument, for in each individual case it has to be established that communication costs stand in the way of an inter-regional equalisation mechanism. Friedmann's analysis is heavily geared to the idea of a dualism of centre and periphery in the sense of two relatively closed circulations. Here, on the other hand, the region is defined from the outset as open and the question is posed why, with basic openness, mobility limitations can bring about self-reinforcing differentiation effects. What is really involved is a shift of emphasis, which has some bearing on the style and manner of the argumentation.

(v)   In the cases considered in (ii − iv) the elements presented are sufficient in each case to clarify a circular causation mechanism. Furthermore, these elements can also be presented as circularly interlinked with one another. In this way the emergence of permanently self-supporting growth processes is also to be explained. The more immobile the induced growth determinants are, the more sharply is this process polarised spatially.

The process of circular causation finds expression in a series of innovations whose support capacity varies, so that the power activities as well as others do not remain the same throughout the process.

The medium of the polarised growth process is the settlement structure. So asserts Kaldor (70, 340): 'Thus, the fact that in all known historical

20

cases the development of manufacturing industries was closely associated with urbanisation must have deep-seated causes which are unlikely to be rendered inoperative by the invention of some new technology or new source of power.'

Similarly for Friedmann, the city is a communication field in which the probability of an exchange of information is high, and generally the social interaction relations are relatively close. This leads to a spatial concentration of innovations (Friedmann, 72, 89). Similarly also Ritter: 'Economic development is a process that occurs in villages, towns and conurbations. These form a system whose structure influences the course of the development process just as strongly as this influences the formation of the settlement structure' (Ritter, 70, 163). Nevertheless, little research has yet been done on the question of the connection between city development and general economic growth (Lasuen, Lorca, Oria, 68, 6).

To sum up, the polarisation hypothesis formulated at the outset can be set out as follows: General economic growth is the result of successive development thrusts within sectoral-regional identifiable concentrations of economic activities, from which adjustment movements are diffused throughout the general economic system. This hypothesis has now been further specified, but has yet to be verified.

(b)   The preliminary assessment of the principle of circular causation should take account of three still open questions.

(i)   The first of these is connected with the fact that little has so far been said with explicit regard to the equalising effects of expansionary tendencies. It could thus be objected that the presentation has unilaterally emphasised the centripetal effects of spatial polarisation, so that relevant conclusions should not be drawn regarding the net results of centripetal and centrifugal forces.

This objection can easily be refuted by reference to the starting point of the presentation. For this purpose reference was made to a simple inter-regional convergency pattern, the Ohlin-Heckscher theory applied to regional connections, whose basic assumptions relate to the mobility of goods and factors. The mechanisms of this pattern explain the convergency effects, and thus the expansionary effects. Nothing more is advanced by Myrdal either.

The considerations can be set out rather in connection with diffusion effects to the effect that withdrawal effects can be induced on the basis of authority-dependency relations even where the conditions for their appearance seem to be good: improved transport conditions for goods and factors can speed up the polarisation process owing to the immobility of complementary growth determinants. In the same way a diffusion effect

21

such as the release of delivery effects at the periphery can promote the domination potential of the centre.

(ii)   The second question arises in connection with the fact that the spatial dimension of the polarisation process has not yet been delimited. The manner in which the adopted concept of spatial proximity lays down this dimension is imprecise. The difficulty can be ascribed to the fact that the concept of proximity has not the same dimension for all activities, and that from the communications point of view, the locations of competing suppliers and customers are decisive for the optimum locality for an activity. The expression in specific terms of economic distance, within which 'proximity' falls, assumes the measurement of communication costs. This is the subject of attraction analysis, which will be discussed later. At this point it is sufficient to recognise that, for purposes of regional policy, the identification of a polarisation region is cardinal for the instrumentalisation of the polarisation hypothesis. The example of the industrial growth pole is to be investigated on this point again.

At the same time, these conclusions give rise to the problem of the direct conclusion of the observation of the spatially polarised circular linkages to regional growth differences:

The centre-periphery pattern is an analytical construction which cannot be applied direct to those spatial dimensions on the basis of which regional income differences are measured. In economic history it is indeed true that the problem of income differentials was first noted in the form of a clear 'North-South' differential (South-West of France, South of Italy and North-East of Brazil); however, the simple North-South correlation cannot be applied in every national economy in which inter-regional differences in the welfare position are found to exist.

The polarisation thesis set out above accordingly makes no reference to regional welfare differences. They may be, and often are, the result of spatially polarised growth thrusts taking place. They should not be so, however, for in that case every conclusion from the observation of minor regional income differences on the small empirical relevance of polaris-ation theory would be incorrect. The importance of this viewpoint will be shown by discussion of the space concept in the polarisation theory.

In this connection, the thesis presented in this work is that under otherwise equal conditions, the more differently developed are the settlement structures of the particular sub-areas, the greater the call of the polarised growth processes for the emergence of regional income disparities. This can be explained by the medium character of the settlement structure for the growth process (Ritter 70, 163). Behind this general statement there are again considerations in connection with the limited mobility of growth determinants. In cases in which predominantly

22

positive urbanisation effects exist, they lead to the fact that bigger and — in the supply of central services — higher quality centres tend to be preferred to smaller and lower quality centres. The transport cost argument may further support this tendency.

It follows from the medium character of the settlement structure that regional development policy has always to be a settlement structure policy at the same time.

(iii) The third question relates to the assessment of the process of circular causation. In the literature this is disputed. First the dualism argument comes to the fore, followed by the role of the urbanisation process in relation to economic growth.

In his analysis of cumulative linkages, Jochimsen comes to the following conclusion: 'The linkage of external effects and rigidities leads to economic dualism and also to a check to the proper utilisation of the factors of production, so that the social product does not attain the level that might be possible in its absence . . . Immobility of the factors of production, possibilities of employing them only in limited proportions, and discriminating treatment can lead in particular to the formation of economic dualism in the form of disintegrated factor and product markets' (Jochimsen, 66, 85).

On the other hand, in view of the phenomenon of 'hyperurbanisation' the urbanisation process is seen in the development theory as a negative result of polarised growth processes.

The polarisation theory in its modern form would reject both final consequences as false, without neglecting the disfunctional effects of the dualism, or the 'social costs' of the urbanisation process. Both points of view will have to be taken up again later in the discussion of the strategy of decentralised concentration, in connection that is with the integration aim on the one hand, and the discussion of the optimum or minimum size of towns on the other.

Lloyd Rodwin (61) and Friedmann would regard Jochimsen's assessment of the circular causation process as a piece of romanticism in the field of competition. They would oppose the critique of urbanisation by reference to the need for growth as part of this process. The common basis for both arguments is obtained from the fundamental explanation of the spatial dimension of the growth process '. . . in which the principal variable is the pattern of authority-dependency relationships that characterises any organised social system' (Friedmann, 72, 84).

Kaldor, too, considers that the polarisation process is inherent in the historical course of the development process: 'I am sure that this principle of cumulative causation — which explains the unequal regional incidence of industrial development by endogenous factors resulting from the process of historical development itself rather than by exogenous differences in "resource endowment" – is an essential one for the understanding of the diverse trends of development as between different regions' (Kaldor 70, 343). Consistently with the implications considered here, this means that neo-classical bases for the clarification of regional growth processes are probably not only in need of revision but are basically of little substance.

On the basis of the considerations for the (partial) immobility of growth determinants and their circular causation effects, Jochimsen's result cannot be accepted without qualification. 'The linkage . . . leads altogether to a reduction in the appropriate utilisation of the factors of production . . .'. Rather is it to be assumed that the location with the minimum communication costs and consequently the optimum spatial allocation of activities can require polarisations in the availability of communication costs. Furthermore the authority-dependency relationships must not be regarded exclusively as disfunctional for general economic growth to a similarly limited extent. New methods of dualism-interpretation only exist on a putative basis (cf. Körner 70, 208 et seq.).

2.2   Sectoral polarisation

It can be shown that the theory of growth poles as conceived by Perroux is no specific spatial economic theory. In consequence it serves to explain thoroughly necessary but not sufficient conditions for the emergence of spatially polarised growth.

This thesis is to be established in the present section; then in Section 2.3 the conditions under which sectoral polarisations can lead to spatially polarised growth will be discussed. Finally, it will be represented in Section 2.3 that the existence of sectoral polarisations in a region is not an indispensable requirement for the emergence of regional polarisation.

1   There is in existence something approximating to a legal definition of the concept of a growth pole, but that stems from the time when the Institut de Science Economique Appliquée took the lead in the further development of polarisation theory. The definition runs: 'An industry constitutes a growth pole which, by the flow of products and of incomes that it generates, conditions the development and growth of industries technically linked with it (technical polarisation), determines the prosperity of the tertiary sector by the incomes that it generates (polarisation of incomes) and produces a growth in regional income thanks to the concentration of new activities in a given zone, in view of the prospect of

24

being able to dispose of certain factors of production (psychological and geographical polarisation) (Paelinck, 65, 12).

It is not surprising that the number of definitions has increased in proportion to the number of contributions to the theory and policy of growth poles. In Lasuen, however, the definition is put straight: 'Yet, there seems to exist general agreement among specialists about the central ideas within the concept. They are: A growth pole is a large group of industries (a), strongly related through their input-output linkages (b), around a leading industry (c), and clustered geographically (d). The leading industry itself (e), and (through its inducement (f) the whole group), innovates (g) and grows (h) at a faster pace (i) than the industries external to the pole' (Lasuen, 71, 2).

In both cases it is a question of functional definitions of the growth pole, for they already contain statements of the effects that can be expected from it. In order to identify a growth pole *a posteriori,* this is the way to proceed.

The growth pole theory requires for itself, however, that accelerated regional[4] economic growth should be explained. It may therefore be enquired why a growth pole expands more rapidly than the rest of the system. For this reason it is useful to break down the expressions used in the two definitions into structural and incidental components. Structural expressions, for example, are 'large groups of industries',[5] and 'strongly related through their input-output linkages', while incidental expressions are those marked (e) – (i) in the definition quoted from Lasuen.

To answer the question as to why a growth pole grows more rapidly than the rest of the system, the structural causes of the incidental effects claimed for the growth pole must be analysed. The identification of a growth pole must be restricted to the structural expressions, for only then can the growth pole concept be used as an analytical category which can be evaluated for forecasting purposes.

In both definitions a necessary condition for the identification of a growth pole is the diagnosis of 'important' input-output relations between industries. The attribute 'important' is used in the literature on the subject inconsistently, sometimes in a structural sense and sometimes in a phenomenological and incidental sense. In the structural meaning it is a question of heavy flows in terms of value of high input-output co-efficients. For Hirschman, on the other hand, the meaning is dependent on induction effects. '. . . in the form, for instance, of the net outturn of new industries that are called into being . . .' (Hirschman, 67, 94). An industry that is important when measured by its contribution to the national product can be called into being by reason of the additional regional supply of an input which, while unimportant for it in terms of

25

value, cannot be obtained from outside the region because of high communication costs.

Another necessary condition is the presence of important inter-industrial input-output relations. Under both definitions these represent the strategic core of the growth pole. From this is derived the concept of the *industrial growth pole.*

As stated above, both definitions imply a spatial dimension of the growth pole, but the conditions discussed so far do not suffice to substantiate this. That is to say, if communication costs between all[6] the activities connected by input-output relations are nil, then there will be no connection between sectoral and sectoral/regional polarisation; that is to say the growth pole, in so far as it can be sectorally identified in accordance with the above definitions, is not to be assigned simply to a definable spatial dimension.

The necessary conditions referred to characterise sectoral polarisations, and the addition of the requisite condition, the existence of communication costs, leads to the determination of sectoral/regional polarisations. In no case is a *specific* sub-spatial dimension of a sectoral pole established thereby. The increasingly employed concept of the spatially localised industrial growth pole does not derive sufficient basis from the mere existence of communication costs.

Sectoral poles are thus designated as a cluster of activities linked by an important input-output relationship independently of their spatial allocation connection. If the elements of a sectoral pole decline towards a spatially neighbouring settlement, this gives rise to a sectoral/regional pole.

2   In essence, the specifically sectoral polarisation argument lays down that economic growth makes for sectoral inequality. Inequality means here that the sectoral growth rates develop at varying tempos. If a 'leading sector' is designated as a sector of above-average growth (in relation to the general economic growth rate), the growth-process can be characterised as the reflection of leading sectors.

This statement is still incomplete and, as will soon be shown, quite unspecific. However, it still says no more than that general economic growth implies sectoral structural changes. To describe this structural change as a polarised process amounts to nothing more than talking about the emperor's new clothes. It can further be shown that the definition of non-uniformity is not specific, but can coincide completely with the definition of balanced growth used in the development theory since Nurkse (Nurkse, 53); when, that is, the sectoral structural change corresponds to the change in the income elasticity of demand.

26

The specific significance of the growth pole theory must therefore be assessed by what it adds to the accepted definitions of non-balanced growth and the 'leading' or 'motor' sector.

The sectoral polarisation argument has its origins in Schumpeter (Schumpeter, 12, 463 et seq.), was taken up again by Perroux (Perroux, 55), and finds its best-known formulation as growth strategy in Hirschman (Hirschman, 67).

(a)   Recourse to Schumpeter's interpretation of the economic development process permits a first definition of the concept of inequality connected with the idea of sectoral polarisation: 'The third general sentence dealing with the phenomenon of economic development − the first being that there is really a purely economic development in our sense, and the second that this development is essentially a disturbance of equilibrium − reads: Economic development is no organic unit in its entirety, but consists of part developments that complement one another but are relatively independent . . . Consequently the development of the economy takes place as it were in waves, each of the waves having a life of its own' (Schumpeter, 12, 490). The really independent element to put these part developments in motion is innovation. This leads to a disturbance of equilibrium 'without any tendency to restore this or any other position of equilibrium' (ibid. 489). In particular, the development of demand is not regarded as an independent cause of development, since it is primarily the result of the development itself (ibid. 485).

Two conclusions can be drawn: First, the definition of dynamic disequilibrium given by Schumpeter is not consistent with Nurkse's definition of balanced growth. Secondly, and this supports the general argument regarding structural change referred to above, these disequilibria stem from the supply side. The polarisation theory is therefore essentially a supply-orientated growth theory. Innovations release waves of partial developments connecting up with one another but still relatively independent in individual sectors or clusters of activities.

The 'own being' of the innovation waves can be described as a sectoral polarisation process.

(b)   Among the Schumpeter-type innovations Perroux refers in particular to the production of new goods. Development for him is thus characterised by the emergence of new industries and the decline of old ones. New activities, especially those facing a high income elasticity of demand form (sectoral) growth poles. A growth pole is first defined in principle without laying down a geographical dimension: 'all these concepts are utilisable and can be handled whether their localisation is specified *or not* [in italics in the original]' (Perroux, 60, 203).

A growth pole is a power unit (*unité motrice*) which can be simple or complex:

Power units	{	1	The undertaking
		2	Non-institutionalised groups of undertakings
		3	Institutionalised (private and semi-state) groups of undertakings

A power unit, which because of the indeterminate nature of the sector concept can here be equated to a leading sector, must satisfy three criteria. These are: a higher degree of inter-industrial linkages, a higher degree of dominance, and quantitatively significant 'sizes' (Darwent, 69, 6).

The degree of inter-industrial linkage can be defined as the sum of forward and backward linkage. Forward coupling is the relationship between sales to industries and total turnover, backward coupling is the relationship between purchases from industries and gross output value (Chenery and Watanabe, 58, 483).

Dominance of i over j occurs according to the most usual definition of the growth pole theory when the size of the real flow valued in currency units of j to i, in proportion to j's gross production value, is greater than the size of the corresponding flow from i to j in proportion to the gross production value of i (cf. Aujac, 60).

The argument regarding sizes is difficult to grasp, as different possibilities are available. For instance, size could be measured in relation (absolutely) to gross output value or (relatively) to the market share, or to a combination of both criteria.

It is still not clear how integrated, dominant or large a sector must be to deserve the description of 'power sector'. Neither is it clear what connection exists between the three criteria. Finally, there is no systematic analysis available of the substance of each individual argument for the establishment of the power character of a sector.

— The dominance definition would, if applied automatically to unilateral supply conditions, imply a dominance effect of the demander over the supplier. If, for instance, a supply monopoly prevails the definition becomes quite meaningless.

— The direct conclusion of input-output relations on potential coupling effects is ruled out at once by the openness of national economies. 'The interdependence relations are only very rough indices for potential coupling effects . . .' (Hirschman, 67, 101).

— Size and dominance are, according to the existing definitions, not generally speaking mutually independent criteria. The greater under otherwise constant conditions is i, the greater must be the dominance of i over j.

The examples suffice to endorse the criticism of the imprecise comprehensibility of the growth pole theory. The criticism of Perroux can go even further in the direction of Blaug's argumentation, in that it enquires what is really original about the Perroux version of the growth pole theory. Nevertheless the analysis should be restricted to the sectoral polarisation argument.

On this assumption it may be asked what induction mechanism Perroux observed in order to arrive at his identification criteria for power sectors. Besides the link-up with Schumpeter, the orientation towards Scitovsky's (154, 143 et seq.) external monetary effects is especially surprising (Perroux, 55, 3111 et seq.). On this point Darwent (Darwent, 69, 7) may be followed, who from a comparison of the statements of both authors concludes: 'Perroux adds little to this concept of external economies in explaining the mechanics of polarisation ... None of this, however, is either precise or rigorous. Moreover it is oversimplified.' One is wise therefore to adopt Hirschman's presentation of the development process in the matter of sectoral polarisation as a basis for the polarisation theory.

(c)   Hirschman too refers expressly to Schumpeter and Scitovsky. He defines development as a series of inequalities, which are signalised by the existence of profits. Like Schumpeter he discerns the decisive stimulus to development in the possibility of making a profit. Development is thus a succession of sequences leading away from equality (Hirschman, 67, 62). Sequences of inequalities arise from the fact that 'the expansion of industry A leads to advantages which are external to A but can be availed of by B ...' etc. (ibid. 62/63). Investments prompted by such complementary effects assume that 'the projects falling in these categories must *have recourse on balance* to external savings' (ibid. 67). Consequently a general clarification of the fact that the development process is sectorally polarised is sought.

Hirschman's analysis of the coupling effects illustrates that the problem of identification of efficient sequences, i.e. of sectoral poles, is not solved by the accentuation of higher input-output relationships. His experiment in ideas, by which he equates input-output relationships and coupling effects, obscures this fact. The observation of purely inter-industrial relationships says nothing about the probability by which forward- and backward-linked activities in the concrete case of a pole are actually established in the pole or its 'hinterland' in this way (ibid. 95). If it is already difficult to define sectoral poles plainly from the observation of input-output relationships, the identification problem can only be made more arduous if sectoral poles should be given a regional dimension. For the (hitherto unknown) probability of the emergence of a sectoral pole still says nothing about the probability of a sectoral pole being established in a particular region. This means that Perroux's contribution is material precisely in this connection. 'In brief, the net contribution of Perroux to the basic Schumpetarian argument was that he took Schumpeter's toolbox of concepts and hypotheses from its original sectoral-temporal setting and applied it to a sectoral-temporal-geographical universe' (Lasuen, 69, 139). Consequently the space concept of the growth pole theory has now to be examined with regard to its effectiveness for the identification of sectoral-regional poles.

3   Perroux starts from an abstract space concept. The abstract, topological, economic space is a geographically indeterminate interaction field of economic relationships. Three basic types of economic space are distinguished: homogeneous, polarised and planned (Perroux, 50, 89).

(a)   The emergence of a sectoral pole leads to the development of a polarised space in that, in connection with the fact that the elements of the pole must be geographically localised in some way, a sectoral pole also requires heterogeneity in the geographical space structure. Nothing has been said there so far on the localisation conditions of the elements. Consequently, a sectoral pole can be distributed over as many space points as it has elements. These space points must not in any way be clustered in any regions demarcated on the basis of geographical, historical, sociological or other criteria.

Agreement accordingly exists today on the fact that *Perroux's growth pole theory is no localisation theory* and certainly not a theory of sectoral-regional polarisation. (Paelinck, 65; Hansen, 67; Darwent, 69). Neither does it show why a sectoral pole first begins to grow at particular space points, nor on what the spatial distribution of induced growth effects depends. In the 'Note sur la notion de "pôle de croissance" ' there is to be found only a very general indication that a sectoral pole grows faster when its elements are established in spatial proximity. 'In a complex industrial pole which is geographically clustered and growing, effects are recorded of the intensification of economic activities due to proximity and to human contacts' (Perroux, 55, 317).

(b)   Boudeville has attempted to bestow on the concept of polarised space a clear geographical dimension: the polarised region. 'In short, it [the functional or polarised region, F.B.] is defined as the place of exchange of goods and services the internal intensity of which is superior at every point to their external intensity' (Boudeville, 57, 7). This definition asserts that, at least in tendency, sectoral poles can be clearly demarcated geographically. Sectoral and sectoral-regional polarisation are equated.

Because a sectoral pole is also spatially polarised, the existence of communication costs is a necessary condition. Communication costs are not systematically examined, however, in the work of the French schools. It is noteworthy that Scitovsky's externality argument, which is linked with the appearance of declining average costs, is taken over without any discussion of the mobility restrictions on external effects that are decisive for the emergence of regional polarisations. Therefore, all the polarisation arguments so far developed only apply to the establishment of sectoral polarisations.

(c)   The confusion in the discussion of growth pole theory and policy arises from the fact that Perroux and his successors have tried to apply the essentially still vague sectoral polarisation argument direct to concrete spatial dimensions.

The empirical studies of the French School have dealt with particular regions, especially more concentrated areas.[7] Their object was thus limited in each case by the tacit assumption that a pole must be regionally identifiable. The fact that sectoral poles were to be found within the selected regions is no cause for surprise, but in view of the manifold demarcation possibilities for sectors this proves nothing. The studies are consequently essentially descriptive and phenomenological-systematic in character. In the strict sense they are also unsuitable for testing the sectoral polarisation argument, for they reduce it unduly to the input-output basis (Hansen, 67, 715). In particular, the connection between urban development and economic growth, and consequently the effects of urbanisation, have not been examined (Lasuen, 69, 141). Since it was specifically due to the presumed effects of general urbanisation that proof of the existence of sectoral polarisations in the regions examined was probably not possible, it is interesting to consider the assessment of the methods of operation of the sectoral pole in the Department of the Basses Pyrenées, where no account has to be taken of the emergence of severe urbanisation effects.

In the Department of the Basses Pyrenées the occurrence of a sectoral-regional pole was expected following the discovery of a gas field and in connection with the Lacq exploitation project. Before the discovery of the gas field the Department was a typical peripheral region, of which little has changed. From this it was concluded that the Lacq project had failed as a growth pole because the expected induction effects on the growth of the Department or of the South West Region of France had not materialised. Growth pole was again identified in this case with sectoral-regional polarisation. 'Yet this discussion is almost entirely misconceived. There is nothing in the original growth pole notion to suggest that the exploitation of gas in Lacq should attract growth *at that location;* this notion claims only that the gas field will induce growth in the economy (without reference to geographic space) ... Growth has undoubtedly

31

taken place — but not in S.W. France' (Darwent, 69, 8).

Like the problem of southern Italy and the failure of the growth pole policy in problem areas of traditional industrialisation such as the Ruhr, Lothringen, Asturias in Spain etc., the Lacq project proved to be *the Cannae of the French school.* The school failed from the fact that it failed to analyse, at least sufficiently, the conditions of the identification of a sectoral-regional pole — the minimisation of communication costs — that is required for the regional policy instrumentalisation of the growth pole concept.

2.3   Sectoral-regional polarisation: the attraction problem

The space-differentiating significance of communication costs has been argued above. The object of the attraction analysis is to measure communication costs. The attraction theory sets out in substance to satsify the need to clarify both sectoral-regional and also purely regional polarisations. Attraction models developed so far (van Wickeren, 71) confine themselves to regional allocation connections arranged through input-output relationships, that is to the clarification of the emergence of sectoral-regional poles.

The reasons put forward to account for the occurrence of communication costs, and in particular for the circumstance that these costs are not settled partially by market process, have so far meant that communication costs have not been directly assessable. An indirect method of assessment consists in interpreting the significantly frequent occurrence of the neighbouring establishment of activities connected by input-output relationships as an indicator for the existence and intensity of the effectiveness of communication costs (Klaassen, 67, 116 et seq.).

1   A preparatory step for this consists in examining the question as to whether any connection can be established empirically between input-output relationships and spatially neighbouring establishment. Under the rules of empirical science this requires a test against the hypothesis that no such connection exists.

The works of Richter (69, 19 et seq. and 70, 37 et seq.) and of Streit (69, 177 et seq.) provide a first answer. Both these authors have used regression analysis to determine whether sectors connected by input-output relationships are more inclined to geographically neighbouring establishment than are sectors which are not so connected. This is confirmed by Richter for United States data and by Streit for the Federal Republic of Germany. On the other hand, Streit's investigations for

France have produced no significantly positive results. They conclude that connected sectors tend to settle in the same neighbourhood more than unconnected ones (Richter, 69, 24), and that in part at least the establishment of industries in the same neighbourhood can be explained by coupling effects (Streit, 69, 182 et seq.).

Both authors are agreed that for certain industries at least, more intensive input-output relationships lead more readily to establishment in spatial proximity than do less intensive ones. This result also supports one of the basic hypotheses of the attraction theory, namely: '. . . the larger the money flow from one industry to another, the more intensely these industries will be connected with each other and *thus* the stronger the tendency for the two to be located in close proximity' (Klaassen and van Wickeren, 69, 249).

For Spain, Angelet Cladellas and Clusa Oriach have employed a similar process (72, 474 et seq.). They find significantly positive correlation coefficients for only a few sector pairs: for the energy sector and the building industry, for raw materials and the metal-processing industry, for the paper industry, printing and the textile industry.

The regression analysis processes of the authors quoted are not of far-reaching consequence when it is realised that the results obtained – especially in the Spanish case – may reflect a sub-optimum industrial location structure. Otherwise it would also be less correct, as was postulated at the outset of the present enquiry, to refer to the failure of the market as a dynamic spatial allocation mechanism. For Spain, however, one of the principal results of the study by Cladellas and Oriach is a strong indication of the sub-optimum state of the establishment structure. The authors find a relatively high degree of industrial diversification in Spanish towns, irrespective of their size (ibid. 487). This finding supports the thesis of too little inter-regional integration and of 'industrial small-holdings'.

The process stands to be further refined, if only because one cannot rest content with establishing the mere existence of communication costs, but must seek to assess them as a means of weighing the attraction power of alternative locations against one another. Finally, it is not enough to investigate the attraction for individual sector pairs in each case; rather is it necessary to judge the attraction connection of alternative combinations of sector complexes as a whole.

2 So far the attraction theory has also been unable to define in concrete terms how an optimum industrial establishment structure should look. Comparative international studies should provide criteria, if it may be assumed that because of its comparatively higher inter-regional degree of

integration, the spatial allocation connection of the sectors in highly industrialised national economies is less distorted by market inadequacies than in semi-industrialised countries. Such studies are under preparation in the Netherlands Economic Institute.

The attraction patterns produced to date are nevertheless suited to meeting the further objections to the processes so far discussed, since they aim at the quantification of the attraction coefficients for sector pairs and the preparation of attraction matrixes (van Wickeren, 71, 88 et seq.), also their utilisation for the whole of the sectors in a particular region. How important this is can be demonstrated by an example. Let us assume that industry A is inclined to establish itself in the vicinity of industry B, but that industries C, D and F are also attractive to it. It is also assumed that in regions j and k, sectors B, C, D and F are established to varying extents (measured by the level of gross output value for homogeneous output in each case). How can we reach a decision on a location for A without knowing the differential attractive intensity of both regions in relation to industry A?

Attraction analyses so far conducted have produced positive results. The first comprehensive investigation for thirty sectors has been conducted in the eleven Dutch provinces (Klaassen and van Wickeren, 69). In Spain, too, a start has already been made with an attraction analysis for Asturias (van Wickeren, 72). Finally, an attempt has been made to develop a dynamic attraction pattern for Holland, for which variations in the attraction coefficients were to be explained in time (van Wickeren and Smit, 71, 89 et seq.). The attempt failed, however, because employment figures had to be used in the pattern instead of gross output values. This process, which is adapted to work with static patterns, is ruled out when different sectoral growth rates are assumed for labour productivity.

3   It seems worth while to turn the experience gained with attraction analysis to use in Spanish planning, and thereby to arrive at a refinement of the existing attraction patterns. Thus in 1972 Klaassen, Paelinck, van Wickeren and the present author submitted to the Planning Commission a proposal for an attraction analysis for the whole of Spain. An opportunity was provided by the final considerations regarding the Asturian attraction analysis. From this it transpired that on the basis of the existing industrial structure, it would be possible to draw up a list of sectors which could be used for new establishments or expansion in Asturias. The list was to serve the purpose of helping to establish sectoral promotion priorities for the new pole in the area. In drawing up the list two criteria were observed, namely regional import substitution ('filling in') and attraction through available activities in the region (existence of communication costs on the

basis of input-output relationships).

Objections to this procedure for the preparation of the lists were raised in the Planning Commission, on the grounds that the results of an attraction analysis relating to a particular region certainly showed that particular activities are attracted, but not whether the attractive pull is strong enough to stand up to competing regions. Consequently the list only indicates which sectors might establish themselves for preference in Asturias, but not whether the general economic spatial allocation is improved thereby. This objection is basically correct, but the extent of its relevance would have to be clarified by an attraction analysis taking in all the regions.

The attraction analysis for Asturias also had a static character. This means that the activity structure of the region existing at a particular time (represented by the regional input-output tables, cf. for Asturias Pinera Alvarez, 72, 537 et seq.) must be taken as a starting point, and only the additional activities directly attracted by the given production volume are considered. Neither the development of the existing activities and of those to be attracted, nor the consequences for the attraction of others, are investigated. It was therefore proposed, within the framework of the entire Spanish investigation, to use dynamic pattern versions also, especially as statistical data problems such as had arisen in the case of the investigation by van Wickeren and Smit seemed capable of solution in the Spanish case.

4   The attraction theory has a wider claim than the attraction models (cf. the author's work on this, 72, 409) discussed here so far, more especially as the claim of the attraction theory — explanation of communication costs — can only be satisfied in the patterns presented hitherto to the extent that the attraction exerted is explained by input-output relationships. The reduction of the clarification claim of the patterns becomes clear when the following definition of communication costs (cf. Part I) is considered: the existence of communication costs means that the production and/or utility functions of an economic subject i in a region j is influenced by whether the economic subjects standing in relationship with it are active in spatial proximity, independently of whether or not the relationship is arranged by the market mechanism.

For the question raised in this section — the identification of sectoral-regional poles — the explanation basis of the attraction patterns considered so far is of course sufficient.

2.4   Regional polarisation, not necessarily sectoral as well

Once the defects of the concept of industrial growth poles had been made clear, the discussion of the regional-political significance of the polarisation theory was revived: in the concept of growth centres the unilateral emphasis on industrial relations as the motive power of regional polarisations was dropped, while other polarisation factors whose effects are closely linked with those of the settlement structure of the national economy moved into the foreground, for example the so-called general effects of urbanisation, and the differential effects resulting from indivisibility in the production of goods with simultaneous partial immobility of supply and/or demand, as set out in central place theory.

The theory of central locations shows that from the existence and significance of central goods and services a hierarchical and accordingly polarised structure of settlements can be established in the district (Berry and Garrison, 70, 121). Further general urbanisation advantages — concerning for example the diffusion of innovations, of housing and leisure values etc. — have the effect of reducing communication costs and so of strengthening agglomerations. On the other hand, the disadvantages of urbanisation produced by an accretion of new activities and inhabitants (congestion) are ineffective as location decisive factors in these respects, unless and until some compulsions exist to internalise them.

Thus regional polarisations also arise independently of the existence of complementarities of the input-output type. Regarding the two differing declarations of a basis for spatial polarisations Lasuen asserts: 'In central place theory, the geographical complementarities which create the geographical cluster, select the sectoral cluster and its organising principles. In growth pole theory, the sectoral complementarities which determine the sectoral cluster, select the geographical clusters and their organising principles' (Lasuen, 71, 9).

Klaassen (70, 125) has represented how the polarisation processes described in the two declarations serve to reinforce one another.

All the polarisation concepts, down to the one concerning industrial growth poles, provide for a connection between spatially polarised growth and the urbanisation process. This applies both with regard to the minimum requirements of a corresponding potential of the localisation selected for a pole (Klaassen, 70, 132 et seq.), and with reference to the role of the town in the acceleration of innovation processes (Friedmann, 72, 90). In the growth pole strategy of the traditional type the element of town development policy is incorporated, but not the role ascribed to it. A decisive urbanisation policy is held to be necessary on the other hand in connection with the reinterpretation of the Schumpeter-Perroux develop-

36

ment theory by authors like Darwent (69), Hansen (71), Hermansen (70), Klaassen (70), Lasuen (71) and in particular Friedmann (70) and Rodwin (61).

1   The pros and cons of a decisive urbanisation policy are seen in particular in connection with two complexes of questions. One concerns the discussion of the optimum or minimum size of the town, and the other the role of urbanisation policy in the development of the social system and so in the social pre-requisites for economic growth.

(a)   The idea of an optimum size of town is regularly based on the hypothesis of a U-shaped course for the social marginal costs of agglomeration. Various attempts have been made to test this hypothesis.

In the event (cf. for example Stanford Research Institute, 68 and Neutze, 65) empirical evidence has so far been adduced only for the descending and not for the ascending arm of the U-curve. Although the thesis of hyper-urbanisation cannot be regarded as falsified thereby, it seems appropriate to base polarisation policy less on the immeasurable concept of an optimum size of town than on the concept of a minimum size of town.

(b)   By the supporters of a decisive urbanisation strategy three particular points of view are presented in justification of the minimum criterion. These concern the connection between the size of towns on the one hand and function, diversification and innovation potential on the other hand.

(i)   A minimum town size is necessary if the town is to rank as 'full grown' (Colin Clark) for the purposes of its urban functions. Apart from the possibility of a horizontal specialisation of centres of equal status and the differentiation of urban functions connected therewith, it can be assumed *a priori* that the particular status conferred by the central functions of a town will first expand rapidly with the increasing size of the town, but thereafter at a steadily declining rate. According to this a medium-sized town can be described in essence as fully developed for the purposes of its central functions (Klaassen, 70, 137 et seq.). In 'The Economic Functions of a City in Relation to its Size' (1945) Colin Clark puts the size of such a medium-sized city at 200,000 inhabitants.

(ii)   A minimum city size is also necessary for the leading town in a polarisation region, since the possibility of a diversification of the industrial production structure connected therewith increases the attraction of the town, and so of the region, to dynamic national and international sectors (on these ideas see Mennes, Tinbergen and Waardenburg, 69). The success of the polarisation policy depends essentially on the success achieved in establishing these leading sectors from a general economic point of view (Lasuen, 71, 20). A work carried out by the Netherlands Economic Institute (1961), quoted by Klaassen (70, 139), laid down for the Federal Republic of Germany in this connection that cities of over 275,000 inhabitants not only showed higher growth rates in their contributions to the national product but that the rates hardly differed at all between them. With regard to the minimum diversification rate to be achieved by a town, Klaassen conjectures that a size of under 500,000 inhabitants should suffice. In his study Clark put the size at which a city could be regarded as 'full grown' in relation also to its production structure at 500,000 inhabitants.[8]

(iii) A minimum city size seems necessary in the third place because the city, in its capacity as a field for the consolidation of social interaction (Friedmann, 72), acts as a catalyst for the development and diffusion of innovations. Hägerstrand (1953), and Friedmann and Pedersen (1969) point out that innovations appear first in the big centres and are then diffused throughout the hierarchy of the settlement system. The following quotation from Pedersen sums up the results of his investigations in Chile under this head: 'As the country develops the transportation and communication network improves. This improvement in communication in general will increase the speed of information diffusion, but it will tend to benefit the largest towns most, and the information diffusion process will therefore change from being a spatial process to the small towns' (Pedersen, 69, quoted by Hermansen, 70, 79).

(c) According to Friedmann, the identification of potential development regions can not only be directed at the settlement structure but must include the social prerequisites for economic growth in the regions as a criterion. Whether a potential polarisation region in this sense also deserves the qualification of a ('social') development pole depends according to Friedmann on two factors, the so-called objective conditions for and the subjective attitudes to social change. To the first belong, for example, vertical mobility and the level of education, the existence of a potential management class and so on.

A social development pole can be seen as the complement or the first stage of an economic development pole. Taking this category into account in the polarisation strategy means that the urbanisation concept is used in a double sense, namely in the sense of the geographical concentration of the population and the secondary and tertiary activities in settlement units of different size and form ('Urbanisation I'), and in the sense of the geographical diffusion of urban values, attitudes, organisation forms and institutions ('Urbanisation II') (Friedmann, 70, 3).

The linking of polarisation and urbanisation policy seems mandatory.

38

As modern economic growth cannot be regarded as distinct from the urbanisation process, an active regional policy in another form is not possible. 'If national policy is unable to roll back urbanisation during periods of active industrialisation, the only alternative left is to direct this process into channels which will promote national development' (Friedmann, 70, 62).

2   In this connection the question which must be looked into is that of the rôle the medium-sized towns can play within the scope of a polarisation-oriented regional policy. For on the one hand the concept of a minimum-sized town seems to be a special requirement for the establishment of medium centres, and on the other hand such centres often form the peaks in the hierarchy of the settlement structure of peripheral regions.

The discussion of the optimum size of towns was obviously stamped with the idea that the optimum was to be found where the marginal disadvantages of agglomeration just balanced the marginal advantages. For an individual town this calculation is valid, and the same applies to a given more or less fixed number of towns in the area, though not necessarily to all the towns in the collective area as a whole. Here the strategy which attempts to maximise the difference between the advantages and disadvantages of urbanisation as a general economic average, is likely to be more efficient. Of course additional agglomeration in larger centres may still yield net advantages, but these could be even greater from similar expansion in medium centres. 'The case for the intermediate-sized city is based on considerable evidence that it has most of the external economies of a big city but that it has not yet become a generator of significant external diseconomies' (Hansen, 71a, 84).

From this point of view, the concept of a minimum-sized city is not only an auxiliary arrangement but it acquires independent significance in the field of growth-orientated regional policy. The development tendencies observable at present go in another direction, however. Thus in the development countries in particular it can be seen that the tendency towards accelerated urbanisation is leading to a decidedly sharp growth in the metropolitan zones, while the intermediate cities are losing in importance. This is primarily due to the fact that the expansion of the infrastructure in these cities is relatively slow, so that with the increasing stagnation many of them are becoming unattractive even in the eyes of former residents (Barbancho, 68, 17). Secondly, migration movements from the peripheries into the centres not only take place for this reason to the avoidance of the intermediate cities, but also because: (a) in the larger cities the chance of finding employment is regarded as greater; and (b) in the calculations of the individual immigrants, account is taken of the disadvantages of agglomeration which they see for themselves, but not of those which they cause to other city dwellers (Ritter, 72, 106).

The policy often observed of 'worst first', by which excessive increases in the metropolitan population prompt the public authorities to remove the most extreme examples of decay in the cities first, has the unintended consequence of giving relative preference to the metropolitan zones within the framework of infrastructure policy and tends thereby to increase the trend rather than to re-direct it (Hansen, 71a, 85).

If we just assume that it so happens that in a particular size of city the disadvantages of agglomeration increase more rapdily than the advantages it confers, the strategy of the 'worst first' takes up a defensive position with its back to the wall. It is also understandable, therefore, if despite prior assistance for metropolitan zones in certain countries a 'silting up' is to be discerned even in the big cities (Ritter, 72, 57). The end result can be a situation in which: (a) the intermediate-sized cities by structure and function will become less attractive for lack of public assistance, while (b) the big cities despite massive assistance are still unable to meet the requirements of an abnormally high growth in the population.

The policy of providing public assistance for growth centres thus represents an improvement in the general economic settlement structure in accordance with the object of the maximisation of efficiency in the national economy. The development pole concept recast in this form can consequently be adopted as an instrument of general economic growth policy. Its adoption in this form corresponds to the notion, for example, of the Spanish regional planners whereby the region is considered as a field of operations (operative unit) for the global development policy.

At the same time the concept of the growth centre holds promise of a certain harmonisation of the general economic efficiency target with the traditional regional policy aim of inter-regional income equalisation. Of course it requires the (decentral) concentration of scarce resources and so cannot be applied by renouncing inter-regional discrimination. An abnormal proliferation of assistance areas is known from experience to put the success of the entire programme at risk. This is corroborated also for the Spanish growth pole and development centre policy.

2.5 Two approaches to a general theory of spatially polarised economic growth

In the author's opinion, Friedmann's and Lasuen's attempts to generalise the theory of spatially polarised economic growth are the most important contributions to the future discussion. A feature common to both is that in their explanation of the growth process they break away from the exclusive consideration of the spatial incidence of sectoral polarisations. They differ in the emphasis they place on various further determinants of spatial polarisation. In this differentiation there is basically no contradiction (Lasuen, 71, 22). Their presentation enables it to be shown that the problem of identification of development poles is presented in essentially different terms from the growth pole concept which has been shown to be too narrow.

1   Friedmann's approach, which is briefly summarised here, is based on a domination theory (cf. below Friedmann, 70 and 72). Spatial polarisation is explained as the result of authority-dependency relations. Authority is defined as legitimate power. The possession of legitimate power denotes the possibility of exercising influence on the basis of autonomous decisions in a particular social sector. This sector can be defined as a spatial system consisting of a centre and the periphery surrounding it. The centre is the place of maximum interaction potential; the periphery is governed by the dependency relationship with the centre. The centre-periphery relationship is further internally structured hierarchically by the existence of intermediate centres.

The centre exercises its authority on the basis of successive innovations which permanently assure its comparative advantage in relation to the periphery. In detail, each advantage achieved is reduced according to the adoption of the innovation by the periphery, yet the centre can retain its overall position since it is there that a self-generating process of innovations takes place. The requirement for this is that the centre should hold its position as the place of maximum interaction potential.

A spatial system is essentially a social system, the integration of which is achieved by the authority-dependency relationships. It operates by means of institutions being introduced by the centre at the periphery. These are controllled by the centre itself. From the viewpoint of the periphery it can simply be a question of innovations, for innovations do not need to be necessarily new organisation forms of a technical, economic, social and political type; all that is required for an organisation form to qualify as an innovation is that it should not have been known or used before in the social sub-system into which it is introduced.

The self-generating character of the central innovation process is rooted in detail in the polarisation mechanisms already set out in the considerations of the present enquiry: (a) in the domination effect in the specific sense of the deprivation effects; (b) in the information effect in connection with city size and settlement structure; (c) in the 'psychological' effect, the consequence of which is the permanent maintenance of a favourable innovation climate in the centre on the basis of positive expectations and the disregard of risks; (d) in the modernisation effect by which, in the centre itself and through the diffusion channels in the peripheral background, permanent changes are produced in the valuations, attitudes and institutions; (e) in the effect of the expansion of the regional input-output matrix ('matrix multiplier') through which the innovations continue in connected activities and (f) in the so-called production effects which can be achieved after the introduction of an innovation in the form of temporary monopoly returns, mass production advantages and external effects of agglomeration.

Friedmann's attempt to arrange a precise assessment is not possible at this point.

The following conclusions seem practical possibilities: [9]

—   The 'general theory of polarised development' is an attempt to establish the polarisation and spatial growth theories on a clearly defined basis. Friedmann's considerations could also be suitable, like Schumpeter's theory of economic development, for providing a general impulse for the development theory; and for that matter not only with regard to the regional economic limitation of the general economic growth process.

—   Friedmann's general theory — as discussed in his categories — is not an innovation in the sense that it contains anything new in itself. For Friedmann is right in the tradition of Schumpeter and Perroux and — not least — of a sociological line of thought as presented by Dahrendorf (Dahrendorf, 57). These authors, and especially Dahrendorf, are also given corresponding prominence by Friedmann. Thus basically he does no more than adopt Perroux's version of Schumpeter's development argument in the space-time dimension.

2   Lasuen's contribution to the problem of identification of development poles, and so to overcoming the narrow growth pole concept, runs in another direction (Lasuen, 69 and 71). Basically he too is concerned to relate the polarisation theory back to the general concept of Schumpeter and Perroux. Unlike Friedmann, however, he tries to base a generalisation of the development theory not so much on *one* basic concept (such as Friedmann's domination theory concept) as on a combination of various aspects of the regional growth theory.

For him two observations are important. The first relates to the fact that regional agglomerations need not necessarily be based on sectoral agglomerations. This is founded on the accepted consideration that the appearance of localisation savings in connection with input-output

42

relationships is only an important element of the polarisation factors. (Lasuen, 71, 11 et seq.). The second observation concerns what is, in Lasuen's view, the declining importance of input-output relationships for spatial polarisations. As demonstrated above, the declining importance of transport costs should not be used as an argument for this, for these may be more than offset by the increasing importance of other communication costs in connection with input-output relationships. Lasuen's judgement is based rather on the observation of the changed organisation structure of the modern leading undertakings as compared with those to which Perroux referred.

For Perroux and again for Paelinck (Paelinck, 65, 44), the aim of a fully integrated polarisation region was envisaged for the structure of the Ruhr district. Lasuen asserts on the other hand that the form of firm organisation (Krupp type) underlying the Ruhr structure represents the prototype of the leading industry of the past, and that the modern leading industries have another form of firm organisation (Litton type). His conclusion that through the development towards 'multi-product/multi-plant/multi-city-firms', general economic growth is less spatially polarised at present than in the past (Lasuen, 69), is not conclusive on the other hand, and is furthermore not repeated in the later contribution (Lasuen, 71). In the latter, the conclusion drawn from this observation is not that the modern growth process is less polarised but rather that today there are other polarisation factors having decisive significance.

Lasuen seeks to consider these factors in that he bases his generalis-ation of the development pole theory on a comprehensive view of relevant theorems regarding the theories of location, geographical organisation, urban development and regional growth in so far as it concerns the inter-regional connection. He attaches particular importance to the connection between growth pole theory and the theory of central locations. The necessity for and the possibility of this connection have already been adequately commented upon.

Also of special importance to Lasuen is the connection with the inter-regional growth theory. Friedmann has said little on this point, his domination theory concept being unsuited to explaining growth impulses transmitted horizontally between centre-periphery systems. Friedmann does not cover the problem raised thereby, but points expressly to the relative statements by Siebert (Siebert, 67). Lasuen desires to establish the connection by the structural analytical description of regional growth or inter-regional growth differences, and refers specifically in this connection to Perloff, Dunn, Lampard and Muth (1960).

Lasuen is to agree that growth and development poles can be identified not only in connection with the isolated consideration of *one* region. The following quotation of his is valid in every respect: 'The propelling effect on the regions from their different national activities depends, as stated, on the income elasticity of these activities on their previous levels of activity in each region, and their ability to capture a larger share of national demand' (Lasuen, 71, 20). The decisive problem concerning the identification of development poles is only correctly set out here, however, not provided with a solution. The 'ability to capture' can also be rendered as 'attraction'.

It seems that Lasuen has added nothing to the question of sectoral-regional polarisation apart from the argument about the organisation structure of the undertakings. His contribution does not consist therefore in the obviously important allocation to the structure analytical growth theory, but in the emphasis he puts on regional polarisation not based on sectoral polarisation. His most important arguments thus concern the connection between polarised development, city size and urban structure, while the structural analytical argument in its formulation so far contains no new polarisation argument.

The strategy connected with the structural analytical argument of assisting leading industries rather than structurally weak sectors in backward regions, is familiar to every regional planner. The difficulty of knowing how, the probability of a higher regional incidence and the requirement of general economic consistency for such allocation decisions are the real theme of the theory of sectoral-regional poles.

Altogether it can be stated that Friedmann and Lasuen have clarified the thesis of the importance of the urban settlement structure for the emergence of regional polarisations. It is for this reason that they have been included here.

2.6 Résumé

The reader will not have overlooked the fact that the discussions have been very general, and are not yet adapted to the development of concrete regional policy programmes. For this purpose, further criteria will have to be established, for which reason it is necessary to make the polarisation argument plausible and to differentiate between its various steps. It should also be clear that the above arguments relate very specifically to the economic policy discussion on growth or efficiency-orientated regional policy on the one hand, and stability or distribution-orientated regional policy on the other. Finally, the important critical arguments on growth pole theory and policy are related to the old concept of industrial growth poles, which has been understood — partly erroneously — as a practical application of Perroux's doctrine and the 'French school' that followed in his footsteps.

The investigation example dealt with in the second and third part of the work, the seven Spanish poles of industrial development, is adapted to giving a vivid description of the possibilities and limitations of traditional polarisation policy within the framework of regional policy. The following theses combine important points of view which are relevant to the assessment of the empirical findings to be given. When reference is made to growth poles later in this sector, it is this traditional concept that is intended.

1   The statements of the growth pole theory apply altogether for the establishment of sectoral polarisation. The corresponding space dimension is that of abstract space. Sectoral polarisation is a necessary condition for accelerated general economic growth. Growth pole policy can be regarded for this purpose as an instrument for the maximisation of the general economic growth rate.

The identification of sectoral poles – motor activities, more efficient investment sequences – has not yet been satisfactorily solved.

2   In the absence of communication costs the elements of sectoral poles can be distributed equitably over space. Communication costs between pole elements have the tendential effect that the most efficient location of any elements lies in spatial proximity to some (several) other element(s). The geographical-spatial polarisation effect arises from the fact that the determinants of communication costs are circularly interlinked.

A sectoral pole can therefore yield a higher contribution to the national product when its elements are wholly or partly established in proximity than when they are dispersed.

The proximity concept has yet to be put into concrete terms.

3   Regional polarisations can thus be the result of sectoral polarisations. There are also regional polarisations in connection with the emergence of communication costs arising from input-output relationships, which are not determined by sectoral polarisations. This is attributable to general urbanisation effects. These can have the effect that the location of any activity, independently of the location of the activities connected with it by inter-industrial relations in the urban environment, is optimal in terms of communication costs. The decisive factor is thus the structure of the communication costs.

The argument runs that the accentuation of industrial growth poles in the growth pole theory is one-sided.

As communication costs cannot be measured direct, it is difficult to quantify their structure.

4 General urbanisation effects also influence the communication cost structure of sectoral-regional poles. There are no grounds for assuming that the argument about general urbanisation effects only applies to regional and not also to sectoral poles.

From this it follows that the settlement structure is an important determinant for the localisation of sectoral poles. The settlement structure influences both the inter-regional distribution of regionally polarising sectoral poles and also the intra-regional allocation connection (main and subsidiary poles) of such sectoral poles.

The settlement structure will be defined not only by the size distribution of the centres but also by their function.

5 The decisive thesis of the growth pole theory for the establishment of the possible coincidence of sectoral and regional polarisation should run: Innovations normally appear first in urban environments and also become rapidly established there. The urban environment is marked by a special concentration of inter-action relationships. In this way it also fulfils the qualification of the abstract space that is of cardinal importance to sectoral polarisation. Sectoral poles arise first in the urban environment and are thus often essential at the outset for sectoral-regional poles.

The concept of the urban environment is widened in its scope by the duality of the concept of urbanisation. Urbanisation means both urban development in the geographical sense and the extension of urban standards, value orientation, and attitudes.

The thesis is especially important, is disputed and is hardly formulated in operational terms. Its presentation in this form suffices, however, to indicate the decisive converse of the points of view. The points considered so far have been so shaped that first of all sectoral poles were identified and thereafter their geographical and spatial dimensions were discussed. Here it is said that the existence of spatial agglomerations is the prerequisite for the production of a maximum of efficient investment sequences (sectoral poles). Regional poles are consequently necessary for rapid general economic growth.

6 The fact that sectoral poles in a concrete situation are localised without being regionally polarised in no way refutes the fact that they have come into being spatially polarised. The further developed is a given sectoral pole, the more standardised do particular production processes become. Under otherwise equal conditions, the lower the communication

costs connected with these processes, the more easily can they be established in peripheral locations.

The 'dialectic' of the polarisation process is consequently also to be found in the fact that sectoral poles, although they have lost nothing of their own dynamic, polarise regionally less strongly in the course of their development as a whole.

7   The widening tendency that arises on the basis of (6) above can be described as a spread effect in the Hirschman sense. If it is limited to the already traditional elements of sectoral poles, the innovation effect on the region of the new localisation is called in question.

8   Provided its existing operational weaknesses can be overlooked, the regional polarisation argument can be used for the purposes of a growth pole policy. A need for this arises in the field of market economic development when
—   by reason of competitive distortions which are not inherent in the nature of the polarisation process the development of its regional growth potential ceases, although yet in the short run the growth in the national product obtainable thereby is higher than that which might otherwise have been achieved in the key regions with the help of the investment funds available for inter-regional transfer;
—   the market-controlled establishment of new industries in the region to be selected for the new growth pole will only go ahead in consideration of the portion of the growth in the national profit, that can be privately appropriated so that investments will not achieve the level arising from estimates of social values;
—   private and social rates for discounting expected expenditure and income flows are not identical;
—   the private economic risk arising from uncertainty regarding investment behaviour in the case of complementary activities can be reduced by the co-ordination of investment plans.

This catalogue will suffice to explain the planning indication. It does not offer a comprehensive system.

9   Growth pole theory is a theory of unbalanced sectoral and regional growth. Growth pole policy must not necessarily be regarded for this reason as a strategy of unbalanced growth. It could be described as even if by reason of the considerations set out in (8) it promotes the creation of balanced centres. If a given centre/periphery system in a national economy is sub-optimal, the situation can be improved if particular peripheries take over central functions. This could exert a levelling effect

on the regional distribution of income, and in relation to this effect the strategy could be described as balanced.

Growth pole policy can be described as a strategy of unbalanced growth to the extent that it operates on an inter-regionally selective basis in the selection of pole regions as potential central regions. It can also be regarded as such a strategy in so far as it avails itself of the principle of investment sequences not making for balance as a means of developing balanced centres.

The argument in support of the criterion of the general economic acceleration of growth and aimed at the development of countervailing centres, and the principle for the stimulation of inequalities employed for the same purpose are associated in the discussion of regional policy in the expression 'decentral concentration'.

10   The growth pole theory in the form in which it is discussed in this section is too imprecise to support convincing operational conclusions for growth pole policy. As has been shown, the regional polarisation argument is not yet sufficiently operationally based. Even if the attempts at an explanation are only intended to apply to sectoral polarisation they must still be qualified as inadequate. The considerations regarding the relationship between the polarisation and spatial growth theories have at least shown why economic growth is or can be spatially polarised. That being so, the general economic growth theory cannot disregard the polarisation theory.

Notes

1 Defined as $\dfrac{\frac{1}{2}(X^r + M^r)}{Y^r}$, where X^r and M^r represent regional exports and imports and Y^r the region's income.

2 'If factor prices are equalised, the only possible differences between nations (or regions) in incomes *per capita* are those to be explained by differences in the amount of capital per inhabitant or by differences in labour force participation rates' (Olson, 71, 35).

3 As indirect input it is the infrastructure that is mainly being considered. This is on the assumption that in so far as an unpaid factor exists it is financed as infrastructure in the form of a non-earnings related tax.

4 Both definitions refer explicitly to a regional dimension: 'and produces a growth in regional income'; and 'clustered geographically.'

5 In the emphasis on a 'large group of industries' there is also a difference compared with the first definition in the choice of words: 'an industry' is not necessarily identifiable with an individual undertaking, or the term for 'firm' would have been selected in the French writings on growth poles.

6 One point to be considered is that even if no communication costs were to arise between two such linked activities, they could still be established in spatial proximity because they are dependent on a common input of restricted mobility, or because not-common inputs of restricted mobility are established in proximity to one another.

7 Thus for example Aydalot (65) has done work on the Department of the Basses Pyrenées, Bauchet (55) on Lothringen, Boudeville (57) on Minas Gerais, Davin, Degeer and Paelinck (59) on Liège, Derwa (57) on Liège, Labasse and Laferrere (60) on Lyons, and Rosenfeld (1964) on Turin. An exception deserving of special mention is Paelinck's study on Venezuela (unpublished, no date). The same author differentiates the regional dimension of a sectoral pole more than others, and also distinguishes between the localisation of a pole *in* the region and its incidence *on* the region (Paelinck, 65, 14).

8 Such figures are rough guidelines, however. Increasing interest is being shown today in figures of 250,000 inhabitants when minimum 'efficient' city sizes are under discussion (cf. Hansen, 71a, 81).

9 Cf. also Hansen, 71a, 28.

PART II

Regional Development Policy in Spain since 1964

1 Development Tendencies - Objectives of Regional Policy

A theoretical economic analysis of Spanish regional policy since the commencement of the First Development Plan in 1964 should cover the policy's objectives, media and means, but it is not possible to undertake a systematic analysis of the media here. Commencing with an analysis of the objects, two questions must be put at the outset:
— to which diagnosis of the situation do the objects relate?
— what changes may they have undergone in the planning process?

1.1 Diagnosis

The following features and development tendencies in particular distinguish the regional economic structure of Spain: increasing regional income differences; a high degree of inter-regional mobility; the phenomenon of multiple dualism; and a considerable degree of unworkability in the old intermediate cities, plus the increasing disadvantages of agglomeration in the traditional centres.

1   In the period since the Second World War *regional income differences* measured by total and *per capita* incomes in the Spanish provinces have risen.

Gini coefficients	1955	1964	1967	1971
based on total incomes	0.4510	0.4766	0.4857	0.5068
based on *per capita* incomes	0.2490	0.2528	0.2396	0.2230

Sources: Planning Commission, Report . . . , 68, 100/1 and Estimate 71, 154/5.

This is shown in the Gini concentration totals available. Closer analysis suggests three observations. First, the disparities in total incomes are greater than in *per capita* incomes, and secondly the disparities in *per capita* incomes have been declining since 1964. This is seen as a consequence of regional policy, if the development in total incomes is disregarded. Thirdly, the developments of the total and *per capita* income coefficients have run counter to one another since 1964. This can be

53

explained by the fact that the provinces with lower incomes have sustained net emigration losses.

Roughly speaking, the connections can also be presented as follows (Planning Commission, Third Plan . . . , 72, 323): in 1955 the richest province (Guipuzcoa) had a *per capita* income 4.41 times bigger than the poorest (Granada). In 1970 the ratio between the richest (Biscay) and poorest (Almeria) was 2.77. The absolute figures for 1955 were Ptas 24,777 and 5,613, and for 1970 Ptas 85,144 and 30,674. The total income differences between the provinces are dependent on the population density per sq. km. as well as on *per capita* income and size of province. The population density per sq. km. ranged in 1970 from 508 (Barcelona) to 11 (Soria) (cf. Planning Commission, Third Plan, 72, 321).

2   Between 1960 and 1967 inter-regional mobility across the provincial frontiers ran to some 2.6 million persons. Based on the total population in 1967 this works out at about 8 per cent (Instituto Nacional de Estadistica, Migration . . . , 68, 22). Between 1951 and 1970 1.423 million inhabitants emigrated from the five provinces mainly affected by emigration, while the five provinces most important from an immigration point of view received some 2.481 million immigrants in the same period (Planning Commission, Third Plan, 72, cf. 322/3).

As was to be expected, the migration movements were selective in the sense that they produced a reduction in the age structure in the immigration areas and vice versa (cf. Planning Commission, Third Plan . . . , Regional Development, 72, 26 et seq.). Presumably the same applies to the qualification of the emigrants, and certainly there is a close connection between the motivation to regional mobility on the one hand and to vertical mobility on the other. Empirical evidence on this point is not yet available in any quantity.

3   *Regional dualism* does not mean the same thing in Spain as a simple North-South differential (de Miguel, 68, 68), nor is it to be described as a purely spatial reflection of the basic structural division into a market and a subsistence area, as established by Boeke (53), Friedmann (59) and Egner (66) in other development countries. It can be said to be manifold, since it is characterised by a geographical conglomeration of hardly inter-related centres and dispersal areas. In connection with the multiple dualism there is a differential social participation of the population in the development process (de Miguel, 68, 131) together with the so-called 'industrial small-holding', that is to say a business size structure marked by small undertakings — partly craft enterprises.[1] From an infra-structure and business-size-structure policy aimed at the reinforcement of industrial market integration positive growth effects are expected.

4   *The disparity between the size of intermediate cities on the one hand, and their structure and function on the other hand,* is brought out by Tamames and Barbancho. Tamames fears that few of the historical intermediate cities are suitable for the necessary adaptation to the modern urbanisation process (Tamames, 68, 50/1), whereas Barbancho considers the comprehensive development of the social and economic infra-structure to be imperative. He demonstrates, in conformity with the results arrived at by Ritter for other countries (Ritter, 72, 79 et seq.), that owing to the under-equipment of the intermediate cities the migration of the population goes direct from the rural evacuation areas towards the three most important gravitation centres in the country — Madrid, Catalonia and Basque Country (Barbancho, 67, 97 et seq.). He goes on to establish that from period to period more intermediate cities showed a negative migration movement. Out of the fifty provincial capitals, which are for the most part intermediate cities, some twenty showed a negative migration trend in 1960-65 (Barbancho, 68, 16/17). Tamames and Barbancho agree in their judgement that many of these cities have become unattractive to their inhabitants because of their increasing backwardness.[2]

1.2   Objects of regional policy

The list of objects set out at the beginning of this work included that of maximising general economic efficiency and inter-regional distribution on an equitable basis. In view of the scanty nature of the diagnosis this needs to be expanded and to some extent at least expressed in more concrete terms.

1   The connection between the objects of general economic efficiency on the one hand and inter-regional distribution on an equitable basis on the other, played an important part in the discussions during the preparation of the Third Plan. The first result of this discussion was the attempt to regionalise the general economic programming pattern for the Third Plan, for the purpose of determining the alternative costs of the regional policy aimed at an improvement in inter-regional distribution expressed in units of the general economic growth rate in the national product that could be achieved without this policy. This was investigated more closely in Part I, the result of this discussion being left open by the Spanish planners for the purposes of the Third Plan: 'Although the contraposition between "efficiency" and "equity" is not strictly precise, it must be borne in mind in defining the regional objectives and when giving concrete shape to and

measuring the benefits and costs of the opportunity of the said policy' (Planning Commission, Third Plan . . . , 72, 324).

In accordance with the diagnosis and the above-mentioned discussions there is also the list of objects for regional policy.

Fernández-Rodríguez (72, 439) mentions in order of their importance:
- acceleration of the general economic growth process by the optimum spatial allocation of resources,
- inter-regional distribution on an equitable basis,
- improvement of inter-regional integration,
- reduction of fortuitous regional inequality in the choice of work place,
- promotion of Spanish integration in international markets.

These objects assume varying importance in the individual plans, and the aim of integration is shown expressly in the Third Plan for the first time. The object of general economic growth is also given prime importance as an aim of regional policy in the Third Plan for the first time. Whereas general economic and regional aims were seen in a competitive relationship in the First Plan on the lines laid down by the World Bank (IBRD, 62, 431), in the Second Plan the notion of the region as a basis for action (operational unit) in general economic growth policy represented a basic new approach under the doctrine (Planning Commission, Report on Regional Development, 68, 7). This new approach in the Second Plan, however, is of little practical significance (Fernández-Rodríguez, 72, 445/6). Comparison of rating of the objects in the various plans is made difficult by the completion and new interpretation of the list of objects. For at first glance it appears that the general economic growth objects assume first place in all the plans. It is thus not clear how the role of regional policy in the presentation of the plans has changed: whereas regional policy played a subsidiary role as a palliative specifically in the First Plan and in substance in the Second Plan (Buttler, 69, 433 et seq.), and should thus correct the outcome of the general economic growth policy from the distribution point of view, it is now acknowledged to be a keystone of growth policy. This means that the space-dependency of growth policy is more strongly emphasised than hitherto.

The emphasis is closely linked with the newly added object of inter-regional integration which − in view of the fundamental importance of the integration object − will be thoroughly investigated in the next sub-section. This section will be devoted to further remarks on the last two objects in the list.

The fourth object is not an independent one: it can be dubbed an argument within the object function for the determination of the first object or be used to give practical shape to the second and third objects. A decisive factor for the role of the object is in any case the relative importance attributed to those three arguments. That this is specially brought out is due in particular to the fact that it plays an important part in the public discussion, and that Spanish politicians and planners are inclined for two different reasons to minimise the inter-regional migration movement inside the country: the planners because the unmistakable trend of the migration movements into the metropolitan centres (Barbancho, 67, 98 et seq.) aggravates the disadvantages diagnosed as arising from agglomeration in these centres; and the politicians possibly because the consequences for social policy of the development of an expanding urban proletariat are regarded as harmful to the system.[3]

The fifth object — the international integration of the Spanish economy — seems at first sight to have no direct regional political basis. The explanation of this lies in the special interest of the highly-developed regions in North-East Spain in obtaining improved access to the European market by the improvement of the communication system across the Pyrenean frontiers. So the inclusion of object number 5 in the list is a price that the central authority in Madrid must pay to maintain the interest of an economically highly-developed region in regional policy as a whole.

2   The linkages between objects one to three are assessed differently by the planners as compared with the politicians. The ideas on which the plans are based are ultimately politically motivated, therefore it is not proposed to conduct a theoretical economic discussion on the object relationships at this point (cf. for example Richardson, 69, 365 et seq.), so much as to present the corresponding concepts of the makers of regional policy. Since there are also considerable conceptual variations between them, all that can be done here is try to establish a common denominator.

The assessment of the relative importance of the objects can be described in the following observations:

(a)   In the official presentation of the policy, the object of inter-regional distribution on an equitable basis assumes a prominent place for propagandist reasons. Its prominence assists the spread of understanding for regional policy and the development plan alike. On the other hand, the fact that no quantification of the object results shows that concrete assurances are avoided as far as possible. The dilemma that the politicians face lies in the fact that they are obliged to canvass the widest possible understanding, while unable to provide more than minimal interest from which this understanding might stem. Consequently it is assumed that the resources available to the regional politicians are limited, and that owing to polarisation theory considerations, the limited means cannot be applied without renouncing discrimination against particular regions if the concept of the maximisation of general economic efficiency is to be offset by the optimum spatial allocation of the resources.

(b)   The object of inter-regional integration is derived from the diagnosis of an unsatisfactory settlement structure in the economy, of which, as has already been indicated, three features specifically have been found to hamper development:

— the low integration level of the main consolidation centres with one another and with their hinterland, and the consequent multiple dualism,
— the disparity between the size distribution of the intermediate cities on the one hand, and their structure and function on the other hand, and
— the fragmentation of the rural settlement structure which entails a high degree of remoteness from markets, under-supplying with public goods and altogether a low level of social participation by the rural population.

(c)   The settlement structure policy aimed at the integration object sets important public requirements within the framework of the infrastructure policy. It is therefore accepted that the long-term integration policy for the maximisation of efficiency depresses the growth rate of the privately available income, at least in the short term, below the level which would otherwise have been possible. Quantitative proposals for this have yet to be worked out.

The integration object is also closely linked with the inter-regional distribution object. The distribution object is reinterpreted in this connection, however: it relates not only to the immediate reduction of the regional *per capita* or total income disparities but also to the supply of public goods — in particular infrastructure equipment — which raise the possibilities for satisfying requirements in peripheral regions with the same monetary incomes of residents and/or further the regional and social disposition to and capacity for mobility. The integration object thus embodies altogether three components: market integration within the framework of the existing settlement structure, changes in the settlement structure, and the expansion of social participation.

As social participation designates the share of both private and public means of satisfying requirements, the relative argument regarding the integration object is basically more comprehensive than the traditional inter-regional distribution object. Moreover, it leaves open the possibility of alternative strategies for different regions, according to whether the component of the raising of the possibilities of satisfying requirements in the region or that of the raising of regional and social disposition to and capacity for mobility is the more prominent. Passive reorganisation in individual peripheral areas and active reorganisation in others can be advocated at the same time provided criteria are laid down to support such discrimination in detail.

(d) Thus certain important points of view discussed by the Spanish Planning Commission are presented in connection with the integration object. The author inclines towards subordinating the distribution object in its traditional formulation to the integration object in general. On the other hand it must be admitted that in the public discussion the distribution object is still so predominant that the politicians, who cannot put forward an indicative plan on a mandatory basis but must promote the social preparedness for its acceptance, are not in a position to renounce the current placatory object formulas.

It must also be assumed, however, that the politicians will themselves fall victims to the pressures to which they have exposed themselves by the formulation and public presentation of the undifferentiated traditional distribution object. It will be shown that the political pressure for the fulfilment of the promises given leads — even in the absence of democratic control as in the present case — to the politicians' trying to achieve too much in too short a time, so that a decisive abandonment of the principle of dealing with all the provinces simultaneously in the same way does not work out. In this way an attempt at a strategy of decentralised concentration on the general economic plane would also be likely to fail at the outset.

2 The Programme of Spanish Development Poles

It has been demonstrated above that since the beginning of Spanish development planning the role of regional policy has more and more frequently been a subject for discussion. In the three preceding plans, however, the growth pole programme has been a constant, even though its relative importance in the formulation of all the regional policy measures has changed.

This change in the relative importance of the growth pole programme within the framework of regional policy can be clearly demonstrated if the passages in the planning documents regarding the poles are compared with one another.

Thus in Plan I it is stated: '. . . having regard to the budget restrictions the regional action programme ('acción regional') is concentrated in Plan I mainly on the instrument for the creation of growth poles' (First Development Plan, 63, 150). Moreover, in Article 6 of Law No. 193/1963 by which the First Plan was put into effect it is stated: 'The state's action programme for improving the standard of living of the economic zones or regions of low income per inhabitant will be achieved by promoting industrialisation, improving agriculture and modernising the services . . . and the furtherance of industrialisation will be effected by the creation of development poles, growth poles and industrial estates'.

At that time two industrial growth poles were established (at Burgos and Huelva), five development poles (La Coruña, Seville, Valladolid, Vigo and Zaragoza) and five deglomeration poles (Aranda de Duero, Alcázar de S. Juan, Guadalajara, Manzanares and Toledo). The first were established in districts which were still regarded as non-industrial, the second in districts where an existing industry could be expanded and the last were designed to reduce the excessive bunching up of population in the capital city of Madrid. In the Second and Third Plans five further development poles were established (in Córdoba, Granada, Logroño, Oviedo/Gijón/ Avilés and Villagarcia de Arosa).

In the Third Plan, the growth pole policy was of a different order; it was clearly adapted to the concept of a national urbanisation policy and brought into line with other action programme sectors. This emerges, in the first place, from the way in which the pole programme is set out in the planning document according to its place value (Planning Commission,

Third Plan . . . , 72, 327 et seq.), and in the second place in the following concise assessment of the programme itself: 'The regional action programmes in Spain have resorted to many expedients, . . . in the industrial sector the development poles, like any programme that is aimed at correcting tendencies that have been deeply embedded for decades, have come up against numerous obstacles, but on balance they have been clearly positive in effect . . . Now the policy of growth poles has reached a point approaching saturation' (Panning Commission, Third Plan . . . , 72, 337/8).

2.1 Theoretical bases of the pole programme

The pole programme is quite clearly a product of the adaptation by Spanish planners of the lessons of the French School in Perroux's wake. For this purpose an attempt has naturally been made to use the hypotheses and results already established empirically on the regional growth incidence of poles, as provided in more general form in a systematic manner by SEMA (Société d'Economie et de Mathématique appliquée) and by Paelinck (63, 32 et seq. and 65, 5 et seq.).

1 The SEMA system concentrates on analysing the income effects of a sectoral pole on the region in which it is localised. In the case of the Lacq project the elements of the sectoral pole localised in the region were easier to identify, since newly instituted and developed activities only came into question in connection with the discovery and exploitation of the gas reserves. For this it was assumed that the project represented the core of a sectoral pole, and that the geographical dimension of this pole was the region of South-West France. Consequently, since new and expanded activities outside the region were not analysed in relation to their connection with the project, the latter's effects were not examined in direct relation to general economic growth. Growth effects in the other regions might possibly have been measured in connection with inter-regional flows of goods and income induced by the project.

The so-called direct, indirect and induced income effects are described as follows:

— the direct effects denote the contribution of the pole industries to the net regional product at market prices, whose recipients are residents of the region;
— the indirect effects emerge as the part of the contribution to the net regional product at market prices obtained from residents of the region — which has arisen in addition in all the other undertakings in

the region by the utilisation of their products as intermediate inputs of the pole industries;
— the induced effects arise as a multiplier effect of the factor incomes accruing in the region as a result of direct and indirect effects in so far as they are spent in the region itself. It is a question of a simple regional multiplier, for which inter-regional repercussions are disregarded.

Effects on the income of other regions are only calculated directly in so far as a distinction is made between internal and residents' incomes when considering the effects for the pole region procedure analogous to the determination of the indirect effects and the utilisation of an inter-regional multiplier pattern seems possible, but has not been adopted.

SEMA has carried out its calculations for only one year. The result is an action shot which, on the whole, seems suitable for evaluation in connection with the additional regional income that has arisen in connection with the activity of the pole industries.[4] Conclusions regarding the growth rate of the contribution of the pole to the net regional product can only be obtained by a comparison of the results over several periods. In connection with the total regional account the statement of the regional pole definition, which contains a more rapid pole growth in comparison with the rest of the system, might be examined in the present case.

2   Paelinck's explanatory system of polarisation effects (Paelinck, 63 and 65) follows the incidental criteria set out in the first-mentioned growth pole definition for technical, income-related, geographical and psychological polarisation.

Technical polarisation. First of all, the power centre of a growth pole must be determined, and for this Paelinck refers to Chenery and Watanabe and the linkage effects in Hirschman. The power centre can be determined by reference to the trilogy of high inter-industrial relations, significant size, and dominance, and is bound to show high inter-industrial interlocking, because the probability of the attraction of new activities is intensified thereby. It must consist of large units, for these alone can afford the research and development expenditure needed to cover further innovations, and it must consist of dominant units, because these exert special development impulses on the establishment of branch undertakings, on sub-contracts, on capital tie-ups and so on.

Polarisation of incomes. This concerns the effect of the regional income multiplier, which basically applies independently of whether a single regional multiplier or an inter-regional multiplier (with retroactive effects) is involved. It follows from the multiplier theory, however, that a polarising — that is to say a self-reinforcing — effect can only be obtained when there are income increases induced increasingly in other ways (e.g., by technical polarisation). This means that the effect concerned can increase polarisation effects produced in other ways, but does not produce a self-reinforcing effect on its own account.

Psychological polarisation. Here it is a question in essence of simulated and information effects. Paelinck lays down that the success of polarisation effects is completely independent of whether the creativity of the power units is sufficient to encourage small and intermediate undertakings to make complementary investments, whether the exchange of special information of strategic value to a sector works, and whether the overall planning makes available valid and sufficiently concrete general economic guidelines. This point of view is extremely important from the standpoint of theory concerning communication costs, but has not been expressed in sufficiently concrete terms (cf. however ibid. 23 et seq.).

Geographical polarisation. This is not a question of the conditions under which a sectoral pole is regionally polarised but of the internal spatial organisation of the polarisation region under consideration. As Paelinck agrees that the polarisation theory is not a localisation theory (ibid. 45/6), so he does not consider that a spatial concentration on a point pole is compulsory: 'It will simply be said here that it is a question of one aspect of polarisation and that the theory of polarisation can be combined in a flexible manner with the regional arrangement of space, for it is not a question of a theory of concentration' (ibid. 38).

In particular, the argument embraces the distribution of a sectoral/ regional pole over various areas within the pole region. In this way, geographically identifiable main and subsidiary poles are distinguished.

A further important view of geographical polarisation in the Paelinck sense concerns the so-called employment multiplier, which proceeds from the development of basis activities to that of non-basis activities. The employment multiplier established a connection between the numbers employed in the basis sector and the number in employment in the non-basis sector. Basis activities are those which produce for regional export, while non-basis activites produce only for the regional market. The distinction corresponds essentially to that between national and international goods on the one hand and local and regional goods on the other.[5]

For further simplification it may be assumed that the pole centre, like the activities stemming from it in the first, second and subsequent generations, is to be attributed to the basis sector. Under the export basis theory, these basis activities have the consequence of promoting complementary activities in the non-basis sector (building industry, services), without high input/output coefficients existing in detail between each branch of the (expanded) pole centre on the one hand and of the non-basis activities on the other. In this case, despite the lower intensity of the flows of goods and services, the high frequency yields a result similar to the mode of operation of strong inter-industrial relations.

As long as local goods are concerned, non-basis activities can be used for the clarification of the intra-regional spatial production structure, which shows a certain connection with the geographical polarisation argument of Paelinck. It can also be argued that non-basis activities can be induced, independently of the existence of input/output relations with input/output activities, via the final demand effects produced by basis activities.

2.2 Prospects

In the public view great expectations have been aroused by the programme as regards the results of industrialisation, including those realisable at short term. New particulars regarding the success of the pole policy, which is mainly to be measured by the growth rate of *per capita* income in the pole provinces, have now become part of the policy. It is not only in Spain that this is based on the observance of a faulty assessment: 'The growth pole concept has often been wrongly interpreted. It has often been confused with that of the key industry, the basis industry, and the industrial complex. From this stems the erroneous impression that a growth pole is something of an industrial monument, erected to the glory of future regional industrialisation, a guarantee of safer economic growth' (Paelinck, 63, 10, translated by the author).

There are three main objectives, whose rapid and lasting achievement was expected to be attained by growth pole policy: that by their sectoral structure the growth poles should facilitate self-sustaining growth; that in consequence of the technical polarisation they should exert irradiation effects on their hinterland and extend the self-sustaining growth process over the entire region; and that by the creation of industrial jobs they should keep in the neighbourhood a working population who otherwise would be obliged to migrate.

These general objects are not expanded in the planning document. In the period of the First Plan which could be described as an experimental phase, no aids were provided for quantifying the objectives, and even today, when experience of more than two planning periods is available, one hesitates to draw specific conclusions. Moreover, in the initial phase the criteria for assessing the plan were more or less uncertain.

However, it was obviously hoped that the time span prior to the production of a self-sustaining development process in the pole regions would last no longer than six to eight years, and it was in this way that the protection period for the poles was originally measured. Only in the Third Plan was this period extended, in the light of the experience gained, to a maximum of ten years (Planning Commission, Third Plan . . . , 72, 338). There is considerable doubt as to whether even this period is sufficient. However, present tendencies are moving towards the incorporation of the first-established poles in the planning of the metropolitan and urban zones (ibid. 331/2), and carrying the process even further.

The expectations can be formulated somewhat more explicitly if specific reliance is placed on the effects formulated by SEMA and Paelinck. The following hypotheses arise regarding the regional growth incidence of the poles:

(i)   The poles will create a favourable investment climate in the region, and in particular will mobilise local capital. This can be tested by determining the production proposals and the share of local, regional, national and international capital in the pole activities.

(ii)   The poles will give rise to a substantial increase in jobs, an increase in regional labour productivity and an expansion in the proportion of industrial net product to the total net product in the region. Corresponding indicators can be established in connection with enquiries into the pole industries and the regional overall accounts.

(iii)   The lower the regional income which can be attributed to non-residents in the region during the investment phase, the stronger the impact of the income effects produced by the poles. The difference between regional internal and residents' income depends for example on the import content of the demand for investment goods and the financing structure of the new activities including the infra-structure. Corresponding values can be determined in the enquiry into the pole industries and their suppliers and into the financing institutions.

(iv)   Similar considerations to those under (iii) can be derived for the production phase of the directly productive activities, and these can be investigated in the same way; for this the SEMA system can be referred to.

(v)   In the production phase, strong linkage effects emanating from the pole industries will have an attractive effect on new activities. This can be firmly established by drawing up input-output tables for the poles and their comparison for different years.

(vi)   The pole activities will exert strong growth impulses on the hinterland as a result of intensive input-output relations with their hinterland. This can be checked on an estimated basis by corresponding disaggregation of the pole imports and exports.

(vii)   As pole pairs (Huelva-Seville, La Coruña-Vigo, Burgos-Valladolid), the poles will allow development axes to arise between the poles of any pair, with the consequence of strong inter-polar linkages. The checking can be effected as under (vi).

(viii)   The poles will promote an improvement in integration of the pole regions with the rest of the national economy by an intensification of the exchange relationships, thus also providing substitutes for former regional and national imports. In this case also the checking can be performed as under (vi).

(ix)   A substantial regional income incidence is to be expected from the pole activities, and of particular interest in this connection is the calculation of a regional income multiplier and a basic/non-basic activities multiplier. A regional multiplier pattern permits first answers to be given to both questions, as the second type of multiplier is closely connected with the additional demand in the pole regions produced by the income effects of the poles.

(x)   The regional welfare level will increase more than proportionately to the general economic growth rate, and a self-sustaining development process can be produced in the pole regions within a period of up to ten years. Indications of the examination of this expectation are provided by the aforesaid tests, but are insufficiently conclusive. Additional data could be obtained from the long-term application of a system of social indicators as first employed in the Third Plan, the preparation and comparison between periods of statistics of personal income distribution in the regions, the analysis of newly established non-basic activities, etc. The analysis of the third part of this work is confined to a limited number of particulars only.

The hypotheses referred to are the subject of the empirical analysis in the third part of the present work (mainly in the order in which they are mentioned), where they are investigated more thoroughly and rearranged in detail according to their systematic relationship.

2.3   Methods and instruments of pole promotion

The planning of growth poles was so conducted that the region to be promoted was first selected, then the sectors whose development in the region was to serve the promotion object (region-first alternative). A different procedure could have been adopted whereby it could first be considered which sectoral poles in a given situation most strongly promote general economic growth, and then which of these can best be established in which peripheral regions (sector-first alternative).

If the growth policy has as its object — as in the First and Second Plans — the assimilation of regional *per capita* income differences, then it would at first sight be better to select the region-first alternative.

1 *Regional selectivity.* The *per capita* income criterion is for this purpose the first selection criterion:

Table 1
Per capita income of the pole provinces, 1964 (Ptas)

Burgos	30,702
Huelva	21,180
La Coruña	21,358
Seville	22,683
Valladolid	31,634
Vigo[6]	25,563
Zaragoza	32,392
Spain	31,036

Source: Banco de Bilbao, 67, 20.

First it is to be noted that two or three of the seven poles are not to be numbered among the relatively poor provinces according to the *per capita* income criterion, in so far as the average national income is selected as the dividing line between relatively poor and rich provinces. The five relatively poor among the pole provinces are for their part not so poor as to match the regional inequality criterion of the United Nations Commission for Europe which the Planning Commission adopts. According to this, regional inequalities are held to exist in a province when parts of the population live in zones with less than two-thirds of the average national income (Planning Commission, 63, 149/50). This applied to none of the pole provinces in 1964, but on the other hand it did then apply to eight provinces which still have no pole.

In accordance with expectations, the *per capita* income criterion is thus insufficient. So far it can only be maintained that, measured by relative *per capita* income, below-average provinces were selected preferentially.

A second principle is that of the *development axis,* which has a connection with the objective of a stronger internal economic integration. Integration is interpreted as a geographic-economic linkage, in which sense an intermediate function is allotted to poles which lie along an assumed connecting axis with economic centres. The axis principle has a number of variations:

68

- an additional control point should improve communciation between two or more centres;
- 'localisation according to the principle of axes enjoys many of the advantages of agglomeration — intensive utilisation of the infrastructure and of the equipment available, facilitation of transport and of contacts between undertakings, advantages of mass production — without incurring all its disadvantages' (Plaza Prieto, 68, 254);
- the neighbouring establishment of two or more poles, between which a circular causation process should set in.

The third principle is the promotion of such provinces as rank as the natural centres for larger regions. While the concept of the natural centre is undoubtedly difficult to specify, Seville can nevertheless claim this attribute, as can also Burgos, La Coruña and Zaragoza.

Among the relatively poor provinces, a similar function is performed by those of Córdoba, Granada and Murcia. Córdoba and Granada were established as poles in Plan II, and Murcia has been the centre of a major agricultural project since 1973. Budget restrictions were largely responsible for the latter's non-inclusion in the first plan.

The fourth principle is that of the availability of natural resources on the one hand, and of a high degree of adaptive capacity to the change in economic structure on the other hand. For Huelva the former certainly applies, and similarly the importance of the fish industry had to be taken into account in the case of Vigo and La Coruña. A high degree of adaptive capacity ('capacidad de respuesta') was also expected in Seville, Valladolid, La Coruña, Vigo and Zaragoza. Since the argument is hard to grasp, it is contentious in detail.

The fifth principle is that of the creation of compensatory centres. The starting point is the observation that the economic gravitation centres of Spain are tending to shift to the North East in the quadrant demarcated by the centres of Madrid, the Basque country, Catalonia and Valencia (Tamames, 68, 124 et seq.).

The alternative in this case is either an extension of the present system of centres or the creation of a counterpart, and in this respect the establishment of the poles is not uniform. Nevertheless the compensatory argument applies to the four poles, for which the axis argument in its first form is not applicable. For this reason, provinces like La Coruña, Vigo and Seville were sought out, where the total income is above the average level (Banco de Bilbao, cf. 67, 18).

Once the pole province is selected, discussion centres on the selection of the central place or places in which the settlement of new activities is preferred. As the Spanish government had decided on the promotion of point poles, the next step was to select the economic gravitation centre of the province, and except in the case of Vigo this choice fell on the capital. The idea behind this point pole system is the use of general urbanisation advantages, especially with regard to the technical minimum capacities of the new infrastructure.

2 *Sectoral selectivity.* For those industries wishing to establish themselves in a growth pole and to have the benefit of the promotion measures, there is a special authorisation procedure ('Concurso'). The basis of this procedure is an application which must provide particulars of the investment planned, the number of jobs to be provided, financing arrangements, production capacity, gross output value and normal cost structure. In addition, it is necessary to give details of special social contributions, the import content of the investment goods demand, and foreign financing.

(a)   Under the authorisation procedure the promotion value of the industry in a particular pole is assessed, and if the result is favourable it is further valued and graded in one of four groups A-D. Independently of this grading, the level of investment incentive to be given would depend on whether a growth pole or a development pole was concerned. Growth poles (in Plan I for Burgos and Huelva) are those for which the province had very little industry involved as yet, while development poles are those for which industrial ventures already in existence should be encouraged (La Coruña, Seville, Valladolid, Vigo, Zaragoza). Today this distinction has been lifted, and all poles are treated uniformly as development poles.

The promotion measures − apart from indirect promotion by infrastructure policy − are as follows (Consejo Económico Sindical Nacional, 67, 142):

Promotion Measure	Promotion Group			
	A	B	C	D
1 Depreciation allowance for first 5 years	Yes	Yes	Yes	Yes
2 Preferential treatment in the provision of State loans	Yes	Yes	Yes	Yes
3 Compulsory expropriation of necessary industrial sites	Yes	Yes	Yes	Yes
4-7 Relief of between 50 and 95% from taxes and dues in a transitional phase graduated according to the promotion group	Yes (for 4)	Yes	Yes	Yes
	95% (for 5)	95%	95%	−
	95% (for 6 & 7)	50%	50%	−

Promotion Measure	Promotion Group			
	A	*B*	*C*	*D*
8 Reduction of customs duties and equalising taxes on imports of investment goods not obtainable in Spain	95%	50%	25%	—
9 Reduction of local taxes on the construction and extension of undertakings up to 95%	Yes	Yes	No	No
10 Investment subsidy on fixed capital				
(a) Growth poles	20%	10%		
(b) Development poles	10%	5%		

Measures 4 – 7 have not been set out in detail here because they relate to very special requirements of the Spanish tax system and are immaterial here. The same may be said of measure 9, and in the case of individual poles also measure 3. For further analysis we can concentrate our attention on measures 1, 2, 8 and 10.

(b) The question can now be put as to what criteria should be used to size up, firstly the promotion value of concerns in general, and secondly the promotion value in connection with the classification into grades A, B, C and D. It was to be expected that behind this qualifying scale might lie an ingenious polarisation theory concept, which does not make for any absolute clear measurement of promotion value but simply permits an estimate to be made of the relative rating of an investment. This, however, is by no means the case.

The general promotion value is arrived at in accordance with a list where those activities which can be authorised are set out for each individual pole. Inclusion in the list provides no claim to authorisation, but is merely a question of a qualifying provision. No list was prepared for growth poles, all activities being permissible which 'contribute directly to the economic and social development of the region' (Consejo Económico Sindical Nacional, 67, 58). This is an empty formula, however, the only condition for authorisation being a minimum investment of Ptas three million and a minimum provision of twenty new jobs.

There were also minimum requirements for development poles, in this case investment of Ptas five million and thirty jobs. As it is only a question of permissive regulations, the additional criteria for authorisation are of decisive importance. However, these are not strictly laid down, and basically are not systematically measurable. One complication is that several ministries are involved in each decision, each ministry being guided, furthermore, by its own criteria. It is to be assumed that non-disclosure of the criteria is due to tactical considerations or that no systematic criteria whatever are available. How far the additional criteria were quantitatively relevant is shown by a comparison of the applications submitted and granted:

Table 2
Comparison of applications submitted and
approved for relative shares on:

	Number	Investment total	Jobs
Huelva	66.6%	54.8%	58.6%
Seville	64.6%	50.9%	66.8%
All poles	64.1%	56.8%	68.1%

These comparisons apply to the first authorisation (1964) (calculated from Tamames, 68, 120).

If it is accepted that, on the question of the general promotion value of undertakings, systematic criteria are not available, it is reasonable to conclude that this is even truer of the promotion values arrived at in accordance with the classification into A, B, C and D. In particular, an important part is played here by empirical values, intuition, the influence of interest groups and general development strategy considerations of entities involved. Nor should it be overlooked that, especially in the first phase of pole promotion policy, recourse was not to be had to a systematic appraisal of operational criteria. In any case the polarisation theory in the form developed by the French school provided none at all.

Three examples should finally serve to clarify the unease felt by the Spanish planners with regard to this system:

(i)   The selection lists are often found to be too narrow. On this account it is complained both that the minimum requirements were drawn up too arbitrarily and that too little consideration was given to the criterion of inter-sectoral interdependence (Planning Commission, Report on Regional Development, 69, 235).

(ii)   The selection lists were too concerned with the viewpoint of the purely quantitative, intersectoral unstructured agglomeration. It was only for the new poles in the Second Plan that input-output studies were systematically undertaken (e.g. for Córdoba). A start was also made on industrial complex analysis, on the analogy, for example, of the industrial triangle formed by Bari, Brindisi and Tarent in Southern Italy, for Huelva, Seville and Cadiz in Andalusia (cf. Planning Commission/Italconsult, 68).

(iii) Finally, it has been recognised that owing to neglect of the communication cost argument, the input-output studies for the planning of sectoral-regional poles do not suffice. Consequently, for the Asturias (Oviedo) pole an attempt was made for the first time to utilise attraction analysis (Netherlands Economic Institute, 71). The result is unsatisfactory, however, because such attraction analysis must be carried out with the incorporation of all the competitive locations.

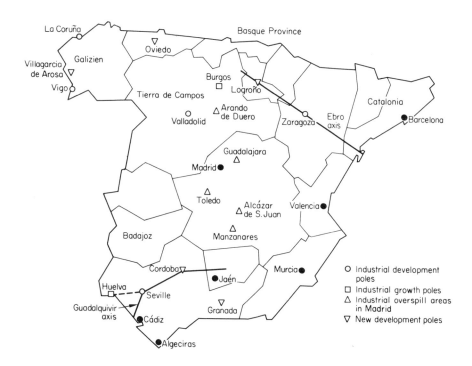

Geographical layout of the promotion districts and of the other zones referred to in the text. (Taken from : Consejo Económico Sindical Nacional, 67, supplemented by the author.)

3 The Incorporation of the Pole Programme in the National Urbanisation Strategy of the Third Plan

It has already been pointed out that the existing pole programme, while generally speaking satisfactory, is also regarded by the Spanish planners as in need of improvement. More precise requirements for this will be set out in the results of Part III of this work, where it will undoubtedly be shown that the traditional growth pole concept based on the ideas of the French school is not completely unassailable. Nonetheless, it must be granted to the Spanish planners that this does not amount to a fundamental repudiation of polarisation-orientated regional policy, merely a recognition of the necessity for basing the polarisation concept on a broader footing. A starting point for this is underlined in the considerations set out at the end of Part I. At this point, therefore, the discussion of growth poles and growth centres will be taken up once more, together with some of the problems of Spanish regional policy which arose in Plan III. This can be accomplished all the more smoothly because it can undoubtedly be established that the urbanisation concept in Plan III clearly derives the characteristics of its development policy ideas from José Lasuen and his followers. This concept is depicted below as one of general urbanisation, in which it must not of course be overlooked to what extent (cf. Planning Commission, Third Plan, Regional Development, 72, 217 et seq.) this is distinguished by the features of the fifth French Plan (with reference, for instance, to the metropoles of equilibrium).

3.1 Identification of the metropolitan, urban and rural zones in the Third Plan as a starting point for the general polarisation concept?

By the general polarisation concept on the basis of previous considerations the promotion of regional polarisation is understood, either by means of sectoral polarisation or independently thereof.

According to the ideas of the planners a development pole is to be identified in this sense in connection with the settlement structure. The pole region is described as part of the national settlement system, and at its head stands a metropolitan or urban zone as part of the regional sub-system.

A metropolitan or an urban zone is a closed settlement unit of more than 750,000 or 250,000 inhabitants respectively (Planning Commission, Third Plan . . . , 72, 331), for which an expectancy value is entertained for 1980.

1   The establishment of the urbanisation concept follows essentially the considerations set out above for the inter-regional integration goal in its various versions. Furthermore, the connection between the polarisation theory notions of Friedmann and Lasuen is very clear: 'The planning of urban development, within a policy for the revalorisation of the territory, raises in the first place the idea of "cities as protagonists of political, social and economic change" in the countries. These aspects emerge ever more closely linked, and the linkage has to be reaffirmed with the planning of urban development' (Planning Commission, Third Plan, Regional Development, 72, 223).

2   Criteria for the identification of Metropolitan Areas (MAs) and Urban Areas (UAs) are based on the connection proposed by Lasuen between growth pole theory, central place theory and structural analytical inter-regional growth theory. Particular difficulties arose from the adjustment of the seemingly plausible size criteria to the Spanish situation, the demarcation of the zones one from another and the coordination of the urban with the metropolitan zones.

While some metropolitan zones such as Madrid, Barcelona, Valencia and Seville could be distinguished to all appearances on the basis of the traditional settlement structure, the demarcation and coordination of the urban zones required a greater iteration procedure. Finally, use was made of a combination of relatively unexacting groundwork from Reilly and Friedmann and Muller (ibid. cf. 228/9) as a first approximation, and the results were partly modified on the basis of additional criteria introduced. The utilisation of this groundwork naturally suggests that the identification of the UA is primarily determined by the concept of central place functions, while the significance of the industrial settlement structure in the sense of an independent space-forming factor barely seems to be reflected.

A second objection arises out of the fact that, in view of the number of MAs and UAs to be incorporated in the promotion, the polarisation concept utilised is in fact watered down, since the general budget restriction will not permit the realisation of a polarisation programme of national proportions on the proposed scale. Owing to the difference in strategy for rural and urban regions, and among the latter for metro-politan and urban zones, an intra-regional selectivity criterion comes into operation, though no explicit inter-regional selectivity criterion really exists. It can be assumed that the strong point formation by means of axes in the Second Plan (Fernández-Rodríguez, 72, 445) along the coasts, in the valleys of the Ebro and the Guadalquivir, the link-up between the North and Madrid via the Burgos and Valladolid poles, and the overspill from Madrid still apply. It will be shown, however, that the poles which are all established in the path of such axes have so far contributed little to the intensification of the axis relations.

With the execution of the Third Plan it will be seen whether and which strong point formations result, and in particular what political ideas have been called for by the functional division planned in the total area. Streit (71, 674) rightly stresses the importance of such perspective, but points at the same time to the difficulty of developing it. Firstly it must be expected that for want of sufficient concentration of the means applied the decentralisation programme leads to the 'proliferation' of growth centres (Hansen, 71, 1, shows that this tendency is not restricted to Spain) and so to self-cancellation. A comparison with the institution by the French of 'métropoles d'équilibre' provides a first indication of this: in their Fifth Plan, which sponsored the conception of the Spanish Third Plan, 'only' eleven counter-balancing centres were founded, whose urban zones showed substantially higher population figures than is the case in Spain (cf. Hansen, 68, 235 et seq. on the one hand, and Planning Commission, Third Plan, Regional Development, 72, 251 on the other hand). Without explicit analysis of the political decision processes it will consequently hardly be possible to pronounce on the chances of imple-menting such a strategy (cf. for France on this point Cohen, 69).

3   In view of its attraction theory background, our first objection under (2) is deserving of special clarification. The Spanish planners have naturally tried to establish sectoral polarising activities (industrial complexes) as possible centres of metropolitan areas, for which they make use of a method proposed by Streit (Streit, 69, 177 et seq.), but the attempt proved unsatisfactory. A short note on this may help.

(a)   The forty-three sectors of the processing industry shown in the Spanish input-output table for 1966 are arranged according to the intensity of their mutual linkages. For measuring the intensity of an inter-industrial input-output relationship, L_{ij}, between two sectors i and j, in Streit the following symmetrical relationship is selected (Planning Commission, Third Plan, Regional Development, 72, 243/4):

$$L_{ij} = L_{ji} = \frac{1}{4}\left(\frac{O_{ij}}{{}_iO_i} + \frac{O_{ij}}{{}_jI_j} \pm. \frac{O_{ji}}{{}_jO_j} + \frac{O_{ji}}{{}_iI_i}\right),$$

where O represents the gross output value and I the inter-industrial input. Although the identical weighting expressed by the quotient is arbitrary, this would be true of any other weighting so long as the aim is a general measurement like the one proposed.

(b)   In order to identify groups of linked sectors or sectoral poles two criteria are employed, and these must be satisfied at the same time:

— The elements of sectoral poles are linked by 'relevant' input-output relationships. A relationship is relevant when it has a higher L_{ij} value than the average of all the L_{ij} values in the sector. This means that relevant relationships must satisfy the condition

$$L_{ij} > \frac{i}{n} \Sigma_i L_{ij} ;$$

— The sectoral poles are formed by $n(n > 2)$ sectors, for which each pair of sectors must satisfy the condition of relevant relationships between one another. In the Commission's view, sectoral poles are adequately identified in this way.

(c)   Furthermore, by reference to Richter (Richter, 69, 24), the superiority of sectoral/regional as opposed to purely sectoral polarisation in the matter of general economic efficiency is generally postulated. It is consequently considered right that steps should be taken in principle to establish sectoral poles in proximity within an urban region.

As will shortly be shown, Streit's procedure has changed in some important respects; he will only designate as elements of sectoral/regional poles or of industrial complexes those activities which incline to establishment in proximity. The criterion for this, which must be satisfied together with the requirement of the relevance of input-output relations, means that the only activities which can be regarded as complex-forming are those which display as between themselves a positive significant correlation coefficient between linkage and establishment in proximity (Streit, 69, 182).

It has to be recognised therefore that the problem of identification of sectoral/regional poles can not yet be adequately solved by this procedure. The preceding considerations have also demonstrated that this would not succeed even if Streit's method had been followed completely. It therefore seems reasonable to adopt the instrument of attraction analysis for the planning of urban regions as well.

3.2 Principles of decentral concentration policy and adaptation of the growth pole concept

The two preceding sections investigated the basic open questions of the identification of regional and sectoral/regional poles and their incorporation in a consistent planning connection from the point of view of polarisation theory. Since the planning cannot be subordinated to the solution of these problems, the planners are often able to offer the politicians no more than rules of thumb to be observed when the strategy is expressed in concrete terms. These particularly concern the interregional selectivity of the public promotion measures, the sectoral allocation policy in the selected regions, and the relationship between direct measures such as subsidies, credits, orders and prohibitions, and indirect measures such as economic and social infrastructure. Other planning sectors seem to have been fairly precisely prepared, apart from the fact that the repercussions of alternative solutions to the open questions referred to above do not produce any effect. The Planning Commissions for the metropolitan and urban zones have thus submitted detailed lists of criteria for the differentiated promotion of varying types of metropolitan and urban zones (Planning Commission, Third Plan, Regional Development, 72, 247/8 and 252 et seq.). These planning data represent a considerable advance compared with those to which the decisions for the implementation of second plans could relate. In particular, the reception and further development of the planning consequences are to be obtained from the concept of the central place functions.

Hence, in what follows only two arguments are to be emphasised, namely the necessity for the pre-eminence of infrastructure policy, and the adoption of strict regional selectivity criteria.

3.2.1 Principles

1   The first principle is evolved as a consequence of the fact that, as established above, the planners cannot recommend the politicians to concentrate the brunt of their activity on the short- or medium-term direction of industrial allocation. The emphasis is thus to be placed on the long-term delineation of infrastructure policy. At the same time, however, the determinants of industrial settlement structure arising from intersectoral integration should be further investigated, otherwise the infra-structure policy signals cannot be directed at the allocation requirements of sectoral/regional polarisations.

Since results will be available for the Fourth Plan on the last point at least, the priority given to infra-structure must at first be still more pronounced. The author consequently agrees with the following recommendation of Richardson (72, 39/40) without any reservations whatsoever:

> My main point is that long-term planning is much easier to carry out than short-medium-term planning, given the degree of intervention by the Spanish Government in the economy, the instruments available to it and the general characteristics of the institutional environment. In particular, it is much easier to influence regional development goals by long-term planning using the spatial allocation of urban infrastructure by the public sector rather than to co-ordinate sectoral and regional planning within a four year planning period.

This opinion also contains a vote for the subordination of the industrial growth poles concept to general urbanisation policy.

2   The second principle sets out the necessity for selective – discriminatory – and differential promotion.

(a)   The requirement that the development pole policy must be keyed to the scheduled functional organisation of the total space (Streit, 71, 674) has to be underlined. For corresponding long-term planning elementary bases for decision are still lacking. In the Planning Commission discussions were consequently held on the promotion of studies, analogous to the French enquiries regarding the long-term planning of national development (cf. e.g. Development Commission . . . , 69). For the Third Plan this could not of course have produced further effect. Consequently, in succession to the former concentration of emphasis two selection proposals are of particular importance, namely the typology of problem regions employed in the Second Plan and the 'main lines of the long-term organisation of the total space' given prominence by Fernández-Rodríguez (72, 445) (see also Buttler, 69, 453 et seq.). The axis principle should be preferred to the typologically established selectivity criterion, that is to say the promotion of provinces differentiated by type (to which the typological method related) is differentiated for its own part according to whether or not the provinces are related to one of the aforesaid axes.

(b)   The differentiation of problem regions by type (Planning Commission, Project . . . , 69, 62 et seq.) presents the following picture:
–   provinces with a predominantly agricultural structure, a negligible amount of industry, a low population density and an undeveloped pattern of central place functions (1),

80

- provinces with a predominantly agricultural structure, a higher population density and a workable net of central places (2),
- provinces with a flourishing agriculture and a developed industry (3),
- predominantly urbanised provinces with heavy industrial concentrations (4).

This typology can be adopted in a revised form, for which purpose the fourth group can be broken down further into those whose industry consists of traditional and structurally weak activities, and others. The former are designated 'crisis regions'. The corresponding differentiation of the main strategies shows the following composition:

Type	Strategies
(1) Underdeveloped provinces	Improvement of the social infrastructure, agricultural promotion
(2) Backward provinces capable of development	Polarisation strategy for integrated groups of provinces, otherwise as in (1)
(3) 'Balanced provinces'	Integration-orientated infrastructure development, no further promotion
(4a) 'Crisis' provinces	Polarisation strategy most probably in connection with provincial groups under (2)
(4b) Traditional metropolitan zones	Town clearance and urbanisation policy in the vicinity

As regards (1), these provinces include Estremadura, most of the southern sub-tableland and Aragon. Their economic and social development potential is too low for any attempt to be made to initiate a self-supporting growth process. The mainstay of the strategy is the promotion of agriculture, which comprises the first industrial processing and more especially an improvement in the marketing of agricultural production. Processing industries of this order do not polarise regionally. The extensive credit financing of objects recognised as worthy of promotion, together with the corporate organisation of undertakings, are capable of increasing the regional income incidence of the value creation achieved. This is confirmed by experience with the Badajoz plan. A complementary factor is the social infrastructure in relation to the object of promoting an improvement in the social participation of the rural population.

With regard to (3) and (4b), the limitation to few strategies[7] for the provinces of these types — the cost of which can nevertheless be very high, especially in the case of town clearance — is unlikely to be disputed. The interest factor in the provinces concerned is naturally another consideration.

As regards (2) and (4a), it is a question in this case of the provinces which are suitable for a purposive polarisation strategy when general consideration is given to the typology existing to date. For the polarisation strategies to be applied to the various types, however, there are various directions of impact. Whereas in the first case the main objective is to first of all concentrate the planning region to be formed at the 'conurbation point', the chief problem in the second place consists in overcoming the traditional structure factors standing in the way of further diversification (Streit, 71a, 227).

3　The third principle makes the existence of metropolitan or urban zones which can be brought to the conurbation point a prior requirement for being worthy of encouragement. If this criterion comes into conflict with the axis principle, because such central zones do not exist along an imaginary axis, the extension of the infrastructure must be so arranged as to minimise the communication costs of covering the space between the axis poles or over particular stretches. As regards the axes mentioned by Fernández-Rodríguez, the minimum criterion should be satisfied, otherwise it will be found that for linking up the Galician and the Andalusian axes with the traditional centres as a whole, and for the connection of the North with Madrid for particular stretches (Miranda del Ebro — Madrid), the extension of the infrastructure should have the object of covering the space at the lowest possible cost, whereas in the zones situated on the axis connection only the social infrastructure is to be promoted.

4　The fourth principle sets out the necessity for the evaluation of the social development potential, and should in consequence only point to the fact that, because corresponding criteria have received insufficient consideration in previous planning discussions, modifications of the long-term guidelines so far followed will only be possible after additional investigation. Attempts made up to now to overcome the concept of industrial growth poles have been slanted one-sidedly towards emphasis on the necessity for incorporating the hierarchical classification of the central place functions. To supplement this, it is necessary in the process of planning to place more emphasis on consideration of the subjective attitude and the objective possibilities for social change in peripheral regions. The works of Friedmann (69), Hansen (71) and Utría (71) are valuable pointers in this direction, and the first conclusions drawn from such considerations are consequently to be found in the list of criteria of the Commission for Urban Zones (Planning Commission, Third Plan, Regional Development, 72, 251 et seq.).

3.2.2   Adaptation of the traditional growth pole concept

At this point an attempt is to be made to link up the elements of the regional policy of the Second Plan with those of the urbanisation policy of the Third Plan. In a general ground-plan, it will be shown how the re-shaping and continuity of regional policy could be illustrated. The selectivity principles considered will be related to the scheme.

1   The typology of the promotion zones in the Second Plan can be combined in a matrix with the action planes of the settlement structure policy in the Third Plan:

Classification in the settlement structure \ Types	Traditional metropolitan zones	'Crisis' provinces	Selected groups of provinces of type (2)	Other provinces of type (1) and partly type (2)
Metropolitan		← → ← → / ← →		(shaded)
Urban	(shaded)	↕ ← → ↑	↕	(shaded)
Rural	(shaded)	↓	↕	

There are twelve possible combinations. Four of these are eliminated as irrelevant (shaded areas). While the elimination of the left-hand lower areas is explained by the definition of the type concerned, the removal of the right-hand upper fields is made on grounds of economic policy. As was postulated above with reference to the necessity for strict selectivity[8], the only measures accordingly justifiable are those of agricultural promotion and the related expansion of the economic infrastructure (EOC), and the raising of the mobility and participation chances by the expansion of the social infrastructure (SOC).

The arrows in the diagram denote the necessity for vertical and horizontal co-ordination of the programme. The horizontal arrows mark the co-ordinating and integrating mechanisms held by the Planning Commission to be necessary for the metropolitan and urban areas, while the vertical arrows relate to the co-ordination of the intra-regional function distribution.

At the next stage, the elements of regional policy in the Second Plan are to be related to the eight strategic fields of action. The following diagram does not consider all the facets of the existing regional policy. A further reason for this is that a number of smaller programmes have to be incorporated in the concept of the promotion of the metropolitan, urban and rural areas in order to obviate fragmentation by reason of the

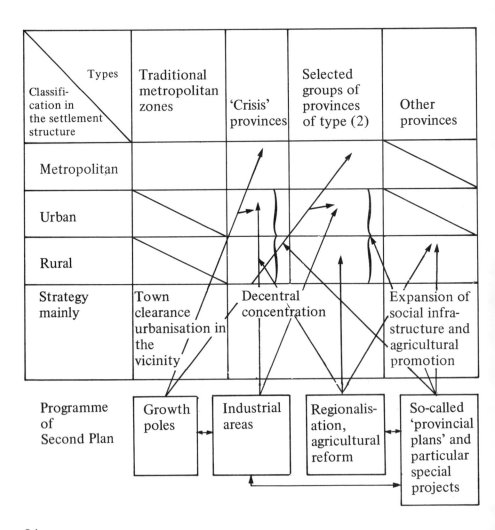

introduction of new elements. This also corresponds basically to the ideas of the Spanish planners.

The arrows pointing one way indicate the arrangement, and those pointing two ways indicate the special co-ordination requirements.

2   The arrangement of the growth policy is illustrated clearly in the same diagram. It is not disputed that the growth policy only comes into question with regard to the second and third types, and to this extent the diagram has nothing to say about additional selectivity criteria.

The co-ordination of the growth pole policy to the development concept for the so-called metropolitan zones and selected urban zones amounts here to a fundamental reorientation, to the extent that the growth pole concept is subordinated to the concept of the economic and social development pole. The most important consequences for the determination of the nature and extent of the utilisation of public promotion means can be set out on the basis of a comprehensive view of both schemes as follows:

(a) *Priority of infrastructure policy.* For this it is required that the risk of the massive supply of previous public work should be specifically taken into account. The more strictly the factual and temporal co-ordination of physical and economic planning can be effected, the lower the risk will be. A suitable instrument for this is the network plan technique. The observer of the growth pole policy in the Second Plan must get the impression that the planners, while trying to establish private initiative in particular activities or abstentions, at the same time were making no binding promises regarding the extent and termination of public promotion measures. This practice contradicts the idea of predominantly indicative planning in principle: it is expected that business investment behaviour provides signals for the direction of public 'successor investments'. For dynamic economic sectors this state investment behaviour is insupportable. An industry which calculates its most important capital goods as having an average depreciation period of between eight and ten years just cannot afford to get established on a site where the necessary infrastructure work will not be finished for several years.

(b) *Necessity for long-term promotion.* Adaptation to urbanisation policy also applies for the planning horizon and the promotion period. As it has been established that a planning horizon of two four-year plans is too short, and since on the the other hand a planning horizon of over twenty years is hard to take in, long-term planning should not exceed twelve to twenty years. This does not mean that the specific planning targets are irreversible.

D

(c)   The above schemes take account of the necessity for incorporating the growth poles in the regional settlement system. This implies recognition of the fact that the point poles — in the geographical sense — have not had their expected expansionary effects, and in particular that there can be no hope of an automatic expansionary tendency in the surrounding area. Consequently, the co-ordination of the promotion measures for the metropolitan pole zones and the related urban zones must be emphasised. It must be considered whether the hypothesis of the relationship between size of business structure and size of settlement structure — the hierarchy hypothesis — permits deductions to be made regarding suitable intra-regional decentralisation criteria.

(d)   The growth pole concept as an instrument for the promotion of sectoral/regional polarisations is subordinated to the general urbanisation concept based on polarisation theory to the extent also that it seeks to transpose strategically an — important — special case of the contingency connection of regional polarisations. This means that the development pole concept is regarded as superior to that of the industrial growth pole because it is more comprehensive. That it is more comprehensive can be attributed to the fact that, with the aid of a uniform category system (communication costs and authority-dependency relationship theorem) it is suited to explaining not only sectoral/regional but also purely regional polarisations. The subordination of the traditional growth pole concept does not mean, however, that it is no longer considered relevant, only that its relevance was over-estimated in the First and Second Plans.

Industrial growth pole policy continues to be an impartial instrument of polarisation-orientated regional policy. Nevertheless, a fundamental new approach is required in the selection of means of promotion. As an analysis of the Spanish growth pole policy in the First and Second Plans will show, the direct promotion measures employed were not suitable for effectively establishing sectoral/regional polarisations. Frequently, it was not merely transitional locational disadvantages which were compensated by these measures, but possibly consequences of inadequate planning. It seems a better procedure:

—   first to establish generally by means of attraction analysis those activities which incline towards settlement in proximity;
—   then to seek out the most suitable peripheral region for their establishment, and
—   finally to organise the establishment of a corresponding industrial complex as a whole, in which
    — the main force of public activity falls on the factual and temporal co-ordination of private investment decision and the timely preparation of the economic and social infrastructure capital,

— while direct promotion measures only serve to even out liquidity shortages with necessary complementary activities and to offset losses arising from one-sided production of external effects through such activities in the initial phase.

3 In this work the foreground is occupied by attempts at planning control and at the formulation of alternative information systems as a basis for planning revision, special consideration being given to the suitability of the polarisation theory for the clarification of the spatial dimension of the general economic growth process. It is not proved that a polarisation-orientated regional policy is the best solution in the case of the national economy when examined in relation to the present group of aims — efficiency, integration and conformity with distribution requirements. On the other hand it has already been demonstrated that according to the proposed considerations and experiences this policy can presumably be regarded as superior. This means that it seems sensible to examine the principles so far established by more intensive study, and that owing to the necessity to proceed with planning even if in a spirit of uncertainty, it is right to select the alternative which is presumably acknowledged to be the most suitable.

The dilemma — and thus the risk — of such a decision lies in the fact that, when the strategy of intensive decentralisation runs into faulty decisions in individual cases, owing to the concentrated expenditure of means, these are of an aggravating nature.

In so far as the traditional growth pole concept is in need of constructive criticism, certain important indications for its improvement emerge from the empirical results of Part III of the work.

Notes

1   'The consequence, and a very important one, is the development of an area with small markets dispersed towards six dense market zones very far apart surrounded by regions that are daily more depopulated' (Perpina and Grau, 69, 643).

2   'It is essential to improve (the) . . . future cities which . . . are towns which sometimes have a natural beauty that would enchant a painter but which display every inadequacy imaginable for the daily life of people. In this sense it must be recognised that many Andalucian towns are very beautiful to visit but inhospitable to live in' (Barbancho, 68, 17).

3   These consequences for social policy ('crisis of inclusion') are pronounced upon positively by Friedmann (68, 366): 'In short, a policy of accelerated urbanization would tend to have disruptive effects on the traditional social system. At the same time, however, it would germinate and build up constructing forces potentially capable of transcending the "crisis of inclusion" that it itself would generate.'

4   The terms of the accuracy of this result are examined in Part II.

5   No attempt will be made here to discuss the viability of the distinction mentioned (cf. Klaassen, 70, 95; Rittenbruch, 68, 48 et seq.).

6   In the case of the Vigo pole the province is Pontevedra. For identification purposes it will be referred to here as Vigo.

7   It can only ever be a question here as in what follows of the central elements. The fact that the provinces have practically no income of their own means that all the tasks arising must be given consideration in the central planning.

8   'The regional action will be based on an eminently strict criterion, a criterion that will be based in the first place on the definition of the network and hierarchy of the nuclei of the population' (Planning Commission, Directives . . . 71).

PART III

The Example of the Spanish Growth Poles (Huelva and Seville)

1 The Field Research Programme

We are concerned here with a work on planning control, that is to say *ex post facto* analysis. As already demonstrated, the expectations of the Spanish planners in connection with the pole programme correspond to the hypotheses of the French school on spatial polarisation, so that it is possible to speak in terms of a test of the growth pole theory.

1.1 Definition of the research programme

As has already been shown, spatial polarisation is the net result of geographically centripetal and centrifugal economic and social forces. Under the growth pole theory the motive power behind the centripetal movements is to be found in the inter-industrial relations. The centrifugal forces signify the growth effect, which exercises a kind of geographically clustered sectoral pole on its hinterland, the pole thus being characterised by an inner and an outer relationship. The differentiating criteria for 'inner' and 'outer' can be established according to Perroux (Perroux, 50) in relation to homogeneity, functional and planning criteria. Since an investigation into planning control must follow the categories on the basis of which the expectancy values for a given planning horizon are formulated, the two central elements of the object of the investigation – pole and hinterland – were defined in accordance with the provisions of the planners in prospect.

1 *Definition of the pole.* The planners define the pole as an administrative unit; accordingly all the industries whose interests are directly benefited by the promotion measures of the pole programme belong to the pole, i.e. those for which applications are accepted in the authorisation procedure ('concurso'). In addition, the present investigation includes all those industries which were established at the place of location of the poles after 1964, at the beginning of the pole programme, even if they were not authorised by the 'concurso'. They must, however, satisfy the criterion which is decisive according to the growth pole theory for the inner relationship of the pole, namely the possible existence of important input-output relationships with such industries as were already available in the pole in the narrowly defined administrative sense. For this

91

purpose it is immaterial whether or not supply relationships actually existed previously; for the rest, this was also the first point to be examined.

In Seville, cases of additional activities in accordance with the expanded pole definition are rare. The majority of the undertakings which either built up new or expanded existing industries have been able to make use of promotion measures. In the case of Huelva, the extended pole definition is for the most part identical with the industrial production potential of the province, if the building trade and extractive industries are excluded. In the case of Seville a certain amount of industry already existed, therefore the pole defined according to the above criterion is not identical with the main bulk of the industrial output potential of the province. Certainly a considerable number of large industries already available have utilised the pole promotion measures to expand their investment.

For the investigation, the deadline for the demarcation of the pole was set at 31 December 1969. The activities permitted for the pole, which were still at the planning stage and for which production could not be expected to commence before 1972, were not recorded. On the appointed date, the pole so defined comprised forty-two industries in Huelva and seventy in Seville.

The concept of industry is used here in a special sense. It embraces independent production units, and is not necessarily to be identified with the concept of the undertaking, partly because many pole businesses belong to undertakings not associated with the pole, and also because some undertakings have established several independent production units in the same pole. One example of this is the Gulf Oil refinery in Huelva and the asphalt factory founded subsequently by Gulf Oil. It is not disclosed whether both production units were combined, or whether the delivery linkages between them were material for the subsequent establishment of the asphalt factory. Admittedly, the criterion according to which such a separation is made is always somewhat arbitrary owing to the disparities between particular situations.

2 *Definition of the hinterland.* The hinterland of the pole can be specified as a functional or nodal region or as a planning region. Fundamentally it would be right to work with the concept of the nodal region, since this can be defined as the geographical projection of a sectoral polarisation. Establishing this could possibly be one of the results of the enquiry. For this reason too the demarcation of the hinterland is determined in connection with the concept of the planning region. In the administrative sense, planning regions do not exist in Spain (Beck, 68, 17

92

et seq.), but the ideas of the planners do permit conclusions to be made regarding the corresponding territorial demarcations.

In the case of the Andalusian pole, the planning region is that of the River Guadalquivir. In order to delineate this, the axis principle in conjunction with the criterion of geographical homogeneity 'river course' is material. In its first expansion stage the planning region embraces the pole provinces of Huelva and Seville, in the second (starting with the Third Plan) the pole province of Cordoba, the province of Cadiz (the Algeciras Bay project) and ultimately the province of Jaén are added. Having regard to the availability of statistics, each regional demarcation must be based on the provincial boundaries (see map, p. 73).

In the enquiry, the hinterland of the Andalusian pole is limited to the first expansion stage.

3 *Choice of years under review.* The first pole industries were established in 1964, but very few of them were able to commence production before 1967. Even in 1967 the gross output value of the industries in both poles attained no more than 20 per cent of the 1971 value for Huelva and 42 per cent for Seville. The first year selected for review was 1967.

The second year to be chosen for review was 1969, since for that year the latest data would be available from the business accounting documents of the various industries. The data for 1971, on the other hand, are drawn from estimates by the undertakings themselves; when evaluating these, the lower of two possible results was always adopted in cases of doubt. Had the enquiry been restricted to using only the data up to 1969, the picture given would have been incomplete, for the 1969 figures for the gross output value of the industries in both poles amounted to no more than some 39 per cent and 72 per cent of the 1971 value for Huelva and Seville respectively.

The years selected for review apply to the *production phase* of the pole industries. In order to ascertain the effects that spread to income and regional external relations during the *investment phase*, the years 1964-66 were also considered in this connection.

1.2 Methods and instruments

1 The control of results under the programme of regional policy has only been effected so far in Spain by means of the observation of simple indicators such as the investment carried out, number of jobs created and so on. To some extent no firm statistics were available to indicate which

industries had already made a start on production.[1] In the face of these estimates which are incomplete in every respect, the author proposed the adoption of integrated accounting systems for the investigation of growth poles. This is the more important in that the observance of unrelated indicators does not permit a critical assessment of the data. An attempt was made on these lines to build an analysis of the results of the growth poles on two basic systems.

(a) In order to examine the development of the pole and its internal relations, and its link-up with the hinterland, with the rest of the national economy and with foreign countries, two accounts were prepared for each pole industry.

The production account provides information on the results of the production phase of the pole industries. It is broken down in such a way that the trade flows with the hinterland, and the rest of the national economy and foreign countries are apparent. From this the corresponding trade balances of the pole sectors can be calculated. Sectors of the pole are groupings of individual pole industries in accordance with the classification of Spanish industry based on the ISIC approach, and a combined classification is used for the poles by the ministries concerned.[2] This procedure is followed here because a precise break-down according to the ISIC classification makes it possible to identify particular industries in the input-output tables. Moreover, this is the only way in which comparison with official statistics on the poles is possible.

The input-output tables were also drawn up on the basis of the production accounts, for which purpose it was also necessary to set out precisely the supply relationships of pole industries to one another. The input-output tables were first drawn up for each review year by showing the values for each industry, and then aggregated by sectors so that the inter-relationships were not cancelled out by consolidation within the sectors. The detailed tables are not suitable for publication because of the need to preserve secrecy regarding the statistics.

The 'capital account' or fixed investment account and its financing provides information on the transactions from which the economic effects of the pole during the investment phase can be analysed. In connection with the data on the infrastructure investment in the pole, the regional outflow effects in particular can be shown on this basis during the investment period.

(b) The pole-hinterland relationships can be described in the frame-work of total accounts for the pole provinces. They enable the importance of the pole to be observed in relation to the total size of the region, and changes to be shown in the total size resulting from the activity of the pole. The total accounts are specifically used for calculating the indirect

94

and induced effects on the regional income in accordance with the SEMA system, much greater accuracy being obtained in this way than by the Lacq project evaluation.

Apart from the connections displayed in the accounts referred to, a range of additional information has been prepared which is relevant to the polarisation theory. This relates in particular to employment and the structure thereof, to inter-regional dominance relationships between parent companies and branch industries, and to the significance of pole industries in the framework of the national economic production structure.

2   Since little material was available in the form of official statistics and documents for use in completing the production and capital accounts and compiling supplementary information, the corresponding data had to be obtained almost exclusively from an enquiry into the pole industries. The main enquiry took the form of a questionnaire which was tried out in some industries in Huelva in the autumn of 1969. After revision, a start was made on the final questionnaire in February 1970.

The questionnaire was deliberately kept simple (cf. Buttler, 73, Appendix 2) in order to guarantee the achievement of a satisfactory return ratio.

The following table shows the return ration achieved and the relative importance of the industries which were not prepared to reply:

Table 3
Return ratio for the main questionnaire

Pole	Number of industries	No reply	Relative importance* in relation to		
			Invest-ment	Jobs	Gross output value**
Huelva	42	4	0.3%	1.7%	1.6%
Seville	70	7	1.5%	1.7%	2.2%

*Value on the appointed day.
**Gross output value 1969, Source: Ministry of Finance, Director General for Indirect Taxes, Madrid 1970.

1.3   Overall system of investigation

The overall system of investigation falls into two main parts, that of the accounts for the investment phase and the accounts for the production phase of the poles. In the investigation of the investment phase two sub-divisions are distinguished, infra-structure investments on the one hand, and directly productive investments on the other hand. At the action phase a subsidiary channel is formed which contains the projects submitted with the applications for admission to the pole and their comparison with the actual values arising from the enquiry. This gives:

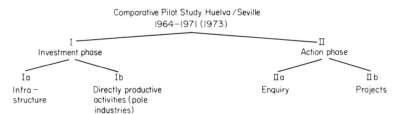

Before the individual lines of investigation are followed through, the sub-division of the flow-sizes of intermediary inputs and sales included in the production accounts – the most highly differentiated part – will be treated separately.

A   Intermediary inputs of the pole industries

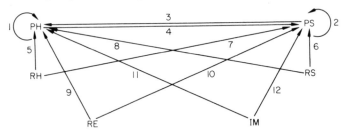

B   Sales by the pole industries

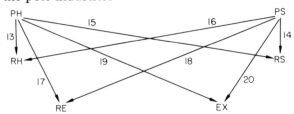

Where	PS	=	Seville pole		RS	=	Rest of Seville province
	RH	=	Rest of Huelva province		IM	=	Foreign imports
	PH	=	Huelva pole		EX	=	Foreign exports

96

The direction of the arrows indicates the flow of goods. Flows 1 and 2 are recorded and shown separately for each industry, flows 3 and 4 are broken down in the additional tables to the input-output tables by supplying and receiving sectors. The same applies in respect of flows 5 to 8. The additional tables are repeated in the Appendix.

Flows 9 to 12 were only set out in respect of the receiving or pole industries. Flows 13 to 20 (sales) were specified in relation to producers and expenditure directions. The breakdown by expenditure — as intermediary input, investment goods and consumer goods — is important, since it is only on the basis of intermediate expenditure that forward linkages can be expected.

The individual currents of the investigation can now be further described, the basis being provided by the diagram on page 96.

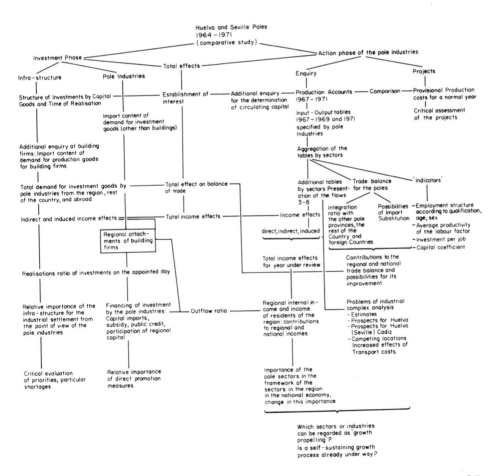

1.4 Objections to the research programme

Objections may be raised in particular to the fact that the definition of the object of the investigation is often based on administrative criteria. Owing to the nature of the data provided this could not be avoided. It might also be objected that input-output tables were not provided for the pole provinces as a whole. This is first of all a time and cost question, but in the second place it can be maintained that with the input-output tables for pole industries in many poles (notably Huelva) the main part of modern processing industry in the province was covered. This is shown by Table 4:

Table 4
Gross value creation of processing industry* (Ptas million)

	Rest of province 1967	Pole 1967	Pole 1971
Huelva	1,607.5	644.7	4,319.4
Seville	8,726.2	1,602.5	3,793.8

*Whole of industry other than extractive industry, building trade and energy industry
Sources: Regional accounts and enquiry.

In addition, all the direct supply relationships of the pole industries with the activities in the rest of the province were shown to be sectorally disaggregated by the additional tables (cf. Appendix).

The degree of information thus achieved is sufficient for present purposes. Special problems arising from ignorance of the extra-polar inner-regional input-output relations will be discussed in connection with the ascertainment of the secondary and tertiary income effects. It must be borne in mind that, because of the time involved, the attainment of the fastest possible knowledge of control data will be impeded by a further perfecting of the planning control procedure in the direction of the periodical preparation of regional input-output tables. Furthermore, the author considers that it might be more useful to expand the existing control system on the lines of a *cost-benefit analysis* of the current promotion programme, especially since the forecasting value of input-output tables for the entire region must remain doubtful in view of attraction theory considerations.

2 General Survey

This section provides guidelines regarding important overall dimensions, compares them with the planning values of the projects and relates them to the corresponding results of the regional and national accounts.

2.1 Investment, production and employment

1 The total *fixed capital investment* in the pole is sub-divided into directly productive (pole industry) investment and infrastructure investment.

Table 5
Fixed capital investment in the pole industries,
1964-69 (Ptas thousands)

Sector		Huelva Pole			Seville Pole		
No.	Description	No. of industries	Investment vol.	Per cent	No. of industries	Investment vol.	Per cent
1	Foodstuffs	4	284,469	1.9	18	785,409	9.3
2	Timber proces- sing	6	1,427,474	9.7	–	–	–
3	Paper processing	0	–	–	7	246,467	2.9
4	Textiles	0	–	–	3	888,219	10.5
5	Chemicals	14	10,081,579	68.6	8	822,983	9.8
6	Building materials	5	241,975	1.6	16	3,431,397	40.6
7	Metal industries	8	1,189,614	8.1	12	1,374,553	16.3
8	Energy .	1	1,209,918	8.2	1	687,003	8.1
9	Various*	4	214,029	1.5	5	207,523	2.5
10	Special cases**	3	54,717	0.4	–	–	–

*Groupings of all the industries which would otherwise have been identifiable. Sectors must comprise at least three firms. Thus two industries are shown in Huelva under 'various' which belong to the textile and paper processing industries. One exception is the energy sector.
**Industries which belong to the pole, are under construction, but had not commenced production before 1972. They are only considered at this point. In all probability the undertakings concerned are to be regarded as having failed.

For the period 1964-69, the proportion of the pole industries which received no direct promotion measures as they were not accepted for promotion under assistance arrangements, amounted to 41 per cent of the total in Huelva and 23 per cent in Seville.

An estimate of future investment in the pole industries can be made for the period up to 1973. This estimate is based on the investment projects in all the industries which − on the scheduled date − planned expansion investments by 1972, or were already authorised to proceed under the scheme despite not having made a start on the project by the date in question.

According to this, additional fixed investment in 1970-73 already approved under the pole arrangements, together with that already available, should amount to Ptas 8,776,200 thousand in Huelva and Ptas 4,321,500 thousand in Seville.

Since as a rule actual investment has considerably exceeded the figure planned, this amount could still rise without any further industries coming into the picture. On the other hand, the values for Huelva still seem on the high side, as according to recent information eight projects with an investment volume of Ptas 3,031,018 thousand were dropped in 1971. These were mainly investments in the chemical industry (approximately Ptas 2.7 million in total), the reasons for which will be considered in Chapter 4. It need only be mentioned at this point that the competing location of Tarragona in Catalonia attracts some of the planned projects in the chemical industry. Consequently, it is impossible to make reliable forecasts regarding further investments in the chemical industry which are not accepted under the aid arrangements.

The total *infrastructure investments* for the period 1964-69 amount to Ptas 1,539 million. The following table shows how these are made up:

Table 6
Infrastructure investments, 1964-69 (Ptas million)

Pole	Industrial areas	Water supply and sewage	Road building	Port instal- lations	Total
Huelva	70	829	138	222	1,259
Seville	154	88	38	−	280
Total	224	917	176	222	1,539

The plan figures for the infrastructure investments in both poles (Planning Commission, Regional Development Report, 69, 226) show that in the framework of the Second Plan up to 1971 the following investments would have to be made if the planning estimates were to be satisfied:

Table 7
Infrastructure investments, 1970-71 (Ptas million)

Pole	Industrial areas	Water supply and sewage	Road building	Port instal- lations	Total
Huelva	267	1,105	642	343	2,357
Seville	188	143	—*	—	331
Total	455	1,248	642	343	2,688

*The plan figures do not show the road-building investment to be effected in connection with the pole separately, but for road and railway construction combined an additional Ptas 1,701 million was planned.

Precise particulars of the situation are not yet available, but it is not to be expected that these investments could all be realised by 1971. Although it must be anticipated that particular positions, especially 'industrial areas', will be sharply reduced, it can be assumed that the projected infrastructure investments can be concluded by 1973.

This leaves the overall position roughly as follows:

101

Table 8
Total investments in fixed assets. Huelva and Seville poles, 1964-69 and 1970-73 (Ptas million)

	Huelva	Seville
Infrastructure		
up to 1969	1,259	280
up to 1973	2,357	331
Pole industries		
up to 1969	14,704	8,444
up to 1973	8,776	4,321
Total	27,096	13,376

The production of both poles and its development are shown for the three years under review in Table 9:

Table 9
Gross output value of the pole industries (Ptas million)

	Huelva		Seville	
	No. of pro-ducing industries	Gross output value	No. of pro-ducing industries	Gross output value
1967	17	3,351.1	45	4,758.7
1969	35	6,500.5	57	8,084.6
1971	41*	16,852.8	69**	11,155.1

*One industry which was shown separately in 1969 was amalgamated with another in 1971.
**One industry which was in production until 1969 has been unable to meet its obligations.

Production and gross value creation are broken down by sectors in Table 10 for the years under review.

Table 10
Gross output value and gross value creation by sectors,
1964-71 (Ptas million)

(a) Huelva

	Gross output value			Gross value creation		
	1967	1969	1971	1967	1969	1971
Foodstuffs	0	15.1	190.0	0	9.0	77.0
Timber processing	415.4	602.0	951.0	201.3	283.7	439.7
Chemicals	2,792.1	5,300.7	9,783.0	420.5	1,136.4	2,786.1
Building materials	22.2	160.7	166.8	13.1	61.9	63.9
Metal industries	23.3	111.9	5,314.9	10.2	68.4	881.7
Energy*	96.7	197.6	353.7	69.9	117.8	212.2
Various	2.4	112.5	138.4	0.1	49.7	71.1
Total	3,351.1	6,500.5	16,852.8	715.1	1,726.9	4,531.7

(b) Seville

	Gross output value			Gross value creation		
	1967	1969	1971	1967	1969	1971
Foodstuffs	1,189.7	1,828.8	2,118.8	107.3	288.9	394.5
Textiles	528.3	667.3	667.3	151.0	176.7	176.7
Paper processing	201.6	359.1	812.7	44.3	74.1	242.5
Chemicals	408.2	999.5	1,100.8	39.0	185.3	225.6
Building materials	892.9	1,474.4	2,827.2	403.4	568.1	1,215.6
Metals industries	1,411.3	2,485.1	3,068.7	795.5	1,307.1	1,422.0
Energy*	68.5	195.0	255.1	43.3	102.6	160.0
Various	58.2	75.4	304.0	18.7	28.0	109.9
Total	4,758.7	8,084.6	11,155.1	1,602.5	2,730.9	3,976.8

*Only includes the value in connection with sales to other pole industries. The undertaking concerned was already in existence before 1964 in both poles. Only increases in investment effected in connection with pole formation and sales to pole industries after such increases are included. Consequently it was also unnecessary to allocate this 'industry' to the sector 'various' on account of the statistical anonymity otherwise to be observed.

For 1973 an attempt was made to estimate the gross production and value creation, the object being to give an outline of the development of the poles on the assumption that the industries already producing in 1971 would continue to operate at full capacity, and the projects available on the appointed day would be fully realised. The outcome is shown in Table 11:

Table 11
Plan figures for gross output value and gross value creation
(Ptas million of 1969) 1973

Sector No.*	Huelva			Seville		
	No. of industries	Gross output value	Gross value creation	No. of industries	Gross output value	Gross value creation
1	7	897.5	255.3	21	4,812.1	1,287.4
2	8	2,131.0	1,037.9	0	0	0
3	0	0	0	8	819.7	245.3
4	0	0	0	4	2,233.2	1,114.9
5	20	13,885.3	4,469.8	16	2,226.0	534.2
6	5	166.8	63.9	20	3,182.2	1,484.0
7	10	5,384.6	983.3	15	3,289.9	1,490.5
8	1	596.7	358.4	2	371.2	233.8
9**	8	4,336.1	1,551.8	11	1,118.0	429.8
Total	59	27,398.0	8,720.5	97	17,052.3	6,819.9

*Cf. Table 5.
**The sharp increase in the values for the sector in Huelva is accounted for by the addition of a further industry in each case in the textile and paper processing industries.

The interpretation of the production results, especially the resulting value creation coefficients, must be made by means of the detailed input-output tables. This is the only way to ensure that obvious inconsistencies, especially those arising from comparison of the sectors with one another, are cleared up in specific cases. Generally speaking, any such comparison must be regarded as highly problematical, because the production structure, or product mix, within the sectors differs sharply between the poles. This can be illustrated by a particularly striking example.

The value creation quota for the metal sector in 1971 was 16.6 per cent in Huelva and 46.3 per cent in Seville. While in Seville this sector consists almost exclusively of processing industries, in Huelva a foundry for the production of electrolytic copper accounts for almost the entire pro-

104

duction and value creation of the sector. The remaining nine industries are small concerns in shipbuilding and metal processing.

Development of the value creation quota within a sector of the same pole can also be thoroughly irregular if the composition of the sector is changed by the establishment of new undertakings. If no new undertakings are established, or if the sector is already so large as to limit their relative importance, then in the first phase of the pole it can be reckoned that the value creation quotas will tend to rise to the level of normal production on account of the higher capacity utilisation. The reason for this lies in the fact that the use of certain intermediate inputs rises in inferior proportion to the capacity utilisation, and that in the initial phase higher reject rates occur in the production. This tendency can be illustrated by the example of three sectors:

Table 12
Ratio of gross value creation to gross output value
(value creation quota)

	1967	1969	1971	1973
Chemicals — Huelva	15.0	21.4	28.5	32.2
Chemicals — Seville	9.6	18.5	20.5	24.0
Foodstuffs — Seville	5.7	15.8	18.6	26.7

To what extent the production conditions of the individual industries are to be considered in the interpretation emerges from the example of the foodstuffs sector in Huelva. In this case the value creation quota declined from 59.6 in 1969, the first year of production, to 40.5 in 1971 and 28.4 in 1973. The reason is that the two industries producing in 1969, concerned with deep frozen fish, handled only the refrigeration, storage and packaging without actually buying or selling the fish. The same thing happened to some extent in a third industry which began to produce in 1971. Lastly, the fourth industry, which also started up in 1971, produces feeding-stuffs. While in the first and second cases the value creation quota must be high, in the third case this can only be expected to apply to the share specifically restricted to the services of refrigeration, storage and packaging; with regard to the remainder, the value creation quota must be lower if — with the same amount of input — the gross production value is increased by the sale of the products for own account by at least the amount of the purchase price of the initial products. For the fourth industry a lower value creation rate must finally be assumed because the production process proper is limited to a mechanical mixing process.[3] The reduction of the value creation proportion for 1973, as compared with 1971, also arises from the fact that two of the three producers of deep-freeze products want to switch their production entirely to their own goods and the appearance of three new industries means that the product mix of the sector is sharply changed.

These examples are given because they show that, in connection with average values of the national input-output tables, the interpretation of the results of so small an aggregate as that of the pole sector is not meaningful. It is not possible to draw any conclusions as to the accuracy of the results of the enquiry from such comparisons.

3   The effects of the pole on *employment* are indicated in the first instance by the newly created jobs recorded in Table 13.

Table 13
Newly-created jobs* in pole industries up to . . .

	Huelva			Seville		
	1967	1969	1971	1967	1969	1971
Foodstuffs	0	55	87	426	612	1,061
Timber processing	592	766	766	0	0	0
Paper processing	0	0	0	176	230	550
Textiles	0	0	0	453	682	682
Chemicals	656	1,356	1,663	222	481	822
Building materials	59	178	178	1,372	1,866	2,689
Metal industry	106	288	1,064	2,052	2,858	2,858
Energy	0	20	20	20	28	28
Various	45	160	160	160	130	357
Total	1,458	2,823	3,938	4,881	6,887	9.047

*Only 'permanent' jobs.

Projections for 1973 on the assumptions so far made for the purpose still show a substantial increase. To repeat these assumptions, it is assumed that all the industries which were admitted to the pole on the appointed day, which belonged to the pole in the wider sense, and whose realisation had to be accepted as probable on the appointed day, are producing normally in 1973, irrespective of whether they were at the planning, construction or production stage at the time.

A notable feature is the high growth in Huelva compared with 1971. Even if one were to eliminate those projects — especially in the chemical industry — whose realisation seemed highly improbable after the appointed day, the result would not be markedly different, for only 634 jobs would be affected thereby. The growth is almost exclusively determined, on the contrary, by two industries in the textile sector (as before, they are shown under the heading 'various') which between them plan to provide 3,000 new jobs. For Huelva, the validity of this forecast consequently depends on the implementation of these two projects, which is doubtful.

Table 14
New jobs, 1964-73

	Huelva	Seville
Foodstuffs	504	1,267
Timber processing	1,227	0
Paper processing	0	711
Textiles	0	2,445
Chemicals	2,431	1,171
Building materials	198	5,030
Metal industry	1,070	2,858
Energy	20	39
Various	3,418	783
Total	8,868	14,569

The effect of the poles on the employment position is thus by no means completely covered, partly because these can be far more extensive owing to the indirect and induced repercussions on income, partly because workers in the region who were formerly under-employed also found employment in the investment phase of pole industries and the infrastructure. To this extent it is only the 'direct' job-creation effect, analogous to the direct income effect of the pole industries in the production phase, that is represented here.

4 On the basis of the data now assembled three *import structure coefficients* can now be calculated, namely average labour productivity (π), capital intensity (ϵ) and capital coefficient (σ). By definition these are related in the equation:

$$\epsilon = \pi \quad \sigma.$$

The average labour productivity is shown below, broken down by sectors for 1969, 1971 and 1973.

Apart from the value for Huelva for 1973, a rising overall tendency can be noted. This rising tendency is explained by the fact that — as set out above — the value creation quota increases, and as production gets under way the number employed is relatively high and expands less rapidly in proportion as capacity is utilised more fully. The explanation is not satisfactory, however, for in particular cases such as the overall result this tendency can be intensified, weakened or over-compensated by the change in the product mix of the sectors, as a result of the varying growth rates of existing industries and the emergence of new undertakings. In the present case it transpires that the total result for the pole in Huelva was sinking because of the high importance of the 'Various' sector in 1973 compared with 1971, despite rising labour productivity in a general situation of below-average labour productivity for this sector.

In order to calculate corresponding sectoral values for capital intensity and the capital/output ratios, the investment planned for the total period 1964-73 must first of all be broken down by sectors. In calculating the capital/output ratios no attempt will be made to establish values for 1969 and 1971 as these would not be very meaningful. In each of the two years under review investments were effected although it had not been possible to start production or provide the jobs concerned, and the measure of temporal correspondence in the development of the two determinants which applied to the development of labour productivity, does not apply here. Necessary restrictions of the forecast values of the projections for 1973, and the consequent coefficients arrived at, are combined again below.

Restrictions of the forecast values of the projections for 1973 arise from the following factors:

— in the case of investments not yet realised on the appointed date, these are determined with prices for investment capital at the time the project was planned, and they are consequently under-valued;

Table 15
Average labour productivity, 1969-73 (Ptas thousands at 1969 prices)

	Huelva Pole			Seville Pole		
	1969	1971	1973	1969	1971	1973
Foodstuffs	164	885	507	472	372	1,016
Timber processing	370	574	845	0	0	0
Paper processing	0	0	0	259	259	345
Textiles	0	0	0	322	441	456
Chemicals	838	1,675	1,839	385	274	456
Building materials	348	359	323	304	452	295
Metal industry	238	829	919	457	497	474
Energy*	—	—	—	—	—	—
Various	311	444	454	215	307	549

*The energy sector was not included because for the calculation of value creation a special process was used (cf. footnote to Table 10 above).

Table 16
Total investments carried out and projected in 1964-73 in pole industries (Ptas millions at prices current at the time)

	Huelva	Seville
Foodstuffs	601.3	1,116.5
Timber processing	1,657.5	0
Paper processing	0	489.3
Textiles	0	1,070.6
Chemicals	15,605.8	1,476.3
Building materials	265.9	4,625.0
Metal industry	1,279.4	1,750.5
Energy	1,812.6	1,811.7
Various	2,257.5	425.3
Total	23,480.0	12,765.2

- for the investments realised up to the appointed date it has been shown that values realised were in excess of the estimates and were only to a minor extent affected by price increases in the capital assets;
- in the same way as for the projection for production and numbers employed, it may be said that after the time of the enquiry investments hitherto regarded as highly probable turned out to be most improbable. This had already been quantitatively established for the sector of the chemicals industry in Huelva which was relevant in this respect;
- in the case of the pole industries examined at the enquiry, investments planned after the appointed day and after the deadline for the questionnaire were not affected.

Altogether, therefore, the projection for 1973 only reflects the values recognised as probable at the time of the enquiry. On this matter it must also be considered that the estimates produced for projects in the pole industries could be faulty in many respects.

Apart from faults specifically affecting projections it may in general be found
- that projected employment figures tend to be set too high because of the *'social' character* of the plan and the authorisation criteria deduced therefrom,
- that the value creation quota having regard to the *income contribution criterion* is put excessively high in the authorisation,
- and that, owing to the lack of opportunity to consider *increases that occur later in the planning estimates* when calculating the subsidies etc., the investments are henceforth calculated more generously on the basis of experience acquired.

For all that, taking into account the fact that the tendency to overvalue will appear in all the basic data essential for the projection of the coefficients, it can be assumed that the resulting coefficients could be more accurate than are the forecasts of the projections of the basic data in detail.

Subject to the reservations indicated, the values for 1969, 1971 and 1973 given in Tables 15 and 17 are designated as normal values for the sectors of both poles, on the assumption that the projects will be completely realised. In this connection, however, there are important general differences between the two poles.

Capital intensity is also the measure for the volume of fixed investment per job. Assuming an approximate exchange rate between the DM and the Peseta of 1:20, it seems that *a job in the Huelva pole cost DM 0.123 million on the average, and in the Seville pole DM 0.038 million.* If it is further considered that the capital/output ratio can be used as an indicator for the speed of recovery of investment capital in terms of 'cash-flow', then it can also be assumed that the essential elements of the industrialisation process in Huelva must be borne by capital – and liquidity-intensive undertakings to a much greater extent than in Seville. If, finally, it is considered that investment resources per head of the population are much lower in Huelva than in Seville, then it must be assumed that the participation of domestic capital in pole investments in Huelva is correspondingly lower than in Seville. This will be examined more closely in future. Similarly the outflow quota, that is the difference between regional, internal and residents' incomes in its direct income effects, is also different (cf. 3.4).

Table 17
Capital intensity and capital output ratios by sectors for 1973

	Huelva		Seville	
	ϵ in 10^6 Ptas.	σ	ϵ in 10^6 Ptas.	σ
Foodstuffs	1.193	2.35	0.881	0.87
Timber processing	1.351	1.60	—	—
Paper processing	–	—	0.688	1.99
Textiles	—	—	0.438	0.96
Chemicals	6.419	3.49	1.261	2.77
Building materials	1.343***	4.15***	0.919	3.12
Metal industry	1.196	1.30	0.668	1.41
Energy*	—	—	—	—
Various	0.660	1.45	0.543	0.99
Total**	2.449	2.59	0.754	1.66

*Because of its special character the energy sector was again omitted from consideration.
**Deviations from the exact product of $\epsilon = \pi \cdot \sigma$ are due to rounding off.
***Particularly problematical value.

Such relationships are so clear that it pays to draw the above comparisons even when the value of the statistical material in particular

111

cases is doubtful. In the following instance, the projections for 1973 are not elaborated further. They have fulfilled their purpose by giving a general picture on particular assumptions of the presumed development of the poles. Later evaluations going into greater detail do not provide a consideration of the projections for 1973, especially as the estimates of certain values for 1971 leave much to be desired from the accuracy point of view.

2.2 Importance of pole activities in the framework of the regional and national accounts

This analysis relates the pole activities to corresponding values in the regional and national accounts. Important amounts set out in the preceding section are measured as to their relative importance in the framework of the pole provinces and the national economy.

The growth pole policy pursues inter alia *the object of increasing the supply of industrial jobs, and of expanding, diversifying and modernising the industrial production of the province. It is interesting to observe the effects resulting directly from the commencement of production of the pole industries in this connection.*

1   At the outset certain structure data for both pole provinces should be given.

(a)   Backward regions are usually emigration areas. Their share of the total population is declining sharply (for Spain see Barbancho, 67, 109 et seq.). The growth pole policy has set itself the task of retaining within the province parts of the population which otherwise would be moved to emigrate.

Both provinces recorded an absolute increase in the population in 1969 compared with 1964. This tendency continued in 1971 (Planning Commission: Estimates . . . , 71, 166).

Whereas for Huelva there was a sharp decline in its proportion of the total population of Spain, the proportion for Seville was increasing. It would be premature to ascribe this result to the pole settlement,[4] but it is interesting to note that while six of the seven growth poles in Spain had a positive population growth in 1971 compared with 1967, only Seville also showed a rising share of the total population (ibid.). This seems due to the fact that Seville is the only 'metropolitan' town among the Spanish growth pole localisation. On the other hand the population movement in twenty-two of the remaining forty-three provinces between 1967 and 1971 was negative.

112

Table 18
Population of province in thousands of inhabitants

Province	Absolute figures			As a percentage of the national population		
	1964	1967	1969*	1964	1967	1969*
Huelva	403.7	394.4	408.5	1.28	1.22	1.21
Seville	1,342.5	1,375.4	1,456.6	4.25	4.25	4.31

*Source: National Statistics Institute, Monthly Bulletin of Statistics, July 1970.

(b) Total income and *per capita* income for both provinces in 1967 were as follows:

Table 19
Income values, 1967

	Ranking among the 50 provinces	Total income (Ptas '000s)	Ranking among the 50 provinces	*Per Capita* income (Ptas)
Huelva	35	11,867,200	40	31,113
Seville	5	46,545,200	34	32,521
Whole Nation	—	1,443,646,400	—	44,681

The table also shows the ranking held by the two provinces in relation to the total and *per capita* incomes of the fifty Spanish provinces.

(c) Table 20 shows the sectoral production structure. Sector I comprises agriculture, forestry and fishing, Sector II industry, and Sector III the services sector. A more detailed analysis of the sectors is to be found in the regional accounts (Regional Accounts, Planning Commission, 70).

Table 20
Sectoral production structure of the pole provinces in 1967 and of the national economy

(a)	Huelva		Seville		Spain	
	Ptas millions	Per cent	Ptas millions	Per cent	Ptas millions	Per cent
I	3,218.5	23.9	10,623.9	20.9	243,535.4	16.1
II	4,428.4	32.9	14,498.7	28.4	523,699.0	34.6
III	5,821.4	43.2	25,769.8	50.7	746,798.5	49.3
Total	13,468.3	100	50,892.4	100	1,514,032.9	100
(b)*	Number	Per cent	Number	Per cent	Number	Per cent
I	52,097	39.7	158,151	34.0	4,176,644	32.0
II	35,356	26.9	134,946	29.0	3,992,765	30.6
III	43,869	33.4	171,561	37.0	4,888,075	37.4
(c)	Ptas thousands		Ptas thousands		Ptas thousands	
I	63.0		67.2		58.3	
II	125.3		107.4		131.2	
III	132.7		150.2		152.8	
Total	102.7		109.5		116.0	

(a) = Gross value creation
(b) = Employment
(c) = Average labour productivity

*Including members of the family working without direct payment.
Sources: For calculation of the values for Spain: Planning Commission . . . , Report on Regional Development 68, 46 et seq. and National Statistics Institute, Accounts, 70, 39.

114

Table 21
Pole/rest of province jobs (without members of the family
etc. assisting)

Sector	Rest of province 1967	Growth rate caused by pole industries in relation in each case to 1967 – rest of province (per cent)		
		1967	1969	1971
(a) Huelva				
Foodstuffs	4,938	0	1.1	1.8
Timber processing	2,340	25.3	32.7	32.7
Chemicals	587	111.8	231.0	283.3
Building materials	628	9.4	28.3	28.3
Metal industry	2,169	4.9	13.2	49.1
Energy	758	0	2.6	2.6
Various	2,469	1.8	6.5	6.5
Total	13,889	10.5	20.3	28.4
(b) Seville				
Foodstuffs	26,870	1.6	2.3	3.9
Textiles	4,634	9.8	14.7	14.7
Paper processing	1,720	10.2	13.4	32.0
Chemicals	2,903	7.6	16.6	28.3
Building materials	3,346	41.0	55.8	80.4
Metal industry	17,556	11.7	16.3	16.3
Energy	2,947	0.7	1.0	1.0
Various	13,922	1.2	1.0	2.7
Total	73,898	6.6	9.3	12.2

2   A certain general picture is thus provided. The importance of the pole
industries relative to value creation, employment, the wage total and
average labour productivity in their province, can now be seen. Since, for
the reasons mentioned, 1967 was the sole year for which an attempt at a
regional account could be made, and as the pole industries only include

processing industries (i.e. industries as a whole other than those of the extractive and construction type), the following procedure is used for purposes of comparison. From the total values for the province in 1967 those of the pole industries are deducted, only the total values of the processing industries being analysed. Following the deduction of the values for the pole industries the value for the 'province in 1967 without the pole' is obtained. The results of the pole for 1967, 1969 and 1971 are then related to this residual value. For 1969 and 1971 and pole/hinterland relationship is then determined on the assumption that no changes have occurred in the hinterland compared with 1967. In relation to an exact delineation of the actual position this assumption is plainly quite un-realistic, nonetheless it makes it possible to explain the relative importance of each pole for its hinterland in the period on the basis of its immediate effects if it is supposed that the 'autonomous' growth rate (independent of the pole) is the same for both poles.

Owing to the uncertainty of the estimated values so far for 1969 and 1971, it seems unlikely that a more suitable procedure can be found in so far as the regional analysis is concerned. The inconsistencies to be noted for the pole provinces in the projections for 1971 are considerable.[5]

(a) For the relative importance of the supply of jobs, related to the supply of jobs in processing industries in the rest of the province, see Table 21.

As it can be assumed that the wages paid represent the earnings of residents in the region as a whole, it is interesting to follow the development of the wage total.

Table 22 shows that, because of the pole activity, the growth rate of the wage total in the poles is between 1.6 and 2.4 times as high as the observed growth rate of the numbers employed. *This relationship is important from the point of view of incomes policy.*

The result for Huelva, moreover, is that the ratio between wage total and growth rate of employees has risen from one year to another under review, that is from 1.65 in 1967 to 2.25 in 1971, whereas the ratio in Seville has moved only marginally from 2.2 to 2.4 in that period.

The over-proportionate increase in the wage total in Huelva in 1971 is mainly attributable to the development in the metal industry field. Generally speaking, the disparities in the growth rates for employment and the wage total are connected with the fact that the pole industries, higher wages are paid on average for the same qualification rating than are paid in the corresponding industries in the hinterland, and that the average qualification rating for employees in pole industries is above that for those in hinterland industries.[6] The first part of the argument is particularly easy to grasp when it is considered that the authorisation of industries by

116

the pole authorities is also dependent on above-average wages being paid.

Table 22
Wage total pole/rest of province

Sector	Rest of province 1967 (Ptas millions)	Growth rate caused by pole industries in relation in each case to 1967 without pole (per cent)		
		1967	1969	1971
(a) Huelva				
Foodstuffs	237.4	0	1.9	6.1
Timber processing	88.1	62.0	99.0	113.7
Chemicals	38.9	236.0	519.3	735.2
Building materials	41.3	7.3	47.2	47.2
Metal industry	161.5	3.5	18.5	87.3
Energy	79.7	0	2.4	2.4
Various	224.0	0.8	6.6	8.0
Total	900.9	17.4	40.0	64.0
(b) Seville				
Foodstuffs	1,458.6	3.5	7.0	7.4
Textiles	239.1	16.1	57.2	57.2
Paper processing	127.2	14.7	16.0	45.4
Chemicals	238.8	10.3	20.4	24.7
Building materials	250.9	69.1	102.0	163.1
Metal industry	1,369.2	30.2	43.5	43.5
Energy	345.2	0.4	0.6	0.4
Various	836.6	0.9	1.0	6.2
Total	4,860.6	14.5	22.4	27.6

117

E

(b) Relative importance of value creation related to the processing industries in the rest of the province:

Table 23
Gross value creation pole/rest of province

Sector	Rest of province 1967 (Ptas millions)	Growth rate caused by pole industries in relation to rest of province in 1967 in each case (per cent)		
		1967	1969	1971
(a) Huelva				
Foodstuffs	630.7	0	1.4	12.2
Timber processing	80.4	250.4	352.9	546.9
Chemicals	66.9	628.6	1,698.7	4,164.6
Building materials	83.4	15.7	74.2	76.6
Metal industry	393.8	2.6	17.4	223.9
Energy	278.6	25.1	42.3	76.2
Various	1,696.8	0	2.9	4.2
Total	3,230.6	22.1	53.5	140.3
(b) Seville				
Foodstuffs	3,616.7	3.0	8.0	10.9
Textiles	361.1	41.8	48.9	48.9
Paper	258.1	17.2	28.7	94.0
Chemicals	619.0	6.3	29.9	36.4
Building materials	231.4	174.3	245.5	525.3
Metal industry	1,876.1	42.3	69.6	75.7
Energy	613.7	7.1	16.7	26.1
Various	1,999.7	0.9	1.4	5.5
Total	9,575.8	16.7	28.5	41.2

(c) Effect on the average labour productivity of the province as a whole.

A comparison between Table 15 and Table 20(c) has already made it clear that there is a substantial difference in productivity between pole industries and those in the hinterland. Table 24 shows the growth rates of average labour productivity which have occurred in the provinces as a whole, as a result of production in the pole industries.

Table 24
Average labour productivity pole/rest of province related to all sectors

	Rest of province 1967 (Ptas)	Growth rate caused by pole industries in each case in relation to rest of province 1967 (per cent)		
		1967	1969	1971
Huelva	99,600	+4.4	+10.9	+31.7
Seville	107,200	+2.1	+ 3.9	+ 5.9

Overall it may be said that here the direct importance of the Seville pole in the framework of its hinterland is considerably less than that of the Huelva pole, which is not surprising if the differing initial situation indicated in Tables 18 to 20 is brought up to date. On the other hand, it is to be expected that the indirect and induced effects of the Seville pole for the remainder of the province will be relatively higher than those of the Huelva pole, since under otherwise equal conditions the outflow effects will be less in a bigger market centre than in a smaller one (cf. under 3.1 and 3.2).

3   The relative importance of the pole industries within the framework of the national industry as a whole and by sectors, shows the establishment value of both the growth poles in the general economic growth process (cf. Table 25).

Table 25
Share of the poles in the gross value creation of processing
industries in Spain

	1967		1969		1971**	
	Total for Nat. Econ. (Ptas million)	Share of pole (per cent)	Total for Nat. Econ. (Ptas million)	Share of pole (per cent)	Total for Nat. Econ. (Ptas million)	Share of pole (per cent)
(a) Huelva						
Foodstuffs	65,840.1	0	78,027.8	0.01	74,911.5**	0.1
Timber	22,964.1	0.84	28,329.0	0.96	37,746.9	1.16
Chemicals	44,642.7	0.87	58,750.6	1.79	93,898.3	2.95
Building materials	25,924.6	0.05	30,945.5	0.20	32,652.5	0.19
Metal industry	135,249.3	0.01	176,743.1	0.04	236,524.4	0.37
Energy	29,640.1	0.24	41,000.0	0.28	44,160.4	0.48
Various	121,164.3	0	144,728.0	0.03	119,158.5	0.06
Total	445,425.2	0.15	558,524.0	0.29	639,052.5	0.71
(b) Seville						
Foodstuffs	65,840.1	0.14	78,027.8	0.34	74,911.5**	0.53
Textiles	67,838.8	0.20	81,923.5	0.20	92,122.9	0.19
Paper	19,267.5	0.19	22,157.7	0.29	27,005.6	0.90
Chemicals	44,642.7	0.07	57,750.6	0.30	93,898.3	0.24
Building materials	25,924.6	1.47	30,945.5	1.74	32,652.5	3.72
Metal industry	135,249.3	0.57	176,743.1	0.71	236,524.4	0.60
Energy	29,640.1	0.15	41,000.0	0.25	44,190.4	0.36
Various	57,022.1	0.03	68,975.8	0.04	37,746.9**	0.29
Total	445,425.2	0.33	558,524.0	0.46	639,052.5	0.62

*At 1967 prices. It would have been better to adopt 1969 prices for a precise comparison, but the appropriate material was not available.
**Other sector classifications than those shown in the INE statistics account for these divergencies, cf. the values for 1969.

Sources: Data for the national economy 1967 and 1969: National Statistics Institute Spanish National Accounts 1966-68 and estimates for 1969, Madrid 1970; for 1971: Planning Commission/Banco de Bilbao: Estimates . . . , 71.

3 Structure of Investments and their Financing

Three things are understood here by the *structure of investments*. First of all, there is the distribution of the investments among the various sectors of the pole on the one hand and the infrastructure on the other hand. This has already been investigated to some extent, when it was shown how this structure operates in the production phase through the capital/output ratio coefficient and factor input relationship on the gross social product contribution of the pole industries. It also became clear that in Huelva the infrastructure investments effected were relatively and absolutely higher than those in Seville.[7] The second element in the structure of invest-ment is the composition of the investment capital in the pole industries by categories, and the third is the regional and national import content of investment goods demand on each occasion.

The structure of the investment capital by categories also influences the import content of the corresponding investment goods demand. It is consequently interesting in the present connection in that the effects on the hinterland arising from carrying out investments — negatively formu-lated, the regional outflow effects — should be presented.

Finally, the structure of the investment capital by categories influences the structure of the financing of this capital. This connection becomes quite clear when, as a financing principle, a correspondence is required between the liquidity of the investment and the period of the financing. In the present case there is also a close connection in the fact, for instance, that the public credits granted for the pole industries are only available for particular types of investment.

The *structure of the financing* of the investments is grouped according to the financing channels. As long as credit financing is available there is a close connection with the period to maturity. Observation of the financ-ing structure makes it possible, in particular, to establish the importance of the public credits and investment subsidies in the framework of the total capital investment. The structure of the financing operates, however, beyond the investment phase proper. It determines — through the operation of the corresponding interest structure — what part of the net value creation pertains to interest income, and also — in connection with the regional grouping of financing sources — what part of the interest income flows out of the region.

On the other hand, by the structure of the financing is also to be understood the participation of regional, national and foreign capital in the basic capital of the industries. On particular assumptions, conclusions can be drawn regarding the outflow quota of the profit income.

3.1 Outflow effects during the investment phase

The starting point for the analysis is the total capital investment in pole industries which was realised by 31 December 1969 (cf. Table 5 above). Corresponding considerations for the infrastructure investments are attached.

1   The first step in determining the outflow quota consists in the establishment of the structure of the investments by asset categories. The asset categories are:
—   developed and undeveloped properties (I),
—   commercial and factory premises and special buildings (II),
—   other fixed assets (III).
Table 26 shows the absolute and relative values for both the poles.

2   The import content of the investment goods demand for asset categories II and III can now be established.
   (a)   The provenance of the investment goods of the 'other fixed asset' (III) variety, that is machinery and mechanical equipment, tools, and factory and office equipment, emerges from the main enquiry. The results can be taken over direct and are assembled in Table 26 together with the result of the calculations for asset category II.
   (b)   As has already been explained, it was necessary to establish the provenance of the asset category 'commercial and factory premises and special buildings' by a more limited additional enquiry at the building firms. This was because the pole industries were unable to supply information on this point because they did not themselves carry out the corresponding transactions.
   In the additional enquiry 40 per cent of the total investments in category II were covered, a level of response which, in view of the relatively homogeneous structure of the basic framework, seemed satisfactory.[8]   The results were upgraded to 100 per cent on the assumption that they were in any case representative.
   The provenance of goods comprised in asset category II is not to be established solely by reference to the fact that the purchases connected with the execution of building investments are regionally grouped with previous work. At the same time the value creation quota corresponding

122

Table 26
Structure of the investment capital by categories

Sector No.*	I		II		III	
	Volume (Ptas '000s)	Per cent	Volume (Ptas '000s)	Per cent	Volume (Ptas '000s)	Per cent
(a) Huelva						
1	374	0.1	99,939	35.1	184,156	64.8
2	29,419	2.0	493,466	34.6	904,589	63.4
5	60,513	0.6	1,335,148	13.2	8,685,918	86.2
6	5,785	2.5	91,327	37.6	144,863	59.9
7	6,920	0.6	360,256	30.3	822,438	69.2
8	2,743	0.3	127,826	10.6	1,079,349	89.2
9	6,563	0.3	52,450	24.2	155,016	72.4
10	21,532	40.0	33,185	60.0	0	0
Total	133,849	0.9**	2,593,597	17.6	11,976,329	81.5
(b) Seville						
1	56,497	7.1	354,278	45.1	374,634	47.8
4	12,372	1.4	271,772	30.6	604.075	68.0
3	15,101	6.1	85,473	34.6	145,893	59.4
5	31,778	3.9	196,807	23.9	594,388	72.2
6	108,371	3.2	1,186,395	34.6	2,136,631	62.3
7	58,187	4.2	282,711	20.6	1,033,655	75.2
8	10,232	1.5	94,835	13.9	581,936	84.7
9	23,829	11.5	61,047	29.3	122,647	59.1
Total	316,367	3.7**	2,533,318	30.0	5,593,869	66.3

*Cf. Table 5.

**The differences between the poles as regards the proportion of investments in land can only be explained by the fact that in Huelva almost the whole of industry in the foodstuffs, chemicals, metal and energy sectors has leased its industrial premises from the Port Authority.

to the investment volume must also be allocated regionally. On the assumption that all building and installation firms were drawn from the hinterland of the pole and there financed themselves too, the total value creation deriving from the execution of the building project could be regarded as a contribution to the gross domestic product of the region. However, this assumption is untenable since in Huelva only about 7 per cent of the investment volume is effected by undertakings in the pole province, compared with about 39 per cent in Seville.

Table 26a
Provenance of the investment goods in per cent of the investment
volume by asset categories shown in Table 26

	Huelva province	Seville province	Rest of Spain	Foreign countries
(a) Huelva				
I	100	0	0	0
II	36	12	50	2
III	2.4	2.8	48.5	46.3
Total	9.1	4.4	48.4	38.1
(b) Seville				
I	0	100	0	0
II	0	53	47	0
III	0	8.7	42.7	48.6
Total	0	25.1	42.2	32.7

A procedure was therefore selected by which the investment volume was broken down into previous work purchases and a gross value creation portion; then the latter was again divided into consumption of fixed capital income from employment and other factor income. The relative proportions were provided by the enquiry. With regard to the regional allocation of the value creation quota, the assumption was made that all the income from employment can be attributed to the pole region in which the investment is effected. In accordance with the quotas of the investment volume, the consumption of fixed capital and other factor income was imputed as a whole to the regions in which the building and installation firms concerned were registered.

(c)   Table 26a shows the result of the determination of the regional structure of investment goods demand for the three asset categories.

The facts condensed in Table 26a demonstrate that the outflow effects of the investment phase (= import content of the demand for investment goods in Huelva (86.5 per cent) amounts to 91 per cent of the total investment of the pole industries, and in Seville to 75 per cent (75 per cent)). The first value given shows the average import quota in relation to the particular pole province, and the figure in brackets shows the quota in relation to the planning region Huelva-Seville.

As regards the polarisation effect within the planning region, the result must be regarded as unfavourable for Huelva in particular. A final evaluation of this result cannot be made, however, purely on the basis of the aim connected with this hoped-for effect of the maximisation of regional income. For in an economy in which inter-regional integration is regarded as a means of general economic growth policy a careful assessment of the aims must be made. In this connection it can be pointed out that the import quotas for the poles in relation to the rest of the economy can be valued in the production phase at 48.4 and 42.2 per cent as a mark of higher integration.

The structural causes of the high and differential outflow quotas in both poles can be sized up in general under the following heads:

If the individual pole provinces are taken as a starting point, for asset category II the difference in comparison with the pole seems high at 17 per cent, although this is evened out if the outflow quota is related to the total planning region. At the same time the import content for both poles in the case of asset category III, compared with asset category II, is in both poles substantially higher. This permits the conclusion to be drawn that in the comparison of both pole provinces, given an almost equal development position measured by *per capita* income, the differential market volume measured by total income suggests that the diversification level of the building and building materials industry is higher in Seville than in Huelva, while at the given development level both pole provinces are not in a position to offer specialised equipment goods.

From this it follows that, in the case of building investment with the given development level, the elasticity of supply is higher on account of its comparatively lower degree of specialisation in the case of the bigger market volume of the pole provinces than the elasticity of supply in the case of equipment investments.[9]

A striking point is that in Huelva, taking the average of all investment categories, the extra-national import content is 5.4 per cent higher than in Seville, while in Seville the extra-national import content for equipment goods is 2.3 per cent higher than in Huelva. This is explained by the fact that extra-national imports in both poles relate almost exclusively to equipment investments, and that in Seville this asset category has relatively less weight (Table 26) than in Huelva.

The axis principle already referred to is fundamental for the strategy of the promotion of double poles established in geographical proximity which is followed in Spain. It is consequently of interest to consider the inter-relationships between the pole provinces induced in the investment phase. *It appears that the relations in this phase were wholly one-sided*: Huelva certainly imported investment and in particular *building investment* goods from Seville to a relatively limited extent, but Seville imported none at all from Huelva. This *weakness and one-sidedness in the axis relationship* is to be noted also in the production phase of the pole industries *at least until 1971,* as is shown below (4).

(d)   The outflow quota on the average for all asset categories is here set out broken down by sectors.

Table 27

Provenance of the capital assets in per cent of the investment volume for each sector up to 31 December 1969

Sector no.*	Investment volume (Ptas million)	Regional distribution (per cent)			
		Huelva	Seville	Rest of Spain	Foreign countries
(a) Huelva					
1	284.5	13.4	5.3	31.3	50.0
2	1,427.5	16.7	4.2	43.9	35.2
5	10,081.6	6.4	3.9	48.7	41.0
6	242.0	18.2	5.0	52.9	24.0
7	1,189.6	16.4	10.4	61.9	11.3
8	1,209.9	10.0	3.3	45.6	41.1
9	214.0	12.2	3.3	27.6	57.0
10	54.7	60.0	7.3	30.9	1.8
Total	14,703.8	9.1	4.4	48.4	38.1

(b) Seville

1	785.4	0	39.2	39.0	21.8
4	888.2	0	22.9	23.5	53.6
3	246.5	0	29.7	44.7	25.6
5	823.0	0	24.1	41.4	34.5
6	3,431.4	0	25.5	45.2	29.4
7	1,374.6	0	21.2	29.4	49.5
8	687.0	0	14.7	77.9	7.4
9	207.5	0	32.2	52.4	15.4
Total	8,443.6	0	25.1	42.2	32.7

*Cf. Table 5.

It also appears that the results by sectors on a comparative basis for each pole display sharp differences, and that the differential product-mix of the pole sectors and the demand structure for investment goods arising therefrom are just as important to the outflow quota as the relative development level and the market volume of the pole provinces. The influence of the differential product-mix is best discerned by comparison with the relative share of imports from foreign countries, for when corresponding goods are not produced in the economy of the country as a whole, the relative development level and the market size of the region play no part in determining the volume of the necessary imports.

The energy sector provides a particularly clear example of the fact that the *results set out in Table 27 cannot for example be used as standard values for sectors in other connections.* In other words, it is apparent that the import content of the investment goods demand abroad has the highest value in comparison with the sectors in Huelva at 57 per cent and the lowest in Seville at 7.4 per cent. It is a question in this case of the same undertaking for both poles, but whereas the investments in Huelva are concentrated on the preparation of new production capacity for electrical energy, those in Seville relate exclusively to the expansion of the distribution network. The corresponding investment goods, especially equipment, are of quite different kinds, and this applies particularly to the degree of specialisation and the technical efficiency of their production. There are similar differences in the import content.

In particular, the sectoral differences in the comparison of the two poles can only be judged on a knowledge of the individual undertakings because in many cases only extension projects are effected by modernisation of the machinery. On the average for the metal industry sector in

Seville, for example, this serves to explain the comparatively high extra-national imports (exclusively equipment goods) in relation to Huelva.[10]

To sum up, it can be said that as regards the differences in the outflow quotas for asset category II, the market volume for the pole region at the same development level is decisive in each case. For equipment investment on the other hand, the product-mix of the investing sectors is also a material factor.

3   In line with the determination of the import content of the demand for investment goods for asset category II, the demand for investment goods which makes itself felt in connection with infrastructure investments can be allocated to supply regions. In this context the results achieved for the pole industries in asset category II are taken over here without modification. Although infrastructure investments in relation to the value creation quota, wage quota and regional structure of the previous work purchases are not necessarily comparable with investments in industrial buildings, a further differentiation on account of the rough character of the calculations of the import content of the industrial demand for investment goods in asset category II did not seem to be called for.

3.2   Financing structure of the pole industries and outflow effects during the production phase

The analysis of the financing structure of the pole industries is designed to show the significance of investment subsidies and public credits as investment incentives in the poles in the framework of total financing, and the weight to be attached to other financing channels (1); in connection with the relative participation of regional, national and foreign capital in the 'social capital'[11] of the industries, the outflow quota of interest and profit income is to be determined on this basis (2). It is not necessary for this purpose to carry out a detailed analysis of the financial structure, but it will suffice rather to adopt the following model:

(a)   The analysis only relates to the income provenance side, and this has two implications. First of all, this question only arises in connection with the financing structure of those outflow effects of the production phase which concern the direct regional and national social product contribution, that is to say the value creation of the pole industries: outflow effects on the basis of previous extra-regional or extra-national work purchases are quite unrelated thereto.[12] In the second place, the portions of income imputed to non-residents of the region are regarded as outflows, although their immediate re-utilisation in the region is possible. However, this only applies to the net income amounts, since the principal of the nominal receipt of capital in the pole industries is adopted henceforth: depreciated provisions are not treated as outflows. There is thus no question of an analysis of business cash-flow.[13]

(b) The analysis distinguishes five financing channels: investment subsidies, public credit, suppliers' credits on purchases of foreign equipment goods, social capital and 'other' financing, the latter including the issue of bonds and recourse to internal credits at the commercial banks. The fourth and fifth categories are furthermore combined as one, and are described below as 'other own and outside financing'; the combination of these two categories has its roots in the fact that reliable statistics were only available for the first three categories, so the last two were treated together as residual items.

1 Relative importance of the financing channels: Table 28 shows the combined result for both poles.

Table 28
Structure of financing of investment capital by sources

| | Investment (Ptas millions) | Proportion of sources of finance (per cent) | | | |
		Subsidy	Public credit	Foreign suppliers' credits	Other own and outside financing
Huelva	14,703.8	6.8	23.7	31.8	37.7
Seville	8,443.6	3.4	22.2	27.4	47.0

This table calls for certain observations. First, the proportion of subsidies and public credits is related to the total volume of capital investment for all the pole industries. An alternative procedure is also possible, since the promotion measures referred to are only applied to those industries that are admitted by the authorities. On the appointed day, their investment volume amounted to Ptas 8,675.2 million for Huelva and Ptas 6,501.6 million for Seville. In relation to this volume, the following proportions emerge:

Table 29
Relative importance of subsidy and public credit (revised)

	Subsidy	Public credit
Huelva	11.4%	40.2%
Seville	4.4%	28.9%

The differences in the public promotion of investment projects in Huelva and Seville are still plainer, stemming from the fact that the proportion of the pole industries not permitted by the authorities to the total investment volume is higher in Huelva than in Seville at 41 per cent compared with 23 per cent. The variations in the comparison between both poles in the case of the subsidy arise from the different character of the two poles in Plan I. In Huelva as a promotion pole subsidies could be granted of up to 20 per cent of the investment capital, and in Seville as a development pole up to 10 per cent. In the comparison between the two poles differences in the case of subsidies and public credits arise further out of the differential classification of the industries in the Groups A-D according to their promotion value. The differences in public credit consist finally in the connection between this financing possibility and particular types of asset, especially asset type II of internal provenance.

It is difficult to say whether the degree of promotion indicated in Tables 28 and 29 is satisfactory. With reference to public credits it should be noted that their allocation is not to be regarded as *specially* preferential treatment of the pole industries, as the pole promotion programme provided, for outside the poles competitive locations are also furnished with the corresponding incentives. It may be said that the Banco de Credito Industrial, which controls the allocation of public credits, has in the course of time applied credit policy in relation to the poles on an increasingly restrictive basis.

Table 30 presents the classification of Table 29 by sectors. As can be seen from Table 30, the sectoral differences in promotion by subsidy and by public credit in both poles are significant. They are here related to total investment including those industries not admitted by the authorities. This emerges as the more correct procedure in so far as it is probable that none of the industries not admitted by the authorities would have voluntarily rejected a subsidy and public credit, nor would they have abstained from applying for admission from altruistic motives.[14]

If, in the view of the Planning Commission, the relative level of the subsidy and public credit is regarded as indicative of the promotion value due to the sectors concerned, then the following sectors seemed to be worthy of promotion to an above-average extent: foodstuffs, chemicals and 'various' in Huelva, and paper, chemicals, energy and 'various' in Seville.

Table 30

Structure of financing of investment capital by sources, sectoral classification

Sector no.*	Investment (Ptas millions)	Proportion of the sources of finance (per cent)			
		Subsidy	Public credit	Foreign suppliers' credits	Other own and outside financing
(a) Huelva					
1	284.5	13.7	30.0	41.8	14.5
2	1,427.5	3.6	8.2	27.4	60.8
5	10,081.6	6.6	29.6	34.6	29.2
6	242.0	5.4	33.8	18.5	42.3
7	1,189.6	16.9	5.3	9.1	68.7
8	1,209.9	0	0	34.7	65.3
9	214.0	8.7	35.0	48.2	8.1
10	54.7	8.7	–	0	0
Total	14,703.8	6.8	23.7	31.8	37.7
(b) Seville					
1	785.4	3.7	20.2	16.9	59.2
4	888.2	1.2	12.8	45.3	40.7
3	246.5	7.7	54.8	21.2	16.2
5	823.0	6.9	31.6	28.1	33.4
6	3,431.4	3.9	13.5	24.8	57.8
7	1,374.6	2.2	22.3	42.0	33.5
8	687.0	0	54.0	6.4	39.6
9	207.5	2.4	31.8	11.6	54.2
Total	8,443.6	3.4	22.2	27.4	47.0

*Cf. Table 5.

This indicator is unsatisfactory however, and does not present a true picture of the promotion background because in addition to the *entitlement* of a concern to promotion by the allocation of credits and subsidies, account must also be taken of its *need* for promotion. If the promotion value is given, the promotion then becomes further dependent on the agreed promotion minimum for the industry to be established; this is known as the 'attraction threshold'. For certain industries this minimum is near zero, the same as for those not admitted by the authorities; of these, it is assumed either that they will none the less settle there owing to the advantages of the locality, or that the mere existence of the pole provides a sufficient stimulus for them. This applies, for example, to the building material industry in Seville and to energy in Huelva. Finally, steps have been taken whereby foreign undertakings have been obliged to settle in a pole without promotion; without satisfying this requirement they would be unable to set foot in the customs-protected domestic market.

2   The basic restriction proposed above, whereby only the income-producing side is considered for the *calculation of the outflow quota* for interest and profit income, has the result that portions of income attributed to persons resident outside the region can be regarded as outflows from that region. An attempt is also made to determine the outflows abroad, since foreign credit financing and participation by foreign undertakings in the social capital of the pole industries means that the portions of income flowing out of the region do not accrue solely to residents in other parts of the national economy.

(a)   In order to calculate the profit income on an inter-regional or inter-national basis, it is necessary to estimate the participation ratio in the 'social capital' of the pole industries. As has already been stated, the precise amount of the social capital is not known in all cases, therefore it has not been possible to show financial sources 4 and 5 separately. Inability to determine the social capital is caused by the fact that it is often impossible to attribute social capital of its own to a pole industry. This is true in particular of the largest industries, which are production plants for undertakings with head offices outside the region.[15] This deficiency is unimportant for the calculation of profit income. In view of the fact that the participation relationships of the undertakings to the pole industries and the offices of the firms concerned are known, as are their link-ups with one another, the proportion of the profit income to be attributed to the regional, national (here meaning the rest of the country) and foreign undertakings can be reliably determined.[16]

In this case the procedure adopted is to distribute the period profit indicated for each individual industry in accordance with the participation relationship. Table 31 shows that in 1971 the regional outflow quota for profit income in the pole industries amounted to 98 per cent for Huelva (!) and to 61 per cent for Seville. The outflow quota to foreign countries in the same year amounted to 30 per cent for Huelva and 11 per cent for Seville.

Table 31
Share of regional, national and foreign undertakings in the profits of the pole industries in 1971 (per cent)

	Regional	'National'	Foreign
Huelva	2	68	30
Seville	39	50	11

As the ratio of period profits and social capital is not constant throughout the period, the outflow quotas shown apply to 1971 only. Corresponding calculations have been made for the other years under review, but they are not shown here as it is not a question of 'normal years' for both poles.

(b)   A precise calculation of the interest income is not possible, since for the reasons already stated financing sources 4 and 5 could not be shown separately in Tables 28 and 30. Consequently, neither could the interest charges in respect of 'other outside financing' be computed. If it is assumed that the share of social capital in the financing of fixed investment amounts on the average to about 25 per cent for both poles, then no interest charge will have been raised in Huelva for 12 per cent of the fixed investment, nor in Seville for 22 per cent. Since the profits of the pole industries were calculated from the final balance of the pro-duction accounts, this means that the profit figures are shown as too high by the amount of this interest charge. When determining the outflow quotas for interest and profit income together this plays no part in practice, as is shown below.

The interest income also includes interest on the circulating capital, and its amount was established in the additional enquiry into part of the pole industries. The interest was put at 8 per cent in accordance with the facts. Interest on the circulating capital represents the sole type of income from interest that could remain in part in the region.

133

This stems from the fact that apart from interest on 'other outside financing' which is not included, interest only arises in respect of public credit and foreign suppliers' credits. Both flow to their full amount out of the region.

For the outflow quota for interest on the circulating capital, the share of the regional banks in the financing of the circulating capital is the dominant factor. It must be assumed in Huelva that the proportion is about 0 per cent. In 1970 the pole industries conducted their bank transactions exclusively with the banking institutions in the locality of the head office of the parent company. The provincial bank in Huelva was not involved in the financing of pole industries at the time of the enquiry.[17] All in all, the commercial banks in Huelva have only one cash office for wage and salary payments and day-to-day previous work purchases which are of minor consequence for the pole industries.

The two regional banks in Seville, on the other hand, participate in the financing of the pole industries there, although precise details were not available. An estimate that about one-third of the circulating capital requirements and also of the 'other outside financing' of the pole industries was provided by them was treated as probably correct at the interviews in connection with the enquiry. Consequently the outflow quota was put in this case at 67 per cent.

For all the interest income the regional outflow quota is as follows:

Table 31a
Regional outflow quota for interest income

	1967	1969	1971
Huelva	100%	100%	100%
Seville	81%	79%	74%

(c) If the two outflow quotas for profit and interest income are considered together, it emerges that the error in determining the outflow quota for 'other outside financing' cannot weight heavily, as in each case the regional outflow quotas for both kinds of income in Huelva and Seville only differ marginally from one another. To that extent it is a matter of indifference that the interest to be apportioned to other outside financing is included in the profits. Nevertheless, the procedure for determining the interest charge and outflow quota for Seville is thoroughly unsatisfactory.

In connection with the outflow quota for profit income, it should strictly speaking be considered that the profit tax on undertakings — which corresponds to corporation tax under the German system — should also be taken into account as an outflow outside the region. That has not happened because the data prepared by the Ministry of Finance for 1967 was insufficient. The tax in question is nevertheless of very minor importance (cf. Commission, 70, RGR, 42).[18]

To sum up, it can be said that the outflow quota for profit and interest income in both poles is very high, but as might be expected the outflow quota in Seville is substantially lower than in Huelva. This is all the more important for the contribution of both poles to the provincial income in each case, in that in Huelva the proportion of profit and interest income to the value creation of industries is higher than in Seville; this is because production is, on average more capital-intensive in Huelva (cf. the input-output tables in the Appendix. In Seville, therefore, a relatively lower proportion of a relatively less important part of the value creation of the pole industries flows out than in Huelva.

In Section 5 the total effects resulting from the outflow quotas obtained here are determined on the basis of the direct effect of the SEMA system. The more important result is represented however by the outflow quotas themselves, for they apply independently of the accuracy of the quantitative ascertainment of the profits shown in the input-output tables, which — as has been emphasised many times — contrary to all reservations are subject to an amount established as a last balance. On the other hand, the value creation category appropriate for the regional income incidence of the pole industries in the sense of the direct effect, the wage total, is directly and correctly included.

4 Input-Output Linkages

In this section, by means of the input-output tables and the additional tables, it is proposed to present the relationships which the pole industries have with one another, with their hinterland, with the other pole and its hinterland, with the rest of the national economy and with foreign countries. On the one hand the preliminary work purchases are considered, and on the other hand the sales of end-products by each industry.

The input-output tables aggregated by sectors are set out in the appendix for the three years under review (Tables 32-41). In this connection, the additional tables should be consulted for information on the previous work purchases of each sector in the hinterland of both pole provinces, and for industries of the other pole in each case classified under the supplying sectors.

Three questions connected with the prospects set out in the pole programme are particularly important:
- the absolute and relative importance of the inter-industrial relationships within each pole;
- the link-ups of the pole industries of both poles with one another and with both pole hinterlands;
- the expected degree of integration with the rest of the national economy and with foreign countries.

Specific prospects underlying these questions are:
- that important inter-industrial relationships within the poles should promote a self-sustaining regional growth process;
- that in the sense of Paelinck's geographical polarisation the hinterland should be included in this process;
- that the establishment of a double pole favours a circular causation process between the poles;
- that the pole industries produce a relatively high positive contribution to the regional and national balance of trade.

4.1 Input-output linkages between pole industries

As is to be expected, the inter-relationship matrix of the input-output tables for 1971 also shows a large number of empty fields, despite the fact that the year in question can be regarded as normal for both poles in the sense discussed above. Further recourse to the detailed input-output tables

137

in order to supplement this section would strengthen this impression: in both poles the number of transactions between pole industries is very modest.

It is not claimed that the inter-relationship matrix reflects every possible transaction of smaller quantity. The questionnaire procedure does not permit the allocation of previous minor work purchases to specified suppliers. In examining the detailed input-output tables, and knowing the products of the pole industries in each case, *a priori* considerations could however be raised regarding the industries between which transactions might have taken place. An express enquiry was made in each case when such an assumption existed.

The picture obtained seems, on the whole, to support one of the working hypotheses formulated by the author at the beginning of the investigation, namely that *in contrast to the declared notion of the Spanish Planning Commission the pole promotion policy to date has been directed primarily to the presentation of a quantitative agglomeration of heterogeneous activities* (Buttler, 71, 184/5). *Declaredly, the industrialisation process should not be seen on the other hand as a purely quantitative but primarily as a qualitative agglomeration process* (Planning Commission/Italconsult, 68, 46).

The extent to which this statement holds for individual sectors will now be discussed (1). The question also arises as to how far it is permitted to draw conclusions from the observation of the transaction matrix regarding the capacity of the pole industries to generate a self-sustaining regional growth process (2).

1 Interpretation of the input-output tables is facilitated by the fact that in Table 42 the structure of purchases of previous work and of sales of end-products of the pole industries is set out by sectors and regional classification. The percentage figures shown can also be described as integration grading, and they demonstrate, again expressed differently, to what extent the linkage effects arising from the pole sectors are regionally reflected.

For purposes of comparison, and having regard to the relationships to be interpreted in sections 4.2 and 4.3, Table 42 does not only show the integration grades relating to the transaction matrix.

At this point, the analysis can be restricted to an observation of the second and eighth column of the table, relating both to previous work purchases and also sales of end-products respectively.

Before going into this, reference must be made once more to the sectoral input-output tables. On this score, it is particularly interesting to note *that in Huelva the intra-sectoral relationships are very much more*

138

impressive than the inter-sectoral relationships. In terms of value, the proportion of the inter-relationships (recorded on the diagonal from upper left to lower right) to the total of the inter-industrial transactions in the pole amounts to 87 per cent in Huelva and 5 per cent in Seville. If consideration is restricted to those transactions which do not concern the energy sector, the corresponding proportions immediately rise to 99 and 54 per cent respectively.

If the proportions of the previous work purchases from the pole industries are compared in connection with the quantitative importance of the same resulting from consideration of the absolute values (column 1), it appears that relevant inter-relationships in both poles are only found in the case of the chemical and building material sectors.

In Huelva there is also an inter-relationship in the timber-processing sector, although quantitatively this is still unimportant. From the investments to be realised up to 1973 it can be concluded that in Huelva the inter-relationships in the chemical and timber processing sectors will increase sharply, because in both sectors investments are planned which arise out of the offer by the existing pole industries of primary products which are substantial in terms of volume and size. Those projects whose realisation seems certain are typically to be ranked as processers of weight-loss materials: although the amount in terms of value of the previous work purchases is high, equally the value/weight unit ratio for the end-products is substantially higher than that for the primary products.

For both poles, the level of the inter-industrial relationships in the pole obviously depends on whether it is a question of deferred or advanced production stages within the sectors, or whether the pole industries are distinguished from one another by different specialisations in comparable processing stages. While this is not an original viewpoint, it does lead to the conclusion that in the chemical, timber and building material sectors in Huelva the existence of the first industries to be established there has had an attractive effect on succeeding activities, while in Seville this only applies to a limited extent to the chemical and building material industries. It is possible to pursue this in detail in connection with the observation of the time lag in the development of the industries in the detailed input-output tables.

In the comparison of the two poles the hypothesis therefore arises almost without qualification for Seville that the pole represents a heterogeneous agglomeration of production units not connected with one another. Huelva can be designated essentially as the pole for the chemical industry. Although when measured by gross production value the metal industry sector in Huelva also asssumes a special position, no attraction

Table 42

Regional structure of purchases and sales in the pole industries in 1971

	Previous work purchase						Sale of end-products					
	Total (Ptas millions)	Geographical distribution (per cent)					Total (Ptas millions)	Geographical distribution (per cent)				
		Pole industries	Rest of province	Other pole province	Rest of Spain	Foreign countries		Pole industries	Rest of province	Other pole province	Rest of Spain	Foreign countries
(a) Huelva												
Foodstuffs	113.1	10.2	14.5	65.5	7.0	2.8	188.0	0	22.5	10.8	48.8	17.9
Timber processing	511.3	6.2	36.9	9.5	45.6	1.8	929.5	0.4	3.3	3.4	87.8	5.1
Chemicals	6,952.0	39.2	5.0	0.1	6.7	49.0	9,736.6	25.0	5.8	8.3	48.2	12.7
Building materials	102.8	13.6	17.4	62.1	3.9	3.0	165.2	3.3	70.1	10.0	16.6	0
Metal industry	4,433.2	0.4	62.5	0.6	8.5	28.0	5,315.5	0	2.2	0.1	95.9	1.8
Various	67.4	1.0	10.5	14.1	74.4	0	134.0	6.9	8.2	14.7	69.9	0.3
Energy	141.5	0	66.0	34.0	0	0	353.7	100	0	0	00	0
Total	12,321.3	22.7	27.9	2.3	9.2	37.9	16,822.5	16.7	5.2	5.4	64.3	8.4
(b) Seville												
Foodstuffs	1,724.3	1.0	61.0	0	7.4	30.6	2,118.8	0	32.8	4.3	44.4	18.5
Textiles	490.7	2.0	74.4	0	7.3	16.3	658.4	0	67.8	1.7	7.9	2.6
Paper processing	570.2	1.0	24.0	0	65.5	9.5	810.5	0.3	23.1	2.1	61.0	13.5
Chemicals	875.2	6.5	59.1	5.0	22.9	6.5	1,109.1	0.3	13.7	1.8	69.5	14.7
Building materials	1,611.6	8.8	41.1	1.7	29.7	18.7	2,813.6	0.4	32.0	4.4	58.1	5.1
Metal industry	1,646.6	2.5	20.9	0	50.8	25.8	3,058.3	0.3	18.4	1.6	71.9	7.8
Various	194.6	4.5	8.8	0	77.7	9.0	304.4	0.5	32.3	6.5	56.5	4.2
Energy	95.1	0	100	0	0	0	255.1	100	0	0	0	0
Total	7,208.2	3.0	44.2	1.0	30.5	20.3	11,128.2	2.5	27.3	3.0	57.5	9.7

impulses are to be expected from there because the total production of the main industry in the sector is subject to a contractual delivery undertaking. Projects requiring capital investment of the order of Ptas 8-9 milliard, which could give the sector a status comparable with the chemical industry, have been known to fail.

2   For the development of the Huelva chemical pole it is a characteristic feature that the intra-sectoral linkage already amounted to 35 per cent in relation to the total previous work purchases. No other sector achieved a comparably high value in the investigation of all the Spanish poles. On the contrary the importance of the raw material basis[19] of the province, which was a very important factor in the location of the first establishment, is at the very low level of 5 per cent.

From this it can be concluded that the chemicals industry in Huelva has already reached a stage which favours the establishment of a further range of activities on the part of the supplier and manufacturer. This could mean that the attraction of the existing chemical industry is so great that a self-generating growth process can be expected in the region.

The position in Huelva, and in particular in the chemical industry, was set out as a model to provide a basis for the discussion of a possible self-generating process (Buttler, 73, Appendix 4).

The example of the Huelva chemical pole was also selected because the whole of the modern chemical production in the province is already tied up with the pole industry. Considerations as to whether the development of the pole industries in other sectors has the character of a self-generating regional growth process could perhaps be taken up in connection with the observation of the inter-industrial pole-hinterland relationship. This will be examined in the following section.

4.2   Pole-hinterland relationships and the Huelva-Seville axis

In this section flows 3-8 and 13-16 presented in 2.3 are examined. The following points of view are of particular interest:
—   the level and structure of the previous work purchases of the pole industries in the rest of the pole province and in the rest of the other pole provinces (5-8) concerned,
—   previous work purchases by the pole industries in Huelva from pole industries in Seville and *vice versa* (3 and 4),
—   sales of end-products by the pole industries in their own hinterland and in the hinterland of the other pole (13-16), and
—   the level and structure of the inter-industrial pole-hinterland relation-

ship in the case of previous work purchases and sales of end-products (parts of flows 5-8 and 13-16).

The first point is of interest in connection with the determination of the indirect income effect during the production phase of the pole industries. Flows 3 and 4, 7 and 8, 15 and 16 denote the contribution of the pole industries to the inter-regional relationships between the pole provinces, the so-called Huelva-Seville development axis. Flows 5-8 and 13-16 are then examined to see which part of the pole-hinterland relationships denoted by them represents inter-industrial relations. This last point of view is connected with the question raised at the end of the preceding section regarding the contribution of the pole sectors to a self-sustaining regional industrialisation process. For this it will be assumed, in accordance with the findings of the growth pole theory, that an effective contribution is only to be expected when the inter-industrial pole-hinterland relationships are significant.

1   In the additional tables to the input-output tables, streams 3-8 are shown as classified by receiving and supplying sectors. Their presentation had to be dispensed with in 1971 because at the time of the questionnaire the industries still in course of construction could not provide the detailed information required. As a whole, however, the pole-hinterland relationships can be obtained as regards their relative importance for 1971 as well from Table 42. This general picture for 1971 is to be considered first.

Table 42 shows the pole-hinterland relationship in each case in the second and third columns of the geographical distribution of previous work purchases and end-product sales. Both in Seville and in Huelva it can be observed that a relatively high proportion of previous work purchases from the rest of their own province contrasts on the average for all sectors with a smaller proportion from the other pole province (27.9 compared with 2.3 per cent in Huelva, and 44.3 against 1 per cent in Seville). An above-average proportion of purchases from the rest of the pole province in each case is represented in Huelva by the metal industry and energy sectors, and in Seville by the foodstuffs, textiles, chemicals and energy sectors. The main inputs of these sectors from the rest of the province are — in the order of importance of the sectors — copper ore and heavy oil in Huelva, and olives and fruit, cotton, industrial inorganic chemical primary products and heavy oil in Seville. This list of the most important intermediate inputs of the sectors having an above-average linkage with the rest of the province concerned shows clearly that industrial previous work played a smaller part than agriculture and mining.

The sales of end-products to the rest of the pole province display other relationships. They are less in both poles than in the case of previous

142

work. This characterises the pole activities on the average as export activities, apart from the building materials sector in Huelva whose products are purchased mainly by the building trade in the province, and from the textile sector in Seville which has strong inter-industrial relations with textile industries in the province that are not included in the pole.

The sales of end-products to the other pole province again reflect the low market volume, in terms of total income at a comparable development level, measured by *per capita* income in Huelva as opposed to Seville. For the pole of Seville not only exports less in absolute and relative terms to the province of Huelva than to the rest of its own province, but the industries of the Huelva pole export more to Seville than they sell to the remainder of their own area.

From this it can plainly be concluded that, on the analogy of the consideration of the delivery flows during the investment phase from pole industries and infrastructure, the inter-relationships that extend from Huelva to Seville (diffusion effects) are greater than those from Seville to Huelva. These axis relationships will now be investigated more thoroughly.

2 The Huelva-Seville axis can be considered up to 1969 by means of the additional tables to the input-output tables. First of all, the direct delivery relationships between pole industries in Huelva on the one hand and in Seville on the other (flows 3 and 4) are of interest. It appears that, measured by the total previous work purchases by the pole industries, the value of the transactions at about Ptas 36 million in 1967 and Ptas 107 million in 1969 is completely meaningless. In so far as it was intended by double pole formation to create integrated sectoral complexes, this must be considered to have failed completely, especially as there is no expectation of any substantial increase in the delivery flows concerned from the start of production by further pole industries in 1971 either.

The contribution on the part of the pole industries to a so-called Huelva-Seville development axis is still to be found perhaps in the delivery relationships of each pole with the hinterland of the other pole. Table 42 shows, however, that with respect to previous work purchases by the poles, the rest of the province of the other pole hardly comes into the picture in either case. For this, purchases in the rest of the province of Seville by pole industries in Huelva are relatively far greater than those by Seville pole industries in the remainder of the province of Huelva. However, at Ptas 73 and 15 million respectively in 1969, these supply relationships are also quite unimportant in absolute terms.

For sales of end-products in the rest of the other pole province, the contribution of the pole industries in each case is greater than for previous work purchases and, as has already been pointed out, is lower as regards

Seville than for Huelva. At Ptas 221 and 721 million respectively in 1969, and Ptas 332 and 904 million respectively in 1971, the sales to the other pole province are of some importance.

Altogether it must be decided, however, that the Huelva-Seville 'axis' hardly existed at all until 1971, and consequently until then the principle of the double pole settlement had virtually no substance.

3   The *industrial* pole-hinterland relationships are set out in Table 45, which shows the purchases and sales which the pole industries in Huelva and Seville effected with the processing industries (in this case all industries other than 'extractive industries') in the rest of their province and in the rest of the other pole province. For the sales it was assumed that the flows shown in the input-output tables for 1971 as sales of production goods went in their entirety to the processing industry. The inter-industrial previous work purchases are shown for 1969, since the additional tables needed to determine them are only available up to that date.

Table 43
Supply inter-relationships of the pole industries with processing industries in the hinterland (Huelva and Seville)

	Huelva pole		Seville pole	
	Industrial sales in % of total turnover 1971	Industrial previous work purchases in % of all previous work purchases 1969	Industrial sales in % of total turnover 1971	Industrial previous work purchases in % of all previous work purchases 1969
Foodstuffs	20.4	0	13.9	0
Textiles	—	—	62.8	2.8
Timber processing	2.9	0.4	—	—
Paper processing	—	—	25.2	30.6
Chemicals	14.1	0.4	9.2	3.8
Building materials	80.1	0	35.0	10.0
Metal industry	1.0	18.1*	19.3	10.0
Various	38.8	0	17.2	0
Energy	0	0	0	0
Total	9.8	0.5	23.7	6.3

*This amount was certainly lower in 1971 because the structure of the end-product compared with 1969 had changed dramatically.

144

For the interpretation of the results of Table 43, it is necessary to quote once more the hypothesis of the growth pole theory by which the speed of growth of the pole is influenced by the height of the inter-industrial linkages with the hinterland; for under otherwise equal conditions the more intensive are the linkages, the higher is the matrix multiplier. In order to apply the theorem to the pole-hinterland relation-ships, it is useful to observe the linkages of the pole industries with one another and with the hinterland in an input-output matrix for the entire Huelva and Seville region. In fact, with the aid of observation of the additional tables and the breakdown of the sales into production goods, investment goods and consumer goods shown in the input-output tables, an input-output table can be prepared for the whole region in which all the inter-industrial relationships based on the linkage-effects of the pole-industries are set out. Only the sectoral classification of the industrial purchasers of end-products in the pole industries is lacking, but they could still be calculated with some certainty from the information available. In connection with such a proposed input-output table for the entire region, first conclusions from Table 43 can now be discussed.[20]

The backward inter-relationship, or proportion of the regional previous work purchases from industries, is small in both poles, though much higher in Seville than in Huelva. The latter result again reflects the higher degree of diversification stemming from the bigger market range in Seville. In neither pole can it therefore be expected that industry in the hinterland is materially influenced by the development of the pole industries by the matrix multiplier; unless, that is, the inter-relationships of the suppliers of pole industries with other industries, which are again extended before them, produce explosive growth effects, namely by previous suppliers to the pole industries established in the pole region. In view of the development situation of the region considered, such a postulation hardly seems justified.

The industrial forward linkage is higher in both poles than the backward linkage with industries, reflecting the fact that in both poles it is generally a question of industries at a low processing level, in which previous work purchases from the primary sector including the extractive industries are predominant. A particular contribution is made to the relatively important forward linkage in Seville by the textile sectors — fibres supplied to other textile industries; building materials — supplies to the main building trade; and paper processing — packaging material. Of above-average importance in respect of the share of the regional forward linkage in Huelva are the foodstuffs sector — refrigeration and storage for other foodstuffs industries; building materials — supplies to the main building trade; and the 'various' category, especially packaging material.

None of these sectors to whose activities the forward linkages in the region are particularly attributable, can be accepted as leading sectors. The foodstuffs industry in Huelva is unimportant and depressed; owing to its remoteness from the market centres its prospects for development are slight, since deep-freeze products require an extensive distribution network. The textile industry in Spain still has little opportunity on the whole to realise above-average growth rates, unless foreign markets can be opened up. In the main, the production of building and packaging materials can be assessed as a successor activity for leading sectors, and their forward linkage is also connected with the fact that their market is limited to a zone bordering the pole region.

This means that it is not to be expected of the forward-linked sectors in the hinterland that they will automatically have above-average growth rates, so that sharp development impulses on the pole industries cannot be expected from them via the matrix multiplier.

This also applies to the chemical industry sector outside the pole, so far ignored, especially in the rest of the Seville province where primary products for fertilisers derived from pole industries are processed. The market for fertilisers in Spain is already overstaffed.

To sum up it may be said that in view of the forward and reverse linkages of the pole industries with processing industries in the hinterland, having regard to the intensity of the inter-relationship and the situation of the inter-related sectors, it is not to be expected that the intra-regional matrix multiplier could be sufficiently high to enable the consequence of a future self-generating industrial growth process in the pole region to derive from it.

This result justifies in retrospect the decision to restrict the investigation to the preparation of input-output and additional tables for the pole industries, and to dispense with an input-output analysis for the entire region; for existing relations connected with the analysis of the regional incidence of the input-output relations of the pole industries are essentially tied up with the selected approach. More comprehensive tables would have had little more informative value for the present problem, and a possible objection that such comprehensive tables are important for purposes of forecasting the further development of the region is not convincing. As has been shown, the utilisation of regional input-output tables is sufficient for forecasting purposes at least in connection with the application of attraction models.

4.3 Degree of integration and trade balances with the rest of the economy and with foreign countries

In the discussion of the Spanish growth poles the following *arguments* play a part in the connection now being considered:
— The growth poles should provide a high positive contribution to the regional balance of trade in accordance with the export basis theory since, in view of the limitation of the regional market, decisive growth impulses must be expected from regional foreign trade ('export-led growth').
— The growth poles should for their previous work purchases restrict themselves as far as possible to products offered within the region; this is the concept of 'external blocking'. In so far as the present structure of the region makes this impossible, a remedy should be provided by means of a regional import-substitution policy — the 'filling in' concept.
— Against a strategy of 'external blocking' and 'filling in' the objection is raised that this is obstructing the aim of the maximisation of the general economic growth rate and a desirable degree of inter-regional integration.

Since the three arguments are too general in scope to be examined in this form, the only aspect to be considered here is the extent to which they might be at all relevant in the present situation to serve as a basis for the discussion of economic alternatives. A start will thus be made by presenting the inter-regional and inter-national inter-relationships of the pole industries (1), then the resulting trade balances will be drawn up (2), and finally the possibility of replacing imported previous work by regional or national products will be examined(3).

1   The level of inter-regional and inter-national linkages between the pole industries is again shown in Table 42. Working on the average for all sectors for both poles, the backward linkage with the rest of Spain and foreign countries taken together is roughly the same and stands at about 50 per cent. Whereas Huelva is relatively more dependent on foreign imports than Seville, however, the latter is more dependent on imports from the rest of the national economy. Huelva's significant dependence on foreign countries turns on imports by the chemical and metal industries, and the greater dependence of Seville on the rest of the national economy hinges on the paper and metal industries.

In the forward linkages the inter-relationship with foreign countries plays a subordinate role as is to be expected. Only the foodstuffs and chemicals industries export in considerable quantities. The paper-processing industry in Seville represents a special case, since this relates almost exclusively to exports from a printing works. Exports of the chemicals industry are confined to fertilisers in respect of both poles, and those from the foodstuffs industry in Seville mainly concern olives and olive-oil.

The important export products are therefore those of a relatively low degree of processing, while the products of a higher degree of processing have only been placed in the international market in exceptional cases. This supports the thesis that in development countries the production of goods for the international market follows their production for the national (and traditionally protected) market after an interval (Egner, 63, 113; Hesse, 68, 679). Normally they are also characterised by the fact that the corresponding export markets offer less chance of growth.

The exports in the rest of the national economy are of prime importance in both poles. In both Huelva and Seville sales of end-products of the pole industries to the rest of the economy represent over 50 per cent of total sales, and the average for both poles is about 60 per cent. The metal and timber-processing sectors make an above-average contribution to this result in Huelva, as do the metal, paper-processing, chemicals and building materials sectors in Seville. In this connection it is interesting to distinguish between the sectors which mainly produce for a narrow zone outside the pole region Huelva/Seville, and those whose market extends over the whole national economy. In the first category in Huelva is the metal sector, virtually the entire production being sold in Córdoba, and in Seville the chemicals, paper processing and building materials sectors. The more important 'national' industries – in the sense that these produce for the entire market throughout the national economy – are thus likely to be those providing an above-average share of the exports to the rest of the national economy measured by total sales. Typical of this is the chemicals industry in Huelva.

2   The results of the forward and backward linkages of the pole industries with their own hinterland, the other pole province, the rest of the national economy and foreign countries are shown together for the average of both poles in Table 44. The net trade balances, shown here for 1971 without sectoral classification, can be culled readily from the sectoral input-output tables, both in their sectoral breakdown and also for the other years under review.

A striking feature at this point is the regional net trade balance on the bottom line, and the balance of transactions with foreign countries on the bottom line but one. As is to be expected, the regional net trade balance in both poles is positive and very high. Exports to the rest of the national economy and to foreign countries, taken together for both poles, are more than twice as high as the corresponding previous work purchases, and it is notable that in neither pole does the value creation quota exceed 35 per cent. This reflects the fact that taking the average for all sectors in both poles the regional previous work purchases are relatively more important than regional sales. On the average, according to this, the pole industries in their allocation ratios are more strongly purchase- than sales-oriented.

Huelva's net trade deficit with foreign countries is interesting in what follows, because its quantitative importance constitutes the primary basis for discussion of the charge on the national balance of payments arising from the pole programme, and the desirability of import substitution.

3   The arguments regarding the charge on the balance of payments and the possibility of import substitution for the previous work purchases of the pole industries have still to be examined.

Because there is a deficit in the balance of trade between the pole industries and foreign countries, it would be incorrect to conclude that there is a corresponding charge on the national balance of payments. The reason for this is that supplies by the pole industries can exert an import substitution effect to the extent that the other sectors of the national economy would otherwise have had to import the corresponding goods. This applies irrespective of whether the new supplies from the pole industries serve to replace imports previously required, or imports which would otherwise be required in the immediate future.

The argument regarding the charge on the balance of payments must now be further defined by saying that there will be some time-lag before the occurrence of the relief effect in connection with the substitution of imports in other sectors, compared with the charge effect in connection with the import content of the demand for investment goods for the production of import-substitution goods. This therefore has nothing to do with the charge in the production phase, only during the investment phase, so it can be seen that, at least during the transition stage between the establishment of the pole industries and the commencement of production, the massive industrialisation policy involves a net charge effect.

But even this recognised argument is less convincing in the present case because of the financing methods employed for foreign investment goods.[21] First it can be observed that the time-lag between the purchase of foreign investment goods and the start of production is not very great. As Table 26a shows, foreign imports of investment goods are confined almost exclusively to machinery and mechanical equipment, and these are often only obtained in the year immediately preceding the commencement of production. Furthermore, purchases of foreign investment goods are financed primarily by means of suppliers' credits, under which 10 per cent of the purchase price is usually payable upon conclusion of the contract, and a further 10 per cent upon delivery of the first items. The remaining 80 per cent is paid in up to five yearly instalments at an average interest rate of about 8 per cent on the outstanding balance.

The argument regarding the burden on the balance of payments thus applies to only a very limited extent, and it does not furthermore apply specifically to the pole industries. Since, however, no comparable information is available as regards the import content of the demand for investment goods in other new industries in the national economy, this assumption cannot be substantiated here.

Table 44
Summarised statement of the balance of trade of the pole industries
in 1971 (Ptas millions)

Transactions with	Huelva pole			Seville pole		
	Previous work purchases	Sales of end-products	Balance	Previous work purchases	Sales of end-products	Balance
Rest of province	3,438.4	880.2	−2,558.2	3,191.9	3,042.3	−149.6
Other pole province	280.2	904.5	+624.3	72.3	331.5	+259.2
Rest of Spain	1,134.1	10,820.7	+9,686.6	2,199.9	6,397.2	+4,197.3
Foreign countries	4,666.6	1,415.1	−3,251.5	1,462.5	1,075.7	−386.8
Rest of Spain and foreign countries	5,800.7	12,235.8	+6,435.1	3,662.4	7,472.9	+3,810.5

The argument regarding import substitution must now be examined more closely. Under this, efforts should be made to replace previous work purchases by the pole industries from foreign countries or from the rest of the national economy — the argument regarding external blocking or filling in — by corresponding internal or regional supplies.

150

The replacement of previous work purchases from abroad depends on whether and to what extent particular production goods can be made available at home, and on whether the use of internal supplies seems advisable at the present development level of the national economy and having regard to the absolute advantages of foreign suppliers. Even if in the analysis one confines oneself to asking which goods could be obtained at all in the country in view of the availability of corresponding natural resources, a sharp limitation arises in the substitution possibilities.

Table 45
Foreign previous work purchases and possibilities of their substitution by internal products, 1971

	Huelva pole		Seville pole	
	Imports (Ptas millions)	Substitut-able portion (per cent)	Imports (Ptas millions)	Substitut-able portion (per cent)
Foodstuffs	3.2	100	525.8	53
Textiles	—	—	80.0	100
Paper	—	—	54.1	100
Timber	9.0	25	—	—
Chemicals	3,405.7	3-20	56.6	100
Building materials	3.0	0	304.2	3
Metal industry	1,245.6	25-30	424.2	100
Various	0	—	17.6	100
Energy	0	—	0	—
Total	4,666.6	16-35	1,462.5	62

In Table 45 alternative values are shown for Huelva in two sectors. First there is the possibility that the chemical industry could use the phosphor deposits in the Spanish Sahara, and then the possibility that the metal industry could utilise the copper deposits in the rest of the economy. Both cases were uncertain at the time of investigation.

It appears that in Huelva and Seville together it is only possible to discuss 41 per cent of imports at the most, because the majority of the previous work imports cannot technically be made available in the national economy.

All in all there does not seem to be very much point in proceeding with the discussion of the possibilities of new industrial establishments in the two poles or in the pole region on the lines of the import substitution argument. In any case this applies in so far as, given the industrial structure of the poles and their hinterland at the time, the further investment chances can only be established to a limited extent with the possibility of replacing regional or national pole imports of the pole industries. This also means that a strategy of external blocking is not very promising. The filling-in strategy must therefore be limited to the supply side, that is to say to the further processing *in situ* of those products which are offered at the time by the poles and the productive sectors of the hinterland.

The considerations will consequently have to concentrate on these two points:
— whether, with the activities promoted in the poles so far, those whose sectoral profile corresponds most readily to the location profile of the pole region have already been affected;
— which activities in the pole region have already been sufficiently increased by the flexibility of the region, thanks to the new supply of the pole industries, to make the promotion of successor activities seem particularly profitable. Here 'flexibility' is an expression for the speed and facility with which new activities are attracted.

5 Overall Effects of the Production Phase

The presentation of the overall effects can now be limited to an examination of the direct, indirect and induced income effects, that is to the polarisation of the income in the production phase of the pole industries. This section is intended to summarise and complete the related results of sections 3.1 and 3.2, enabling the summarised presentation of the Andalusian growth pole results to be rounded off to the extent that, after the presentation of the outflow effects on the basis of the investment and financing structure and of the previous work purchases from foreign countries and the rest of the national economy, the outflow effects for the value-creation of the pole industries are now determined on the basis of the difference between internal and residents' incomes (regional and national).

This means that a certain systematic conclusion is reached whereby, though the regional income effects of the poles are not finally presented, the differential income incidence of the poles is characterised and clarified by the different outflow quotas, by reference to their structure and to the initial situation of the hinterland surrounding them.

5.1 Direct and indirect income effects

1   The basis for the calculation of the direct income effect is the net value creation of the pole industries in the years under review. The input-output tables show the structure of the net value creation broken down into wages and salaries, social insurance contributions (employers' and workers' shares), interest on investment and working capital financed by borrowing, profits and indirect taxes (Impuesto sobre el tráfico de la empresa, which is comparable with sales tax). At the risk of some measure of repetition, the assumptions regarding the applicability of these value creation categories are set out briefly below, but the bases are investigated elsewhere:

— wages and salaries: incomes of residents and internal incomes are equated;
— social insurance contributions: these are attributed entirely to the rest of the national economy;

- interest on investment capital financed by borrowing: interest on public loans is attributed to the rest of the national economy, and interest on foreign suppliers' credits to foreign countries;
- interest on working capital: assuming complete credit financing, attributed in Huelva as to 100 per cent to the rest of the national economy, and in Seville as to 33 per cent to the pole province and 67 per cent to the rest of the national economy;
- profits: distributed to province, rest of national economy and foreign countries according to the participation ratios in the 'social capital';
- indirect taxes: entirely to the rest of the national economy.

The differentiations made enable the regional outflow quotas to be determined; the outflows are then subdivided into those accruing to the rest of the national economy and those going abroad. It should be emphasised that consideration is restricted to the side on which the income arises, no account being taken of where the recipients in fact spend the income attributed to them.

Direct effects on regional incomes: after the above explanations it is now possible to determine the direct effect on the incomes of residents in the regions, that is to say the share of the net value creation of the pole industries in the years under review attributable to residents in the region, by the addition of wages and salaries and the profit incomes from regional participations in the social capital. In Seville the share of the interest on the working capital financed by borrowing has also to be considered. The results are shown in Table 46.

By determining the total regional outflow quota in relation to the net value creation of the pole industries a particularly important result has again been achieved. The corresponding result for the investment phase of the pole industries was given in Table 27, which also gave the investment phase of the infrastructure investments including the assumptions made in connection with section 3.2.1. Table 47 shows a comparison of the outflow quotas derived therefrom with the outflow quota according to Table 46 for the 'normal year' of 1971.

In both poles, the highest outflow quota is thus to be found in the demand for investment goods in the pole industries, and the lowest in infrastructure investments. The differences in the outflow quotas reading across and down need no further clarification in view of what has been said above, since they reflect in every respect the explanations given at the various points for the summarised statements of the Huelva and Seville poles.

To sum up it can be stated that in view of its lower regional and national outflow quota compared with Huelva the Seville pole produces a sharper polarisation of incomes than the Huelva pole. As is to be

Table 46
Direct effect on the income of the province (Ptas millions), 1967-71, and outflow quotas

	1967	1969	1971
(a) Huelva			
Wages and salaries	132.4	305.8	491.7
Profit income	1.0	35.8	53.0
Total	133.4	341.6	544.7
Total outflow quotas related to net value creation (per cent)	66	70	85
(b) Seville			
Wages and salaries	573.3	898.7	1,086.1
Profit income	188.7	404.0	632.6
Interest income	34.8	61.1	87.4
Total	796.8	1,363.8	1,806.1
Total outflow quotas related to net value creation (per cent)	43	43	50

expected, this result is also confirmed for the indirect income effect now to be considered.

2   The indirect income effect is shown in Table 48, which includes in each case the effects of the previous work purchases of the pole industries in the rest of the other pole province.

155

Table 47
Summarised statement of the outflow quotas related to the pole provinces (per cent)

	Huelva	Seville
Infrastructure investments	64	47
Directly productive investments (pole industries)	91	75
Share of income of the residents outside the region in the net value creation of the pole industries	85	50

Table 48
Indirect income effect, 1967 and 1969 (Ptas millions)

	1967		1969	
	In rest of province of		In rest of province of	
Indirect effect of	Huelva	Seville	Huelva	Seville
Huelva pole	153.2	20.4	337.6	109.5
Seville pole	7.4	921.3	18.1	1,577.6
Both poles	160.6	941.7	355.7	1,687.1

The indirect effects of the poles in the remainder of the other pole province reflect in each case the weaknesses and one-sidedness of the Huelva-Seville axis relationship. The importance of the indirect effect of each pole on its hinterland, in relation to the importance of the direct effect, is best demonstrated by a comparison between the gross value creation of the pole industries and the indirect effect on their hinterland, for both are contributions to the gross internal product of the province.

As stated above, it was not possible to follow the lines of procedure adopted for the direct effect in order to determine the net value creation quota and the internal quota of the net value creation from the indirect effect.

The comparison in Table 49 accordingly shows the proportions borne to one another by the gross value creation of the pole industries and the gross value creation induced by previous work purchases in the hinterland. It is impossible to do more than form assumptions from the incidence on the income of residents of which the best founded are set out further below.

Table 49

Contribution of the pole industries and their suppliers in the hinterland to the gross domestic product of the province (Ptas millions)

	1967		1969	
	Huelva	Seville	Huelva	Seville
Pole industries	714.6	1,602.5	1,726.8	2,731.0
Suppliers*	153.2	921.3	337.6	1,577.6
Relationship suppliers/ pole industries	0.21	0.57	0.20	0.58

*Contribution induced only by previous work purchases of the pole industries.

The fact that the relationship is almost constant over the years is surprising despite the fact that it is at the same time also observed that the supply relationships in the individual pole industries are relatively stable; in view of the changes between 1967 and 1969 in the product composition and in the resulting structure of the previous work purchases, this constancy can only be regarded as fortuitous (cf. the additional tables).

While it would have been desirable to calculate the values of the additional tables to the input-output tables for 1971 as well, this was not possible because the 1971 values of the input-output tables are based on estimates. To supplement Table 49, only an estimated reckoning for 1971 could therefore be provided (for methodology see Buttler, 73, 203/4), the result of which is given in Table 50.

Table 50
Supplement to Table 49 for 1971

	Huelva	Seville
Pole industries	4,531.6	3,946.8
Suppliers	2,975.9	2,289.1
Relationship suppliers/ pole industries	0.66	0.58

The supplier/pole industry relationship in Huelva as compared with Seville now seems surprisingly high, although there are two main reasons for this: in the first place, the relationship between previous work from the hinterland and gross value creation in 1971 is only marginally lower in Huelva than in Seville, and in the second place, on the weighted average for the supply sectors the value creation quota is higher in Huelva than in Seville.

Finally, consideration has to be given as to whether it is still justified to assess the incidence of the poles on the regional residents' incomes in Seville in 1971 as being higher than that in Huelva. The first point to consider is that in 1971 the difference between the gross and net domestic product of the suppliers will be substantially higher in Huelva than in Seville, for the capital intensity of the extractive industries — and consequently the depreciation ratio to gross value creation — are known to be high. With ~ 90 per cent, the extractive industries in Huelva in 1971 accounted for an extraordinarily high proportion of the previous work from the rest of the province.

The second point concerns the fact that the outflow quota for interest and profit income related to the pole province will be higher in Huelva than in Seville, and not only for pole industries. This means that the difference in internal and residents' incomes will be higher in Huelva than in Seville for suppliers as well. For 1971 this can be taken as certain, since at least 80 per cent of all previous work purchases of the pole industries in the rest of the province comes from the mines in the Rio Tinto district, which are owned by capitalists outside the pole province. Consequently the indirect effect, now measured as a contribution by the supplier to the net domestic product, was also higher in absolute and relative terms in Seville than in Huelva in 1971.

The result of this section can thus be fully summarised by saying that in Huelva the direct and indirect effect on the income of residents in the province is confined essentially to the wages and salaries paid by the pole industries and suppliers. In Seville also in the last year under review, despite lower contributions by the pole industries and suppliers to the gross domestic product, the contribution to the residents' income was higher than in Huelva.

The *relative* contribution of the Huelva pole to the residents' income in the province is still greater than in Seville, despite the substantially higher outflow quota. This is because, taking the weighted average of the suppliers including their share of the previous work, the wages and salaries related to the gross value creation by the suppliers already amount to just on 30 per cent. Since the total income in the province of Seville is about four times as high as in Huelva, the relative contribution of the pole of Seville does not match that of Huelva. In view of the population development in both provinces a *further* point is that the *per capita* income must show a still higher growth rate than total income in Huelva as compared with Seville.

5.2   The regional consumer expenditure multiplier

The object of this section is to consider the importance attaching to the *induced* income effect, by reason of the expenditure of the provincial residents' income, which is produced by the direct and indirect effect. The additional incomes available in each period by reason of direct and indirect effects give rise to multiplier processes, which can be described by reference to a regional consumer expenditure multiplier. The differences between the multiplier correlation k^H (for Huelva) and k^S (for Seville) provide important information on the pole-hinterland relationship. It is to be expected that $k^H < k^S$ and that correspondingly the result of the considerations in 3.4.1 is to be completed. The 'consumer expenditure multiplier' is chosen as a terminus technicus in order to ensure a clear-cut abstract definition in contrast to matrix multipliers.

First the multiplier relationship has to be developed (1), then the possibilities of its empirical definition and the result will be considered (2). The result is suitable for correcting optimistic estimates of regional multiplier effects.

1   A *simple regional multiplier* could be defined as

$$k^i = \frac{1 - im^i}{1 - c^i\,(1 - im^i)}, \qquad [1]$$

where c^i represents the marginal consumer quota, and im^i the marginal import quota for consumer goods. The symbol i denotes any region. This is a question of a simple regional multiplier, since inter-regional feedback effects are not considered.

If this relationship is adopted, then it will obviously be assumed that those income portions which are spent in the region, again become income in that region to the full extent. However, that cannot be accepted, since incomes of non-residents are to some extent relevant to the consumer goods production of the region and the activities extended in front of it in the region; firstly because the producers of consumer goods and their suppliers within the region will be dependent upon previous work imports, and secondly because parts of the internal income of the region will be imputable to non-residents (cf. Rittenbruch, 68, 55 et seq.). Although it must not be assumed that the same outflow quotas as observed in connection with pole industries apply also in the case of consumer goods production, the results achieved for pole industries emphasise the importance of consideration of the outflow quotas in the present case.

For peripheral regions the consideration of the outflow quotas should from all experience be more important than that of inter-regional feedback effects. The latter flow from outside the region to a peripheral region because increased imports by the region lead to income growth in export areas and eventually to an increase in imports into these areas from the peripheral region. Jansen, who deduces a regional multiplier with feedback effects (Jansen, 68, 49 et seq.), cites very low hypothetical values for the feedback operation, and considers these plausible. For this purpose, however, he does not yet make explicit use of the above-mentioned argument that such feedback effects on peripheral regions will be particularly small with respect to *peripheral* regions.

The use of a simple regional multiplier is therefore proposed here, paying particular attention to the regional outflow quotas. The regional consumer expenditure multiplier takes the form

$$\frac{dY^i}{dA_a^i} = k^i = \frac{(1 - im_c^i)\quad(1 - im_v^i)}{1 - c^i\,(1 - im_c^i)\,(1 - im_v^i)} \qquad [2]$$

Here dA_a is the additional amount of consumer goods expenditure which, by reason of direct and indirect pole effects, is effected ('autonomously') by residents in the region in each period compared with the preceding period, that is the growth in internal income accruing to residents in the region on grounds of pole activity (direct + indirect effects) less direct taxes on such income, social insurance contributions

160

and savings. im_C is the portion of consumer goods imported from outside the region, and im_v is the outflow quota from the production of consumer goods; it concerns the import content of the demand for previous work induced for internal producers of consumer goods and their internal suppliers, as well as the difference between internal and residents' incomes at these stages. c is the marginal propensity to consume and the symbol i indicates here, as with the other expressions, that is is a question in each case of an expression for a particular region.

The extended multiplier relationship can be regarded as a specification of the previous example, $(1 - im)$ being replaced by $(1 - im_C)(1 - im_v)$. This takes account of the fact that the consumer goods produced in the region also include import elements.

2   In discussing the possibilities of the empirical determination of the relationship, recourse can only be had to warranted material in part. Necessary assumptions are examined with regard to their plausibility, and definitive sensibility tests clarify the dependency of the multiplier on any errors in the assumptions.

Generally speaking the idea of working with *marginal* propensities to consume or import must be abandoned; first because there are no time series for the warranted material (from the regional accounts for example), and secondly because in the estimates only approximations are available. As will be shown later, this can be accepted in so far as propensities to consume or to save are concerned. At 8 per cent of the available income in both pole provinces, the savings quota of households is slightly higher than in the rest of the national economy (7.5 per cent for the whole economy in 1967, see RGR, 27). Changes of relatively greater importance will have no marked effect on the multiplier result. The acceptance of the constancy of the import quotas seems more problematical, as the new pole industries whose effects come up for discussion here could indeed have import substitution effects for the region. This does not apply in Huelva to the same extent as in Seville, as is apparent from the supply structure of the pole industries in both provinces. For Seville it has only a weakening effect in that the consumer goods industries there are export-oriented; also, many of them manufacture products which had already been produced in the region in such quantity that it was unnecessary to import them. Nevertheless, it has to be recognised that corrections might be advisable in Seville, and this is dealt with below.

(a)   First the consumer quota must be determined, for which purpose the following reservation must be made: for each period the multiplier analysis gives the induced increase in the income of residents in the region

(dY^i). This is the net domestic product at factor cost, not the available income. Only the available income less savings will be income-effective in the region in the next period, for direct taxes including social insurance contributions are outflows from the region (see also Tiebout, 60, 76). This is a consequence of the centralised financial system of the Spanish economy.

Taxation of the net domestic product at factor cost by direct taxes including social insurance (charge payable) amounts (Planning Commission, 70, RGR, 24) to

$$\frac{T_{dir}}{YH} = 0.088 \quad \text{and} \quad \frac{T_{dir}}{YS} = 0.086.$$

the symbols H and S standing here, as in what follows, for Huelva and Seville. The total savings of households and undertakings in the provinces related to net domestic product at factor cost amount (RGR, 41) to

$$\frac{S}{YH} = 0.100 \quad \text{and} \quad \frac{S}{YS} = 0.099.$$

According to this

$$\frac{C}{YH} = cH = 0.812 \quad \text{and} \quad \frac{C}{YS} = cS \ 3 \ 0.815.$$

This average propensity to consume c^i is treated below as a constant and therefore equal to the marginal propensity to consume.

(b)   At the second stage the proportion of imported consumer goods to the additional demand for consumer goods in the province (im_c^i) is to be determined. Here the difficulty arises that no regional import-export statistics are available from which the corresponding values could be calculated. Because of lack of information on individual flows of goods and services as in the case of the regional accounts, regional trade balances are often worked out by an indirect process. A start is made on individual groups of goods for which the difference between inner regional supply and regional demand is determined, the difference then being recorded as a regional export or import.

Such a procedure could also be adopted here if, as is the case, the structure of consumer expenditure by products or product groups is known. The Spanish statistical office (Instituto Nacional de Estadística) carried out an investigation in 1964/65 into the structure of consumer expenditure in all the provinces (INE, 65), and it may be assumed that this structure has not undergone any material change. This assumption is necessary, since comparative data for the calculation of the elasticity of demand by product groups are lacking. An attempt could be made to use the data for those provinces which in 1965 had a similarly high *per capita* income as the pole provinces had in the years under review. It is difficult to interpret the result of such a cross-section analysis on the lines of a development time path for individual provinces, however, since regional consumer habits, differences in personal incomes distribution, availability of services provided and so on have a substantial effect on the structure of consumer demand.

In the concluding section of its tables the regional overall accounts give the basic data for the determination of the net trade balance of the pole provinces regarding inner-regional supply and regional demand for major product groups (ibid., 67 et seq.). These will only be resorted to below, however, in order to determine the import content of demand for consumer goods for part of the products, as the product groups are too highly aggregated, and consequently the availability of the more closely classified material of the investigation by the INE would not be used to the best advantage. It is important to note that the result of the indirect measurement of import flows is dependent on the aggregation level employed for the product groups. If sub-groups show balances with different (plus or minus) signs, the sum of the balances of the sub-groups will be higher than if only the consolidated results of the main groups were recorded. The particulars of the regional accounts can only be compared with those of the INE study for twenty-seven groups, the INE grouping embraces eighty-eight sub-groups, and the sub-grouping often comes down to individual products such as sugar, milk and so on.

In order to estimate the import quotas for the individual groups of goods and services, the eighty-eight varieties of products in the INE study were arranged in four categories, namely:

- those which are not produced at all in the province, as shown in the production statistics; these account for 23 per cent of purchases of consumer goods in Huelva, and 11 per cent in Seville;
- those which are not traded between regions, particularly because they must be consumed at the time and place of production (certain services, usufruct of dwellings); that are indeed traded between regions but are qualitatively undifferentiated,[22] and are so plentifully available in the province that imports would be unimportant (fish in Huelva, olive oil, eggs and milk in Seville for example); these account for 33 per cent of purchases of consumer goods in Huelva, and 43 per cent in Seville;
- those which are certainly produced in the province but of which the

163

supply is either insufficient or is qualitatively so differentiated that even if the supply were sufficient it could not be expected that the only products to be used would be those of the province. The latter would include, for instance, textiles, furniture, household appliances etc. (accounting for 32 per cent of purchases of consumer goods in Huelva and 34 per cent in Seville).

– those which really belong to the third category, but because of the impossibility of arranging them in product groups of the regional accounts no indirect estimate of the imports was possible (accounting for 12 per cent of expenditure on consumer goods in both provinces).

On the basis of this grouping, the following deductions can be drawn: for the first category the outflow quota amounts to 100 per cent, and for the second to 0 per cent. The level of the proportion in the second group in both provinces calls for explanation. It must be realised that provinces with a relatively low *per capita* income are concerned. In these, proportionately more foodstuffs and day-to-day services are required (cf. Table 51). Foodstuffs of a simple kind predominate. High-grade differentiated products, especially durable consumer goods, are of little importance. Thus the proportion of expenditure on durable consumer goods to total consumer expenditure amounted in 1967 to 6.3 per cent in Huelva and to 9.0 per cent in Seville (RGR, 27).

For the products in the third category the import balances were calculated by the indirect procedure on the basis of the RGR data, on the following lines: if for 1967 the RGR showed a deficit for the product or the product group, and if in addition no cover was to be expected from the production of new pole industries for 1971, the expenditure proportions of the corresponding goods were recorded entirely as an imported element. For if, with a given demand, imports had to be made in view of possible import substitution pole activities, the additional demand would be wholly reflected in increased imports; but if a surplus were shown for any product or group of products,[23] it was assumed that no imports took place. Using this procedure produced an import proportion for the products of the third category of some 65 per cent in Huelva and 68 per cent in Seville. The results were also used in the same way for goods in the fourth category, since no other suitable method was available and these goods could have been attributed in themselves to the third category.

It must be admitted that the procedure for groups 3 and 4 is not very satisfactory, due in particular to the fact that the trade which plays an important role for these products (e.g. textiles, cleansing agents and cosmetic articles, durable consumer goods, and highly processed foodstuffs) remains completely unconsidered. This is a serious deficiency, for in the present connection whether a region produces a particular product

164

in sufficient quantity is less important than whether and to what extent this intra-regional supply also becomes effective. Consequently the imports in doubt are undervalued for groups 3 and 4.

This deficiency, however, is not so important in the comparison of the poles, for it can be assumed that the divergence from reality is relatively similar in both. It will also be compensated for if imported consumer goods, in so far as they are sold in the region by retailers resident there, are not recorded as imports at the full amount of their final selling price. Rather are the actual imports smaller by the amount of the value creation of the domestic retailer handling them, less the imported previous work and income of foreign factors required to provide these services.[24] It is not claimed that, because the undervaluation of imports will be wholly or more than wholly compensated thereby, a partial compensation still arises without doubt. As the information required for the measurement of the internal proportion of the flow of imported consumer goods is lacking, it can be assumed that the systematic deficiency is not so great as to dispense with the need for an analysis of the import content of the demand for consumer goods in groups 3 and 4. A sensibility analysis under (d) will show what importance is to be attached to systematic defects in these groups for the result of the multiplier relationship.

If the procedure for determining im_C is accepted, with the reservations mentioned, then values of

$$\frac{dIm_C^H}{dC^H} = im_C^H = 0.510 \quad \text{and} \quad \frac{dIm_C^S}{dC^S} = im_C^S = 0.420$$

for the multiplier analysis can be established. Table 51 shows how this import content is made up.

By and large Table 51 shows the differences to be expected in the consumer structure and the import content of the demand for consumer goods in Huelva and Seville. Only in the fourth group of goods in the table is the import content higher in Seville than in Huelva, which highlights the questionability of indirect methods of determination for category 3 in the preceding classification of a concrete case. The difference arises mainly from the fact that in Huelva a production branch of durable consumer goods, such as the furniture industry, is very strongly represented despite being highly specialised. At the same time this sector is clearly identifiable in the regional accounts, whereas other productions of durable consumer goods, such as household appliances, cannot be separately identified in Seville because of the aggregation of the groups of goods concerned. In both groups inter-regional trade is certainly substantial, which means that it will definitely be impossible to maintain the established correlation of 100 per cent cover for own requirements in Huelva, and 100 per cent imports in Seville.

Table 51
Structure of consumption by main groups with their import content (per cent)

	Huelva		Seville	
	Proportion of con-sumption	of which imported	Proportion of con-sumption	of which imported
Foodstuffs	53.6	48	48.6	31
Clothing	15.1	80	10.8	77
Housing	6.0	0	6.8	0
Energy, equipment, household appliances and repairs	8.4	72	10.5	78
Sundry goods and Services	16.9	44	23.3	44
Total/weighted average	100.0	51	100.0	42

It might of course be possible to correct the result obtained to some extent by reviewing the considerations mentioned. That would be an unreliable procedure, however, for until a systematic additional criterion can be found which covers all the sectors, a partial correction on the basis of more or less random primary experiences must be rejected as altogether too uncertain. In addition, the sensibility analysis will show that the errors in estimation which were discussed are not nearly large enough to suggest any renunciation of the corresponding estimates.

(c)   At the *third stage* it is necessary to determine the import content of the induced previous work demand and the proportion of foreigners' income in the production of internal consumer goods demanded in addition. This is im_v^i. For this purpose the gross output value *(BPW)* created by the inner-regional production of consumer goods is broken down analytically into its component parts:

$$BPW^i = V_i + V_a + W_i + W_a \qquad [3]$$

where

V denotes the previous work, and W the gross value creation. The suffix a denotes the area external to the region, and i the region as before.

The proportions to be determined are expressed in the form

$$1 = \frac{V_i}{BPW} + \frac{V_a}{BPW} + \frac{W_i}{BPW} + \frac{W_a}{BPW} = v_i + v_a + w_i + w_a. \qquad [4]$$

V_a and W_a flow out upon the production of consumer goods within the region immediately. Consequently $Im_v = V_a + W_a$, but this only applies when V_i contains no import components at all. However, it must then be reckoned that the producers of internal previous work also import previous work themselves. If it is assumed that the total import quota Im_v appears not only in the production of consumer goods but at every stage of production of domestic primary products for consumer goods inside the country, and further that the relationship V^i/W or v_i/v_a is equal at every stage, then the total induced import demand for previous work converges on the value

$$im_v = \frac{v_a + w_a}{v_a + w_a + w_i} \qquad [5]$$

The above assumptions should apply in the case of further analysis. Only with the aid of a detailed input-output model could a solution be found in which the assumption of the equality of the previous work quotas at all stages could be abandoned. Additional information on the relationship W_a/W_i for each of the activities concerned would be necessary in order to replace the assumption of the equality of the outflow quotas on the basis of the difference between internal incomes and residents' incomes by realistic values.

In the following v_a, w_a and w_i are to be determined. First of all the relationship V^i/BPW and the relationship W^i/BPW have to be established. According to the regional accounts in 1967 they amounted on the average for all activities in the province to

$$vH = 0.450 \qquad vS = 0.452$$
$$\text{and}$$
$$wH = 0.550 \qquad wS = 0.548$$

There is no doubt that both here and in what follows the utilisation of the average values for the entire province is problematical. Even that would be capable of solution by the utilisation of a detailed input-output model.

w has now to be broken down into its component parts. For w_a the formula can be written:

$$w_a = \frac{W_a}{BPW} = \frac{T_{ind}}{BPW} + \frac{D}{BPW} + \frac{\text{foreign factor income}}{BPW} \qquad [6]$$

$$w_i = \frac{W_i}{BPW} = \frac{L_i}{BPW} + \frac{\text{other internal factor income}}{BPW} \qquad [7]$$

where L denotes the wage and salary total (less the social insurance contributions).

The allocation of T_{ind} and D to the foreigners' income needs to be explained. Owing to the centralised financial system of the national economy the indirect taxes flow out into the area outside the region. They have to be considered here because Y^i in [2] has to be defined as net regional income at factor cost, as set out above. This is also the reason for considering D as an outflow. D cannot of course be treated as a foreigners' income element, but it is an outflow in relation to W, as W here describes the gross value creation. As the deductions from W are not intended to provide information regarding the incidence of the poles on the external incomes, but to restrict the remaining size of the residents' incomes, it is possible to adopt the procedure proposed in relationship [6]. If on the other hand an inter-regional multiplier model were drawn up, D would not need to be considered as a foreigner's income element. W_a is therefore rightly defined as a gross value creation outflow.

For l it is assumed as in previous cases that the full extent of a resident's income element must be taken into acount. w can now be written as

$$w = l + d + t_{ind} + \text{other factor income}/BPW \qquad [8]$$

According to the results of the regional accounts we now have

$$w^H = 0.186 + 0.035 + 0.030 + 0.299 \quad \text{and}$$

$$w^S = 0.209 + 0.038 + 0.038 + 0.263.$$

168

For the 'other factor income', assumptions regarding their imputability to w_i and w_a must be adopted. As has been shown, such assumptions can only be avoided when – as in the case of the pole industries – the financing and participation structure is known. An assumption which could be regarded as plausible might be that 20 per cent of 'other factor income' might be imputed to residents outside the region in Huelva and 10 per cent in Seville. The difference between the provinces can be demonstrated for the experiences now available, since the low outflow quota compared with the values observed in the pole industries supports the assumption that, with regard to the producers of consumer goods in the province it is usually a question of undertakings registered in the province. In addition there are well-established small and medium-sized undertakings to which the explanations for the relatively high outflow quotas in the pole industries do not apply. If these assumptions are accepted then

$$w_a^H = 0.030 + 0.035 + 0.059 = 0.124 \quad \text{and for}$$

$$w_a^S = 0.038 + 0.038 + 0.026 = 0.102.$$

In the same way $w_i = w - w_a$

$$w_i^H = 0.426 \quad \text{and}$$

$$w_i^S = 0.446$$

The determination of v_a and v_i must be effected entirely on the basis of assumptions. It is certain that v_a^H will be greater than v_a^S, and it is also certain that in both provinces the level of previous work imports, measured by the total previous work by producers of consumer goods, will be lower than in the case of the pole industries. This is because the consumer goods which are produced in the provinces themselves are as a rule simple products, the producers of which have a high degree of backward linkage with the primary goods sector in so far as they do not actually belong to it. This has already been indicated.

It is accordingly assumed that the internal producers of consumer goods in the provinces only import 25 per cent of their previous work in Huelva and 20 per cent in Seville. If these assumptions are accepted as plausible, then

$$v_a^H = 0.112 \quad \text{and} \quad v_a^S = 0.091.$$

On that basis im_v can be calculated for relationship [5]:

$$im_v^H = \frac{0.112 + 0.124}{0.112 + 0.124 + 0.426} = 0.356$$

$$im_v^S = \frac{0.091 + 0.102}{0.091 + 0.102 + 0.446} = 0.302.$$

(d)   From the calculation of c, im_c and im_v the multiplier relationship can be calculated.

By insertion in the relationship [2], $k^H = 0.425$ and $k^S = 0.604$.

3   The individual assumptions can now be altered to demonstrate the sensibility of the multiplier relationship to errors in the assumptions made.

For the determination of im_c the method of assessment of the import content of categories 3 and 4 was subject to serious doubts. It may now be assumed for instance that the import content of these categories is 20 per cent higher for Huelva than was first estimated. im_c^H at 0.573 would then be some 12.3 per cent higher altogether. For the multiplier relationship $k^H = 0.353$ is then obtained, and the relative difference from the above result for k^H amounts to -17 per cent.

im_v was determined on the assumption that the domestic producers of consumer goods utilise internal previous work which has the same import content which the consumer goods would have if only direct previous work imports were considered. It may now be assumed that the suppliers of the producers of consumer goods at a previous stage import no previous work themselves, but d and t_{ind} are still to be considered as an outflow quota for them too, and that the foreigner's proportion of the 'other factor income' is the same as was assumed above. For im_v^H a value of 0.220 is reached, which is 38.3 per cent lower than that assumed above. For k^H a value is obtained which is correspondingly 30.3 per cent higher, namely 0.554.

It can also be objected that the foreigner's share of the 'other factor income' is set too low in the case of Huelva. Instead of a proportion of 20 per cent, one of 30 per cent could now be applied. On this basis im_v^H changes by +13.2 per cent to 0.403. k^H then comes down by 9.5 per cent, namely to 0.385.

Finally it is necessary to examine how k^H will react to an increase in the savings quota by 2 per cent. c^H then comes to 0.792. On this supposition k^H would assume a value some 1 per cent lower, namely 0.421.

What conclusions are to be drawn as regards the dependency of the multiplier relationship on errors in the essential assumptions? Will the errors accumulate or tend to cancel out?

(a)   The non-observance of marginal changes in the consumer, tax payment and import quotas is justified, because either the multiplier reacts so insensitively to realistically possible changes or the recording method is so imprecise, that considerations regarding marginal changes have no purpose. There is a tendency to suppose, however, that the savings quota – and owing to the progressive income tax scale the tax payment quota – will rise in the development process. On the other hand the import quota will tend, *ceteris paribus,* to sink because the diversification of the regional production structure facilitates the substitution of existing imports. The effects of both changes on the multiplier will tend to compensate one another.

(b)   As regards the import quota for consumer goods, in view of the considerations set out above the author would be inclined to regard the result as on the whole correct, or at any rate with the exception of the results for categories 3 and 4 in Seville. In this case the import content of the demand for consumer goods might be lower than was calculated. The multiplier is consequently probably undervalued in Seville compared with Huelva.

(c)   The determination of im_y is still somewhat unconvincing. An improvement of the model might first be adopted here, while different previous work and value creation quotas and import quotas for previous work purchases are considered for an input-output model. As regards the determination of w_a the result seems quite plausible on the other hand, so that the author would surmise that the error in im_y consists in too high a quota v_a. This error is strengthened by consideration of the previous stages. In consequence the author would be inclined to regard a correction of the multiplier in an upward direction as probable here also. The sensibility test under 2 has shown, however, that decisive changes are not to be expected on this account either.

(d)   At the outset the hypothesis was adopted that k^H will be smaller than k^S. Has that been validly tested? It could be objected that the result only serves to support the hypothesis because the assumptions were adopted in retrospect in accordance with this prior understanding, but this can be contradicted. If it is assumed that in the case of v_a and w_a no different assumptions were adopted for Huelva and Seville, then having in mind the empirically assured virtually equal consumer quotas in both provinces k^S would be greater than k^H because im_c^H is greater than im_c^S. The difference in the relationship im_c in Huelva as opposed to Seville does not arise merely because of the assumptions adopted, but because of the (empirically assured) differential significance of the consumer goods category 2. Moreover, there is no plausible reason for assuming that v_a and w_a should be no higher in Huelva than in Seville.

4   The result of the analysis of the regional consumer expenditure multiplier provides the relationship by which autonomous expenditure changes are reinforced by means of direct and indirect effects of the pole activities on the induced effects in the pole hinterland. In consideration of the systematic errors it can be established that the multiplier in Huelva will probably have a value in Huelva of between 0.4 and 0.55, and in Seville of between 0.6 and 0.75.

The theory of the regional multiplier is often discussed in the literature on the subject in relation to the export basis theory (Isard, 60, 189 et seq., Rittenbruch, 68, 54 et seq., Richardson, 69, 247 et seq.). Moreover, the export basis theory is also criticised on the grounds that previous work imports are not considered. The reason for the deficiencies in the multiplier relationship of the export basis theory lies in the fact that 'the multiplier process only relates to the expenditure field, and the production side that provides the basis for the income arising is not considered' (Rittenbruch, 68, 56). Richardson also considers the observance of the 'indirect' outflows from previous work imports as extraordinarily important. This is supported by the present result.

However, the difference between the multiplier results for Huelva on the one hand and for Seville on the other hand demonstrates clearly the dependence of the multiplier relationship on the development level and the degree of diversification of the sector structure in the region considered.

It is therefore to be assumed that the multiplier relationship in the poles will strengthen for increasing promotion periods, with the consequence that, the nearer the region can be located to the growth threshold, the more the support effect exerted by the income multiplier will increase for the production of self-generating growth. It would accordingly be wrong to draw conclusions regarding a fundamental rejection of the polarisation strategy from the hitherto low multiplier relationship. On the contrary, the dependence of the multiplier relationship on the inflow volumes referred to demonstrates clearly − in accordance with the statistical trustworthiness of the results arrived at − the validity of their interpretation from the point of view of polarisation theory: a vicious circle of the regional growth process also arises from the fact that the multiplier effects are likely to be greater in central regions than at the periphery. As regards the strategical starting points for specifically influencing the multiplier effects within the region, the variation analyses set out under (3) of this section provide some clear indications.

172

6 Results of the Investigation of the Development Poles of Burgos, La Coruña, Valladolid, Vigo and Zaragoza

At this point some important results of the investigation of the other five poles will be set out. As has already been stated above, these investigations correspond essentially to the procedure adopted for the pilot studies which have been conducted. The results will show that the final conclusions to be drawn on the basis of the pilot studies will serve as a valid foundation for assessment of the entire pole programme. (Cf. in particular Planning Commission, Economic evaluation of the poles ... Vols. I & II, 1972/3).

1 Fixed capital investment and newly created jobs are shown in summarised form in Table 52.

Table 52

Fixed capital investment and newly created (permanent) jobs in the industries of all seven poles

Pole	Fixed capital investment in the pole industries up to 31.12.69 (Ptas millions)	New jobs up to 1971
Burgos	5,164.9	9,681
La Coruña	6,146.6	3,307
Huelva	14,703.8	3,938
Seville	8,443.6	9,047
Valladolid	4,229.2	8,394
Vigo	5,867.8	7,838
Zaragoza	5,460.8	11,331
Total	50,016.7	53,536

It can be seen that half the capital investment in the poles was already covered by the pilot study in Andalusia, but barely one quarter of the newly created jobs. The capital investment per job differs enormously between the poles. Valladolid, Burgos and Zaragoza enjoy extremely favourable positions in this respect, and La Coruña and Huelva extremely unfavourable ones. On the average per pole a new industrial job has cost about Ptas 1 million, that is to say it has called for fixed capital investment to the amount of about £8,000. But these figures do not include:

— working capital requirements,
— interest charges on the fixed capital in respect of credit financing, and
— the proportion of infrastructure investment to be charged.

Therefore the total capital requirement per job is much higher.

2   The infrastructure investment effected up to 1967 and planned up to 1971 is shown in Table 53. The figures for investment realised up to 1971 are not yet available, and the reservations made above in connection with the infrastructure investments in the Andalusian poles, regarding the imputability of the infrastructure investments to new activities, apply here also. It is also true that the estimated appropriations for 1971 are not likely to be realised for any pole.

Table 53
Infrastructure investments in the seven poles (Ptas millions)

	Investment effected up to 1967	Investment planned for 1968-71
Burgos	92	926
La Coruña	27	339
Huelva	1,023	2,593
Seville	301	2,165
Valladolid	120	474
Vigo	100	795
Zaragoza	568	2,005
Total	2,231	9,297

The direct promotion measures that were effective up to 31.12.69 are shown in Table 54, which also illustrates the relative importance of these measures for the financing of fixed capital investment.

It can be seen that the public financial assistance measured by the legally established maximum rates of 10-20 per cent for the subsidy and 60-70 per cent for the public credit was low, for it amounted on the average for all the pole industries to only about a third of the maximum rates. The experience with investment promotion in Western France was very similar. Thumm reports that the graduated 'nominal' promotion premiums of 20 per cent, 12 per cent, 10 per cent and 5 per cent actually come down by reason of the calculation method adopted to 9.9 per cent, 6 per cent, 5 per cent and 2.5 per cent (Thumm, 68, 162/3).

Table 54

Subsidies and public credits paid up to 31.12.69 and their importance for the financing of the fixed capital investment in all the poles realised by that date

	Subsidy		Public credit	
	Ptas millions	Percentage of fixed capital investment	Ptas millions	Percentage of fixed capital investment
Burgos	360.4	7.0	1,164.4	22.5
La Coruña	31.7	0.5	1,783.9	29.0
Huelva	992.0	6.7	3,487.9	23.7
Seville	284.0	3.4	1,876.3	22.2
Valladolid	88.1	2.1	770.7	18.2
Vigo	61.6	1.1	1,334.4	22.7
Zaragoza	97.9	1.8	650.4	11.9
Total	1,915.7	3.8	11,068.0	22.1

7 Do the Spanish Poles comply with the Definition of a Growth Pole?

First let us repeat the basic definition of a growth pole: a growth pole is a large group of industries (a) strongly related through their input-output linkages (b) around a leading industry (c), and clustered geographically (d). The leading industry itself (e), and (through its inducement (f)) the whole group, innovates (g) and grows (h) at a faster pace (i) than the industries external to the pole.

7.1 Identification and incidence criteria

As set out in the first part of the investigation, the terms included in the definition can be classified as identification and incidence criteria. Here it will be demonstrated to what extent the Spanish poles meet the requirements according to the results available. For this purpose the characteristics will be dealt with in the order in which they appear in the definition.

7.1.1 Identification criteria

1   The size requirement is most suitably quantified in connection with the other requirements by reference to the gross output value or turnover. Table 55 shows that with an average gross output value for the poles of about Ptas 13 milliard in 1971, that is to say about DM 0.65 milliard, the quantitative importance of the output of the poles is low. To be precise the values range from about £0.14 milliard for Huelva £0.1 milliard for Zaragoza.

The relative importance of the pole industries in relation to industrial production in the Spanish economy as a whole is shown in Table 55.

According to this a total of 3 per cent of the gross value creation of total Spanish industry was produced in 1971 by the pole industries. In the national scale of things the poles are therefore of minor importance from the point of view of size. On the other hand, with an average of 27.3 per cent in the industrial value creation of the pole provinces in the same year, they are of considerable importance to the individual provinces. In the order of the poles, the corresponding value proportions came to 48.5 per cent, 21.3 per cent, 66.9 per cent, 18.3 per cent, 29.5 per cent, 35.1 per cent and 16.0 per cent. As is to be expected, moreover, the two former poles of industrial promotion, Burgos and Huelva, show the highest values, while Valladolid and Vigo occupy an intermediate position.

Table 55
Contribution of the pole industries to the industrial gross value creation of the national economy

Pole	Ptas millions 1971	Percentage contribution to total Spanish industry
Burgos	3,367.1	0.380
La Coruña	3,606.4	0.407
Huelva	4,531.6	0.512
Seville	3,946.8	0.443
Valladolid	3,671.4	0.415
Vigo	4,725.4	0.534
Zaragoza	3,446.3	0.389
Total	27,295.0	3.080
Total Spanish industry*	884,891.0	100.000

*Source: Planning Commission, Estimates . . . , 71, 87.

The criterion of size, which can be very easily quantified in this way, is not so easy to evaluate, and this was indicated early on in the first part of the work. Precisely how big must a pole be to be entitled to the qualification of growth pole? No attempt should be made to establish a particular standard, for the criterion of size cannot be usefully applied to heterogeneous agglomerations like the Spanish poles, only to complexes interlinked with one another. Of these it is required that the industries forming them must be altogether substantial, since the assumption of a higher degree of attractivity or flexibility is linked with them. Consequently it is necessary to examine first of all whether there is any question of complex formations in the sense of the growth pole theory.

2 The input-output criterion, as has often been explained, is of exceptional importance in connection with the growth pole theory. Table 56 shows, however, that with the exception of the poles of Huelva and Valladolid the inter-industrial relationships within the pole are very limited. This confirms the thesis of the predominantly heterogeneous agglomeration in the poles, the cause of which could lie less in the attraction of planned complexes than in the incentive effects of the promotion measures.

(a)   First the inter-industrial linkages in the other five poles can be commented on:

—   In Burgos the inter-industrial relationships in the pole are confined to the sector of the foodstuffs industry, but even there they do not amount to 1 per cent of the total previous work purchases. Altogether the result for Burgos is wholly negative in relation to the input-output criterion. The reason could well be that the industries in Burgos are often subsidiary undertakings of industries in the North of the country. In the Basque provinces with the exception of Alava, the severe shortage of land means that the formation of new industries is only possible on payment of very high prices for premises. In recent times this has resulted in the establishment of new activities in the province of Alava adjoining Burgos to the North. Since the difference in transport costs would be insignificant compared with running an establishment in Alava, the promotion measures proposed in Burgos have led to a partial redirection of investments otherwise intended for Alava.

—   In La Coruña, which shows the third highest — albeit extremely modest — degree of inter-relationship, almost 50 per cent of the inter-relationships are attributable to the circumstance that as in Huelva and Seville, the electricity supply industry is one of the activities promoted in the pole. For purposes of the polarisation theory the corresponding flows are irrelevant. An important factor in the pole is the inter-relationship of the chemical industries to one another, but although they concern roughly one quarter of all the inter-industrial relationships in the pole, they are still unimportant, related to the total previous work of the chemical industry at about 3 per cent.

—   In Valladolid the inter-relationships are confined to the metal industry, and more particularly the Fasa-Renault motor-car industry. With a value of some Ptas 1 milliard Renault also has intensive supply

Table 56

Intensity of the regional linkages of the industries of all poles, 1971

	Previous work purchases					Gross output values				
	Total (Ptas millions)	by pole industries (percentage of total)	Pole-hinterland relationships (percentage of total)			Total (Ptas millions)	of pole industries (percentage of total)	Pole-hinterland relationships (percentage of total)		
			Rest of province	Other pole province*	Industrial relationships**			Rest of province	Other pole province*	Industrial relationships**
Burgos	11,939.2	0.3	16.7	4.3	3.9	15,306.3	0.25	6.9	3.1	2.8
La Coruña	9,272.0	6.3	15.3	1.2	6.7	12,878.5	4.5	15.1	3.2	3.9
Huelva	12,321.3	22.7	27.9	2.3	0.5	16,822.5	16.7	5.2	5.4	9.8
Seville	7,208.3	3.9	44.3	1.0	6.3	11,128.2	2.5	27.3	3.0	23.7
Valladolid	12,279.8	16.3	13.6	0.6	1.0	15,951.1	12.6	4.5	0.8	3.1
Vigo	6,034.5	2.4	29.1	5.6	9.1	10,759.9	1.4	16.6	1.4	11.6
Zaragoza	6,461.4	3.8	33.1	–	15.2	9,907.6	2.5	17.5	–	6.4
Total	65,516.5	9.3	23.8	2.4	5.0	92,754.1	6.6	12.0	2.9	8.2

*Corresponding to the pole pairs Burgos/Valladolid, La Coruña/Vigo, Huelva/Seville.
**Corresponding to the values for 1969, cf. for constitution and definition the text on Table 43.

linkages with an industry in the Seville pole, where the production of gearboxes is located. Communication costs for the mass production of such products which are insensitive to transport costs obviously play no part.

— In Vigo the inter-relationships are on the whole unimportant. Most of them represent inter-relationships in the metal industry sector, and with something over 2 per cent concerned with the total previous work purchases of this industry they are again insignificant.

— In Zaragoza some 95 per cent of all inter-industrial relationships are conducted within the metal sector. Since about 7 per cent of the total previous work purchases were by the metal processing industries, they have a certain importance.

(b) It was mentioned above that — except for those of Huelva and Valladolid — the new activities were not attracted by new complex-formations. This was enlarged on in particular for the poles and the sectors established therein. Apart from the poles in Huelva and Burgos, in whose hinterland very little industry was present prior to the establishment of the poles, the position to date is somewhat unsatisfactory, because the new pole activities might well become integrated with activities already present in the province or region, so contributing to the complex-formation. To this extent, the extensive administrative delimitation of the growth poles does not take sufficient account of the bases of the growth pole theory.

Table 57 therefore shows the intensity of the pole-hinterland relationships in the case of each pole in 1971. By means of the additional tables and the classification of sales of end-products set out in the input-output tables, it was further calculated to what extent industrial pole-hinterland relations could be specified. The table corresponds in the first column on each page to the first columns on Table 42, and in the last of each page to Table 43.

Thus the pole demarcation is not made dependent here on the administrative delimitation, rather are the new industries shown in an interdependent connection with those present in the planning region. In each case the pairs of provinces corresponding to the concept of the establishment of double poles are treated as a planning region, except in the case of Zaragoza where the comparison consequently calls for special comment.

Table 57 shows that inter-industrial relations on the side of previous work purchases (backward linkage) by the pole industries with the relative hinterland have a certain importance in La Coruña, Seville and Vigo. In comparison with all poles the value achieved in Zaragoza is particularly high. The forward linkage is marginally above average in

G

Huelva and Vigo, and is of considerable importance again in Seville. This last result has already been commented upon. In all the other cases the industrial backward and forward linkages with the hinterland are unimportant. The summarised result of the inter-industrial linkages in the pole and of the pole-hinterland relationships is shown in Table 57.

Table 57
Regional inter-industrial** relationships of all seven poles in
per cent of the gross output value in 1971

	Industrial reverse linkage pole-hinterland*	Inter-industrial linkage in the pole	Industrial forward linkage pole-hinterland
Burgos	2.8	0.3	2.8
La Coruña	4.8	4.5	3.9
Huelva	0.4	16.7	9.8
Seville	4.1	2.5	23.7
Valladolid	0.7	12.6	3.1
Vigo	5.4	1.4	11.6
Zaragoza	9.9	2.5	66.4
All poles	3.5	6.6	8.2

*On the assumption that the relationships observed for 1969 remained constant up to 1971.
**Processing industries.

The degree of inter-industrial regional linkage of the poles is thus low on the whole. The position of Seville and Huelva is above average, and the regional inter-industrial linkages in Burgos and La Coruña are particularly weak. Owing to the linkages present in the metal industry in all three poles, Valladolid, Vigo and Zaragoza occupy an intermediate position.

The result for Huelva and Seville has already been covered in the fourth chapter. Particular reference was made to the fact that the building material industry — a typical successor activity — accounted for some 40 per cent of the high degree of industrial forward linkage in Seville. In none

182

of the other poles has the building material industry the same importance
as in Seville, apart from Vigo where it still accounts for 10 per cent of the
gross output value in the pole. It is reasonable to conclude that
possibilities of relevant complex formations in the pole-hinterland connection can perhaps be assumed for the metal industry in Valladolid, Vigo
and Zaragoza.

3 With the exception of Seville, the leading sectors can be clearly
identified in all the poles. As the input-output tables show, in each case it
is a question of a sector which has easily the biggest proportion of the
gross output value in the pole, and in four poles produces over 50 per cent
of the total gross output value. The most important sectors, together with
their proportion of the gross output, are shown in Table 58.

Table 58
The most important sectors in the poles in 1971

Pole	Sector	Gross output value (Ptas millions)	Proportion of gross output value of the pole (per cent)
Burgos	Foodstuffs	6,718.6	44
La Coruña	Chemicals	7,225.0	56
Huelva	Chemicals	9,738.0	58
Seville	Metal industry	3,068.6	27
	Building materials	2,827.2	25
	Foodstuffs	2,118.9	19
Valladolid	Metal industry	12,631.8	79
Vigo	Metal industry	6,701.4	62
Zaragoza	Metal industry	5,965.0	60

Under the polarisation theory not all the sectors listed are to be
regarded as leading sectors. The foodstuffs and building materials
industries do not themselves induce any spatial complex formation. While
the foodstuffs industry may be a leading sector on the lines of the export
basis theory, the building materials industry is not a typical export
industry and consequently is not a leading sector within the meaning of
the export basis theory. As leading sectors, the chemicals industry can

thus be identified in the poles at La Coruña and Huelva, and the metal industry at Valladolid, Vigo and Zaragoza. These also have certain linkages with one another although, as has already been noted, with the exception of Huelva and Valladolid this is so far insignificant.

4   The observance of the identification criteria produces as a whole the following picture:

−   So far the Spanish poles, measured by their proportion of the total industry of the national economy, are small, but within their region on the other hand they have secured a considerable strengthening of one industrial production potential.
−   The inter-industrial linkages of the pole industries with one another and with the rest of the region are still of little importance. High matrix effects which would result in a self-reinforcement of growth impulses, can so far only be looked for in Huelva.
−   The leading industries are identical in five poles with sectorally strong polarising industries. The sectoral inter-dependence relationships, however, have so far been reflected regionally to only a limited extent.

7.1.2   Incidence criteria

The second part of the pole definition reads: the leading industry itself and − through its inducement − the whole group innovates and grows at a faster pace than the industries external to the pole.

1   With reference to the relative growth of the pole industries in comparison with the industries external to the pole, no reasoned statements can be made owing to the shortness of the period considered. For in the years immediately succeding the formation of the pole, the latter's still modest extent will mean that new activities require very high growth rates. In these circumstances it is obvious that the poles will grow faster than the average for the industries in the economy as a whole. Taking the average for all the poles, the growth rate for gross value creation at 49.5 per cent in 1971 compared with 1969 was thus almost twice as high as the growth rate on the average for all industries in the national economy in the same period (26.8 per cent. Source: Planning Commission, Estimates . . . , 71, 85 and 87).

Table 59 provides grounds for doubt regarding the dynamics of growth in certain poles. If the absolute increase in production in the poles is measured as between any two of the years under review, then it looks as if the production increase in certain poles inclines to stagnation rather than to self-reinforcement. In Table 59 the first column can be roughly interpreted as a production increase in 1967 compared with 1965, since with certain exceptions in 1964 there was virtually no production at all.

In Seville, Valladolid and Zaragoza the increase in production between the years 1965, 1967, 1969 and 1971 declined continually. In Burgos the increase between 1969 and 1971 was less than in the previous period, and the same is true for La Coruña, Huelva and Vigo in the period 1967-69. In the three last-named poles the increase in 1969-71 was higher than in the previous period, and this outcome was influenced to a large extent by the different investment cycles observed in all the poles and the length of the investment period in each case. Consequently general conclusions cannot be drawn. For all that, there is little doubt that in Seville, Valladolid and Zaragoza additional impulses will be needed after the pole promotion that has already taken place if the growth rate of production is also to be higher than the national average in future. This will also apply when it is considered that the procedure employed in the pole investigation for the assessment of the results for 1971 no doubt led to too low values.

In view of the still modest size of the poles it is by no means surprising that with their assistance success in assimilating the growth rates of the provincial incomes in each case to the national growth rate was probably not achieved by 1971. Table 60 shows the corresponding values.

Reference has already been made to the problem of this computation for the pole provinces.

2   The innovation argument could not be examined systematically in the framework of the investigation, which it would have been necessary to extend considerably in order to do so. In particular, the structural changes caused by the emergence of the pole in the pole cities would have had to be investigated for the purpose. This does not mean, however, that little importance is attached to this argument.

Consequently, at this point only certain considerations and particular observations will be dealt with.

(a)   The poles are themselves an innovation. Their formation has had an important psychological effect, especially in the early years, which is shown by the number of projects submitted to the Planning Commission. In particular, for the first pole formations, capital could be mobilised in the centres for investment in the poles. As experience with the new Córdoba and Granada poles shows, this concept has lost nothing of its attractiveness. Whereas in the poles in the First Plan the number of new applications declined from year to year, with the formation of the new

Table 59
Development of the gross output value of the poles, 1967-71

	Gross output value 1967 (Ptas millions)	Absolute increase	
		1967-69	1969-71
Burgos	2,343.7	8,439.2	4,523.2
La Coruña	3,830.9	2,948.7	6,098.9
Huelva	3,351.1	3,145.4	10,352.3
Seville	4,758.7	3,326.0	3,070.4
Valladolid	11,121.1	2,621.2	2,208.8
Vigo	6,190.3	2,063.6	2,506.0
Zaragoza	3,387.0	3,310.4	3,210.2
Total	34,982.8	23,854.5	31,969.8

Table 60
Estimated growth rates of provincial and national incomes in 1971
compared with 1967 at current prices

	Total income	Per capita income
Burgos	45.15	50.1[25]
La Coruña	47.87	46.7[25]
Huelva	44.40	43.4
Seville	42.70	35.4
Valladolid	45.95	43.7
Vigo	45.13	41.7
Zaragoza	46.68	42.2
'Spain	50.77	43.8

Source: Planning Commission, Estimates . . . , 71, 106 and 115.

poles the same favourable investment climate has obviously been created as in the initial phase of the seven poles here being examined. Furthermore, local capital now seems to be more heavily involved than before.

(b)   As regards the participation of national capital, the pole promotion policy faces the dilemma that high outflow quotas of the regional residents' incomes produced are incurred thereby in so far as the profits are not reinvested in the pole region. On the other hand, the participation of national capital cannot as a rule be turned down, because regional savings are inadequate and sufficiently powerful investors are rarely available in the region; also, with the influx of extra-regional capital new techniques — and as a rule business personalities — come into the region.

(c)   It is difficult to assess how far trade and services in the rest of the province have adjusted to the demand developed by the pole industries. It seems that the adjustment to new consumer requirements has occurred very rapidly, whereas the adjustment to previous work demand is invariably attended by great difficulties or just does not happen. In all the poles, complaints are heard that because supplies of specialised services are lacking, recourse must be had to supplies from outside the region, and that regionally-based trade is not suitable for meeting the new demand. This leads to high costs for stocking up with spare parts and other goods in daily use.

(d)   The effects on the qualification of manpower are also important. Apart from the fact that the pole industries will retain in the region part of the qualified manpower which would otherwise be obliged to emigrate or to accept less skilled work, particular industries allow for reject production months ahead in order to build up their own specialised staff. Thus the book-printing profession in Seville, for example, was not represented at all. The printing works established in the pole — Imprenta Sevillana — reckons with about a year's scrap production to enable it to produce internationally acceptable products. This is a particularly interesting but by no means exceptional case. On the other hand it must be emphasised that essentially the industries only train manpower which was previously unqualified, therefore the aim is restricted to limited qualifying grades.

(e)   Finally it is seen that primary production is also induced to embark on expansion and rationalisation investment by the pole industries. A particularly clear-cut example of this is provided by the investments in the mining district of Rio Tinto in Huelva. It often transpires, however, that substantial investments are only embarked upon when the activities concerned are in the hands of a national undertaking.

These are more or less casual observations which permit no general conclusions. The period since the formation of the poles is too short to facilitate investigation of the innovation behaviour induced and to test the corresponding hypotheses of growth pole theory in the present case.

7.2   Evaluation of growth pole policy in the First and Second Plans

Here there is less to be said for giving a summary of the results already recorded, than for pointing out some of the weaknesses and problems of growth pole policy.

1   In all the poles with the exception of that for Seville, one can observe a clearly leading sector in so far as the proportion of the contribution of the pole to the social product is concerned. Nevertheless, except in the case of the chemical industry in Huelva, the motor industry in Valladolid and the metal industry in Vigo and Zaragoza, it is a question of thoroughly heterogeneous poles which are only marked by inessential sectoral/regional linkages. On the other hand, the growth pole theory aims at the interdependence criterion as a necessary condition for regional polarisation.

As an alternative to the promotion policy followed so far, the formation of sectoral/regional complexes could be adopted. These would not necessarily have to be concentrated on a point pole, but might be located in a spatially integrated set-up of several central places. The industrial triangle Bari-Brindisi-Tarent, in Southern Italy, offers an example of this idea for Spain, and the Planning Commission is aiming to produce a replica of the concept with its plans for the industrial triangle Huelva-Seville-Cadiz.

The formation of industrial complexes has the advantage that it takes account of the necessity to coordinate the growth pole policy. The basis for this is summarised by Streit as follows: 'As has already been demonstrated, the possibility of being able to internalise final demand impulses, and external savings in a narrow space by direct and indirect linkages to any extent, is among the specific location advantages of a growth pole. For private as well as public investments in this integrated set-up it is therefore a fact that for purposes of profitability they depend on one another to a more or less substantial extent. *The complementary relationships in the construction phase of a growth centre are somewhat of a hindrance.* For when the private investor is uncertain whether it will come to the necessary complementary investments, he turns rather to the gravitation centres. . . . The thing that matters for regional policy is thus to initiate a whole batch of state and of private investments.' (Streit, 71a, 228, author's italics, F.B.) This is a vicious circle of the polarisation strategy in peripheral areas.

The dilemma in pole promotion policy which has been referred to is not easily resolved. If one considers the leading sectors of the majority of the Spanish poles, then a strategy for the formation of industrial complexes in this situation could amount to the promotion of centres of the chemicals and metal industries. It will be difficult, however, to promote five potent complexes of the metal industry in addition to those already existing (especially in Asturias and Biscay), either because of the high cost of promotion or because of the regional fragmentation of the supply structure. On top of this it must be borne in mind that the suppliers and specialised service undertakings which are so urgently required in close spatial proximity — especially by the existing industries in the metal sector — can only be active in the pole when the threshold value of low-cost production in each case is at least achieved. Even when it is anticipated that state undertakings of the Instituto Nacional de Industria might take over parts of this supply, their location would still have to be arranged in accordance with a national scale of priorities.

It is accordingly important that the growth pole policy should not be based solely on the accentuation of sectoral/regional input-output linkages, such a type of pole would be best represented by an agglomeration of the Ruhr district type or by an undertaking structure of the 'Krupp type'. On the other hand, it is conceivable that the growth of the poles could be effected by heterogeneous concerns of the 'Litton type', (Lasuen, 69, 146, and also Streit, 71a, 231).

2 The problem of growth pole policy in Spain is connected in the second place with the *promotion system adopted.*

Firstly, it must be noted that the system of promotion measures implies a clear preference for the capital-intensive industries. In addition promotion through subsidies, public credit and tax concessions in respect of depreciation, for example, only relates to investment capital requirements. Consequently, those industries which are labour-intensive and/or have heavy working capital requirements in relation to the need for investment capital are put at a disadvantage. By way of compensation a premium could be granted in respect of the new jobs created.

The weighting of direct and indirect promotion measures is also worth discussing, and on this point there are two main arguments. The first is concerned with the unavoidable dilemma of growth pole policy 'that uncertainty regarding the structure and implementation of a pole calls for caution, whereas the pole strategy requires rather a special measure of regional policy previous work' (Streit, 71a, 230). The second has as its object the infant-industry argument advanced for the pole promotion policy. According to this the Spanish growth pole policy, in accordance with the basic idea, had the declared aim of promoting sectoral/regional agglomerations, whereby subsidies and low-cost public credits are designed to ensure that initial difficulties in the new industries arising from the absence of supplementary activities should be offset.

The uncertainty argument has played a special role in the discussion of the most suitable strategy for the development of the infrastructure, for which it was established with the principle of caution that the development of parts of the infrastructure might follow the establishment of industries. Two observations were made on this. Firstly, this strategy requires a very flexible coordination of state and private investment, and secondly it is based on the assumption that the investment periods more or less agree in both cases. Experience has shown that the coordination was not sufficiently flexible, and because of the number of public bodies involved there was probably little likelihood that it could be so. In the second place, the investment period for the most important infrastructure projects, which also tie up the bulk of the resources available for investment, is so long that owing to the simultaneous commencement of the infrastructure investments and of the directly productive investments in 1964, the first industries still had to reckon on experiencing considerable bottlenecks at the start of production.

Another point worth discussing is the provision of industrial equipment. So far the only part of this procedure to work relatively well has been the fitting-out of industrial units, while the link-up with the transport, energy and water networks has caused bottlenecks. Consideration must also be given as to what extent regional investors in particular could be given an extra incentive by the supply of standardised workshops. By the provision of leasing facilities in particular (Ritter, 66, 1254), it would be possible to reduce the investment risk and financing requirements for these investments.

Subsidies can be justified on the one hand by the fact that they tend to offset losses arising from infra-structural bottlenecks, although this is not a very convincing argument. Then there is the infant-industry argument whereby subsidies and subsidised credits should compensate for losses arising from the lack of complementary activities in the initial phase. But if the dilemma of the growth pole policy that emerges in connection with the necessity for planning industrial complexes is a valid diagnosis, if that is to say the industries primarily dependent on localisation savings by reason of the necessary inter-industrial linkages *in situ* avoid location in the pole from the outset, then to that extent the bridging argument will fall to the ground.

3   A third dilemma of growth pole policy lies in the fact that the

necessity for concentrated investment promotion faces political pressure for scrupulously equal treatment of all the backward regions. It is naturally recognised that not all the provinces in peripheral regions are suitable for the establishment poles, but sufficient alternatives still remain, and the promotion period and promotion intensity in the case of each individual pole is strongly influenced thereby. It is thus to be observed that in Spain the politically based wish to include as many regions as possible in the promotion field prejudices the success of the entire programme.

For the seven poles examined, this dilemma has led in the past to the fact that

- the intensity of promotion has lagged far behind expectations;
- the specification of the promotion terms has become much more restrictive with the passage of time;
- in view of the multiplicity of locations provided with similar incentives, the range of promotion intensity has been narrowed;
- and as regards the promotion of new poles, the promotion period for the individual poles was too short.

Experience of regional programmes in other countries has *also* shown that complete success in the matter of regional policy is not to be achieved over short periods (Richardson, 71, 50).

4   Finally, on the basis of recent studies, the argument in favour of premiums with respect to new jobs created, ought to be reinforced and established in a broader sense. That means, that it will be necessary to co-ordinate future regional development-policy with labour market-policy. However, regional labour market-policy in that sense does not mean job creation policy alone, but must include certain other criteria, as for example diversified and flexible patterns of supply and demand for the promotion of internal labour-markets, and manpower development programmes. Special attention should be paid to the fact that diversification and flexibility of a regional labour market are not indentical with diversification within an inhomogeneous growth pole nor in a sectoral/regional cluster of industries. Even in the latter case, it is possible that the degree of qualification of newly created jobs remains relatively low in comparison with clusters of a similar sector-mix found in core regions. Labour market segmentation as one important source of domination/dependance effects between core and peripheral regions therefore, does not necessarily depend on the sectoral/regional patterns of the distribution of industries (Buttler, Gerlach, Liepmann, 74). Therefore it does not seem hazardous to postulate that traditional growth pole-policy must not only be reformulated in the sense of promotion of sectoral/regional clusters of industries,

191

and accompanied by deliberate urbanisation policy, but has to be combined with special strategies with reference of the building up of workable labour markets in pole regions.

Notes

1   The lack of a results control for regional policy is not only found in Spain. The resultant 'gap in knowledge of effect analysis' (Streit, 71, 689) applies to virtually all countries.

2   Ministerial Order of 1 February 1964.

3   This argument also serves to explain the lower value creation quota for all years in the chemical industry in Seville as compared with Huelva. Reference need only be made to fertiliser production in Seville, which is confined in most cases to mixing processes. This does not apply to the biggest chemical industry in Seville, for which the value is also well above the average, i.e. 32.7.

4   With over 500,000 inhabitants Seville is by far the biggest pole city, and in consequence is subject to the migration tendency which favours the 'metropolitan' zones.

5   The method of projection used there is responsible for this. It is assumed that trends which have been observed in the past mainly continue to operate unchanged. Growth pole policy, however, should have the effect of changing particular trends.

6   Although the qualification rating of employees in pole industries was covered in the enquiry, the validity of this argument cannot be quantitatively assured owing to faulty comparative data on the regional plane.

7   More correctly, the capital output ratio coefficient and factor intensity should have been correspondingly adjusted for the average of both poles. In this way the differences existing between the two poles would have been brought out more clearly. For reasons of defective allocation this did not happen, and in particular consideration would have had to be given here to the degree of employment of the new infra-structure in each case, and to the external effects arising in utilisation. However, it must be recognised that the social (opportunity) costs per job are substantially increased by the infrastructure investments.

8   The homogeneity of the structure of the totality of the building and installation firms in relation to value creation quota and sources of supply for previous work and wage quota is to be treated here as a working hypothesis. Their employment can bring regular faults in its train. In the ordinary way, for instance, both the value creation element and the regional incidence of labour income, also the regional structure of the previous work purchases in the small and intermediate undertakings in the pole region will vary from the corresponding values for the undertakings operating on the national plane. Since, with one exception, the additional enquiry was only answered by undertakings working on the

national plane, in the final reckoning a systematic fault cannot be excluded. When comparing both poles, this fault could be considerable because of the differential participation by undertakings in the pole hinterland. It can be expected, however, that the differences represented are more likely to be increased in tendency than reduced.

9   In a United Nations study, (UN, 63, 12 et seq.), the elasticity of demand in relation to the *per capita* income is described as 'income elasticity', and that in relation to market size (measured by the size of the population) as 'growth elasticity'.

10   For this, as for other results on the regional structure of the investment goods demand, it must however be considered that some industries had not yet concluded their investments by the appointed day. Possible consequences for the import content of the demand for investment goods are made clear by the example of sector 10 in Table 26.

11   In the poles it is mainly a question of joint-stock companies or branches thereof. 'Social capital', by way of departure from other usual definitions, is a comprehensive expression for share or ordinary capital, or in the case of partnerships for partners' deposits. Apart from some exceptions which will be mentioned later, this composite term is adequate for purposes of the present analysis.

12   The latter are dealt with in section 5.1.

13   The rejection of a cash-flow analysis is based on the method of determination of provisions and profits.

14   One exception has to be noted: the major portion of the investment in the timber processing sector relates to a state undertaking. Consequently the relative proportion of the subsidies and public credits is very low in this case.

15   Capital expansion by these undertakings is effected in material and temporal relationship with the formation of pole industries. This was often done too by the Banco de Crédito Industrial, upon credit being granted for the purpose. However, the undertakings do not expand their capital solely in connection with the establishment of industries in the poles, but with their entire investment programme.

16   In the case of public joint-stock companies, it may of course be that part of the shares are held by residents in the region, while the offices of the firm lie outside the region. That aspect was not considered here.

17   A possible alternative would be credit financing by the savings banks. These banks, which perform an important function in the accumulation of funds in both pole provinces, and which operate independently at the provincial level, are not permitted by their statutes to participate in industrial financing.

18   Failure to consider this has also to be emphasised, because regional

per capita income calculations are not made on the basis of available income.

19 This relates to the pyrites deposits in Rio Tinto and elsewhere in the north of the province. It is estimated that about half of the world reserves are situated there.

20 Such an extended table is not shown here. Its presentation would have no informative value beyond the input-output tables of the pole industries, the additional tables and Table 43.

21 Capital imports in the form of contributions by foreign undertakings to the social capital of the pole industries are not considered, because their amount is unknown.

22 This means that it can be assumed that inter-regional trade in goods is insignificant.

23 The balances shown in the regional accounts also allow for a possible intermediate utilisation of the goods.

24 The Bureau of Reclamation of the US Department of the Interior has drawn up rules for the ascertainment of wholesale and retail profits in connection with the valuation of secondary effects of irrigation projects (US Department of the Interior, 52, quoted by Jansen, 68, 53). A corresponding basis would also have been useful in the present case.

25 The difference between the growth rates of total and *per capita* income reflects the change in the population proportions. Positive *per capita* income accompanied by negative total income divergencies point to the fact that the income target was certainly achieved, but the object of retaining the regional population in its home region was not attained.

Appendix

Table 32
Input-output table: Huelva pole 1967 (Ptas thousands)

Outputs	Foodstuffs industry	Timber processing industry	Chemicals industry	Building materials industry	Metal processing industry	Miscellaneous	Energy	Line total
Inputs			Pole industries/sectors					
Foodstuffs industry	0	0	0	0	0	0	0	0
Timber processing industry	0	0	0	0	0	0	0	0
Chemicals industry	0	0	264,656	0	0	0	0	264,656
Building materials industry	0	0	0	0	0	0	0	0
Metal processing industry	0	0	0	0	108	0	0	108
Miscellaneous	0	0	0	0	0	0	0	0
Energy	0	5,325	90,673	429	182	86	86	99,695
Inter-industrial relationship	0	5,325	355,329	429	290	86	86	361,459
Purchases from rest of province	0	75,735	84,568	2,675	2,665	398	20,608	186,649
Imports Seville	0	14,631	0	1,625	7,240	0	6,185	29,681
Rest of Spain	0	111,979	148,807	2,340	1,917	1,878	0	266,921
Foreign countries	0	6,430	1,783,384	2,000	0	0	0	1,791,814
Total	0	133,040	1,932,191	5,956	9,157	1,878	6,185	2,088,416
Wages and salaries	0	45,500	78,155	2,501	4,689	1,546	0	132,391
Social insurance, companies' share	0	9,100	13,673	499	938	328	0	24,538
Interest	0	20,226	302,236	4,771	999	2	15,283	343,517
Profits	0	66,055	−268,971	4,341	2,345	−2,006	54,606	−143,630
Contribution to NNP at factor cost	0	140,881	125,093	12,112	8,971	−130	69,889	356,816
Indirect taxes	0	8,950	29,775	70	136	0	13	38,944
Contribution to NNP at market prices	0	149,831	154,868	12,182	9,107	(−130)	69,902	395,760
Depreciation	0	51,488	265,178	949	1,045	202	0	318,862
Contribution to GNP at market prices	0	201,319	420,046	13,131	10,152	72	69,902	714,622
Gross output value	0	415,419	2,792,134	22,200	22,264	2,434	96,695	3,351,146

CG	PG	IG	Total	CG	PG	IG	Total	Rest of Spain	Foreign countries	Total	Stock changes semi-finished and finished goods	Gross output value
			Sales to the rest of Huelva				Seville		Exports			
0	0	0	0	0	0	0	0	0	0	0	0	0
6,250	6,000	0	12,250	18,750	0	0	13,750	381,712	2,707	403,169	0	415,419
0	118,450	0	118,450	0	234,361	0	234,361	509,671	967,998	1,712,030	696,998	2,792,134
0	16,200	0	16,200	0	3,000	0	3,000	0	0	3,000	3,000	22,200
0	0	16,746	16,746	0	0	0	0	4,500	0	4,500	910	22,264
0	1,300	0	1,300	0	42	0	42	926	0	968	166	2,434
0	0	0	0	0	0	0	0	0	0	0	0	99,695
6,250	141,950	16,746	164,946	18,750	237,403	0	256,153	896,809	970,705	2,379,820	701,074	3,351,146

Abbreviations
NNP = Net national product
GNP = Gross national product
CG = Consumer goods
PG = Producer goods
IG = Investment goods

Table 33
Input-output table: Huelva pole 1969 (Ptas thousands)

Outputs	Pole industries/Sectors							
Inputs	Foodstuffs industry	Timber processing industry	Chemicals industry	Building materials industry	Metal processing industry	Miscellaneous	Energy	Line total
Pole industries/sectors								
Foodstuffs industry	0	0	0	0	0	0	0	0
Timber processing industry	0	3,455	0	0	0	0	0	3,455
Chemicals industry	0	0	760,619	0	0	0	0	760,619
Building materials industry	0	0	0	5,410	0	0	0	5,410
Metal processing industry	0	0	0	0	456	0	0	456
Miscellaneous	0	186	60	0	0	0	0	246
Energy	3,536	9,194	164,547	7,417	748	578	0	186,020
Inter-industrial relationship in pole	3,536	12,835	925,226	12,827	1,204	578	0	956,206
Purchases from rest of province	686	109,634	214,597	17,271	10,691	6,931	52,660	412,470
Imports								
Seville	0	20,186	20,200	63,307	4,453	9,516	27,072	144,734
Rest of Spain	1,929	156,501	307,701	3,129	25,403	45,808	0	540,471
Foreign countries	0	19,182	2,696,541	2,300	1,762	0	0	2,719,785
Total	1,929	195,869	3,024,442	68,736	31,618	55,324	27,072	3,404,990
Wages and salaries	3,942	73,241	175,540	16,038	23,998	11,545	1,550	305,854
Social insurance, companies' share	557	14,168	27,291	3,436	5,884	3,145	350	54,831
Interest	2,439	18,082	216,167	7,765	6,285	7,276	21,305	279,317
Profits	3,697	105,925	219,087	22,950	22,690	15,882	22,659	405,436
Contribution to NNP at factor cost	3,239	211,416	638,085	50,189	58,797	37,848	45,864	1,045,438
Indirect taxes	243	9,930	79,799	1,295	816	928	2,864	95,974
Contribution to NNP at market prices	3,482	221,346	717,884	51,484	59,613	38,776	48,827	1,141,412
Depreciation	5,520	62,327	418,534	10,381	8,775	10,874	68,991	585,402
Contribution to GNP at market prices	9,002	283,673	1,136,418	61,865	68,388	49,650	117.818	1,726,814
Gross output value	15,153	602,011	5,300,683	160,699	111,901	112,483	197,550	6,500,480

	Sales to the rest of Huelva				Seville				Exports			Stock changes semi-finished and finished goods	Gross output value
CG	PG	IG	Total	CG	PG	IG	Total	Rest of Spain	Foreign countries	Total		
3,876	9,446	0	13,322	142	0	0	142	1,689	0	1,831	0	15,153
7,000	0	0	27,000	9,000	8,545	0	17,545	491,120	35,136	543,801	+27,755	602,011
0	405,185	0	405,185	0	672,937	0	672,937	1,254,231	1,977,100	3,904,268	+230,611	5,300,683
0	113,281	0	113,281	0	11,042	0	11,042	24,920	3,500	39,462	−2,546	160,699
0	52,553	59,500	112,053	0	0	0	0	0	0	0	−608	111,901
0	10,981	0	10,981	0	19,663	0	19,663	76,110	408	96,781	+4,475	112,483
0	11,530	0	11,530	0	0	0	0	0	0	0	0	197,550
30,876	602,976	59,500	693,352	9,142	712,187	0	721,329	1,848,670	2,016,144	4,586,143	264,779	6,500,480

Abbreviations
NNP = Net national product
GNP = Gross national product
CG = Consumer goods
PG = Producer goods
IG = Investment goods

Table 34
Input-output table: Huelva pole 1971 (Ptas thousands) at 1969 prices

Inputs	Foodstuffs industry	Timber processing industry	Chemicals industry	Building materials industry	Metal processing industry	Miscellaneous	Energy	Line total
Foodstuffs industry	0	0	0	0	0	0	0	0
Timber processing industry	0	3,455	0	0	0	0	0	3,455
Chemicals industry	0	0	2,429,791	0	0	0	0	2,429,791
Building materials industry	0	0	0	5,410	0	0	0	5,410
Metal processing industry	0	0	0	0	456	0	0	456
Miscellaneous	600	8,518	88	0	0	0	0	9,206
Energy	10,976	19,532	296,205	8,571	17,743	658	0	353,685
Inter-industrial relationship in pole	11,576	31,505	2,726,084	13,981	18,199	658	0	2,802,003
Purchases from rest of province	16,360	188,872	347,563	17,907	2,767,200	7,055	93,471	3,438,428
Imports — Seville	74,023	48,589	9,260	63,886	26,832	9,516	48,052	280,158
Imports — Rest of Spain	7,930	233,352	463,334	4,004	375,320	50,129	0	1,134,069
Imports — Foreign countries	3,182	9,000	3,405,711	3,047	1,245,647	0	0	4,666,587
Total	85,135	290,941	3,878,305	70,937	1,647,799	59,645	48,052	6,080,814
Wages and salaries	12,311	84,029	246,696	16,038	117,003	14,006	1,550	491,633
Social insurance, companies' share	2,188	16,135	39,320	3,436	23,979	4,029	350	89,437
Interest	11,013	17,888	187,768	5,583	165,613	4,039	13,749	405,653
Profits	33,141	229,986	1,611,169	27,019	364,982	36,947	122,220	2,425,464
Contribution to NNP at factor cost	58,659	348,038	2,084,953	52,076	671,577	59,021	137,869	3,412,187
Indirect taxes	3,740	18,754	139,634	1,395	104,823	1,190	5,302	274,838
Contribution to NNP at market prices	62,393	366,792	2,224,587	53,471	776,400	60,211	143,171	3,687,025
Depreciation	14,559	72,860	561,475	10,473	105,303	10,874	68,991	844,535
Contribution to GNP at market prices	76,952	439,652	2,786,062	63,944	881,703	71,085	212,162	4,531,560
Gross output value	190,023	950,970	9,738,014	166,769	5,314,901	138,443	353,685	16,852,805

Outputs — Pole industries/sectors

| Sales to the rest of Huelva | | | | Seville | | | | Exports | | | Stock changes semi-finished and finished goods | Gross output value |
CG	PG	IG	Total	CG	PG	IG	Total	Rest of Spain	Foreign countries	Total		
10,619	31,646	0	42,265	13,629	6,700	0	20,329	91,711	33,718	145,758	+2,000	190,023
27,000	3,671	0	30,671	9,000	23,110	0	32,110	815,845	47,371	895,327	+21,517	950,970
0	565,427	0	565,427	0	809,818	0	809,818	4,692,967	1,238,646	6,741,431	+1,365	9,738,014
0	115,781	0	115,781	0	16,542	0	16,542	27,420	0	43,962	+1,616	166,769
0	52,553	62,500	115,053	0	0	6,000	6,000	5,099,000	95,000	5,200,000	+608	5,314,901
0	10,981	0	10,981	0	19,663	0	19,663	93,710	408	113,781	+4,475	138,443
0	0	0	0	0	0	0	0	0	0	0	0	353,685
37,619	780,059	62,500	880,178	22,629	875,833	6,000	904,462	10,820,654	1,415,143	13,140,259	+30,365	16,852,805

Abbreviations
NNP = Net national product
GNP = Gross national product
CG = Consumer goods
PG = Producer goods
IG = Investment goods

203

Table 35
Input-output table: Seville pole 1967 (Ptas thousands)

Inputs	Foodstuffs industry	Textile industry	Paper processing industry	Chemicals industry	Building materials industry	Metal processing industry	Miscellaneous	Energy	Line total
Outputs → Pole industries/Sectors									
Pole industries/sectors									
Foodstuffs industry	0	0	0	0	0	0	0	0	0
Textile industry	0	0	0	0	0	0	0	0	0
Paper processing industry	0	0	849	0	0	700	0	0	1,549
Chemicals industry	0	0	0	0	0	0	0	0	0
Building materials industry	0	0	0	0	7,309	0	0	0	7,309
Metal processing industry	0	0	0	0	0	11,447	0	0	11,447
Miscellaneous	0	0	0	0	0	0	0	0	0
Energy	5,718	5,753	1,092	2,966	36,568	14,841	1,519	0	68,457
Inter-industrial relationship in pole	5,718	5,753	1,092	3,815	43,877	26,988	1,519	0	88,762
Purchases from rest of province	521,107	289,355	70,929	234,905	210,961	104,269	1,619	25,206	1,458,351
Imports									
Huelva	5,300	0	0	25,819	9,254	0	0	0	50,373
Rest of Spain	95,398	20,202	62,919	38,626	142,812	364,435	32,898	0	757,290
Foreign countries	454,894	62,000	22,300	56,079	82,611	120,130	3,400	0	801,414
Total	555,592	82,202	85,219	130,524	234,677	484,565	36,298	0	1,609,077
Wages and salaries	39,897	28,069	14,886	19,292	118,938	345,923	5,087	1,200	573,292
Social insurance, companies' share	11,186	10,575	3,832	5,294	29,290	66,146	2,525	300	129,148
Interest	20,487	12,927	5,378	8,509	66,393	68,999	4,296	814	187,803
Profits	3,983	54,099	7,919	7,521	64,087	253,155	2,670	29,393	407,785
Contribution to NNP at factor cost	75,553	105,670	32,015	25,574	278,708	734,223	14,578	31,707	1,298,028
Indirect taxes	13,833	12,660	8,371	5,201	23,288	30,176	991	200	94,720
Contribution to NNP at market prices	89,386	118,330	40,386	30,775	301,996	764,399	15,569	31,907	1,392,748
Depreciation	17,906	32,680	3,957	8,224	101,382	31,091	3,169	11,344	209,753
Contribution to GNP at market prices	107,292	151,010	44,343	38,999	403,378	795,490	18,738	43,251	1,602,501
Gross output value	1,189,709	528,320	201,583	408,243	892,893	1,411,312	58,174	68,457	4,758,691

| Sales to the rest of Seville | | | | Huelva | | | | Exports | | | Stock changes semi-finished and finished goods | Gross output value |
CG	PG	IG	Total	CG	PG	IG	Total	Rest of Spain	Foreign countries	Total		
253,357	100,816	0	354,173	27,536	15,004	0	42,540	680,564	99,272	822,376	13,160	1,189,709
25,491	367,125	0	392,616	9,750	2,458	0	12,208	125,271	0	137,479	−1,775	528,320
0	67,972	0	67,972	0	10,163	0	10,163	121,789	0	131,952	110	201,583
13,968	77,061	0	91,029	0	4,071	0	4,071	283,426	29,717	317,214	0	408,893
0	205,842	0	205,842	0	34,039	0	34,039	611,810	19,894	665,743	13,999	892,893
7,550	80,092	78,708	166,350	2,300	10,225	4,000	16,525	1,218,124	7,606	1,242,255	−8,740	1,411,312
0	21,477	0	21,477	0	10,929	0	10,929	21,136	1,440	33,505	3,192	58,174
0	0	0	0	0	0	0	0	0	0	0	0	68,457
300,366	920,385	78,708	1,299,459	39,586	86,889	4,000	130,475	3,062,120	157,929	3,350,524	19,946	4,758,691

Abbreviations
NNP = Net national product
GNP = Gross national product
CG = Consumer goods
PG = Producer goods
IG = Investment goods

Table 36
Input-output table: Seville pole 1969 (in Ptas thousands)

Outputs	Pole industries/Sectors								
Inputs	Feedstuffs industry	Textile industry	Paper processing industry	Chemicals industry	Building materials industry	Metal processing industry	Miscellaneous	Energy	Line total
Pole industries/sectors									
Foodstuffs industry	0	0	0	0	0	0	0	0	0
Timber processing industry	0	0	0	0	0	0	0	0	0
Paper processing industry	300	0	0	731	0	1,300	0	0	2,331
Chemicals industry	0	0	0	0	0	3,161	0	0	3,161
Building materials industry	0	0	0	0	6,498	0	0	0	6,498
Metal processing industry	0	0	0	0	0	3,730	0	0	3,730
Miscellaneous	1,600	0	0	0	0	0	0	0	1,600
Energy	9,450	9,988	1,666	46,901	63,227	·61,929	2,054	0	195,015
Inter-industrial relationship in pole	11,350	9,988	1,666	47,632	69,525	70,120	2,054	0	212,335
Purchases from rest of province	829,416	365,018	98,099	517,119	410,580	164,462	2,017	72,374	2,459,085
Imports									
Huelva	10,556	0	0	42,918	18,406	0	0	0	71,880
Rest of Spain	186,370	35,610	145,190	151,405	221,860	676,264	42,224	20,000	1,472,923
Foreign countries	508,189	80,000	40,000	55,143	185,954	267,202	1,000	0	1,137,488
	699,115	115,610	185,190	249,466	426,220	943,466	43,224	20,000	2,682,291
Wages and salaries	80,362	43,623	16,164	37,397	210,723	503,689	5,088	1,600	898,646
Social insurance, companies' share	21,741	13,584	4,474	11,250	45,111	89,932	3,124	400	189,616
Interest	31,591	40,137	6,648	38,763	63,251	101,478	2,856	10,820	295,544
Profits	108,330	25,372	31,779	48,635	79,351	488,176	11,263	58,511	851,417
Contribution to NNP at factor cost	242,024	122,716	59,065	136,045	398,436	1,183,275	22,331	71,331	2,235,223
Indirect taces	22,471	14,830	10,593	11,190	530,413	51,416	1,440	550	142,903
Contribution to NNP at market prices	264,495	137,546	69,658	147,235	428,849	1,234,691	23,771	71,881	2,378,126
Depreciation	24,434	39,171	4,487	38,029	139,220	72,409	4,360	30,760	352,870
Contribution to GNP at market prices	288,929	176,717	74,145	185,264	568,069	1,307,100	28,131	102,641	2,730,996
Gross output value	1,828,810	667,333	359,100	999,481	1,474,394	2,485,148	75,426	195,015	8,084,707

206

Sales to the rest of Seville				Huelva				Exports			Stock changes semi-finished and finished goods	Gross output value
CG	PG	IG	Total	CG	PG	IG	Total	Rest of Spain	Foreign countries	Total		
440,631	150,626	0	591,257	42,129	23,286	0	65,415	782,728	315,728	1,163,871	73,682	1,828,810
55,200	411,437	0	446,637	9,504	1,895	0	11,399	145,758	16,681	1,173,838	46,858	667,333
0	117,532	0	117,532	0	10,737	0	10,737	217,167	5,320	233,224	6,013	359,100
51,068	76,601	0	127,669	460	16,495	0	16,955	703,551	144,406	864,912	3,739	999,481
39,012	374,075	0	413,087	0	69,220	0	69,220	855,267	75,393	999,880	54,929	1,474,394
16,035	296,901	0	312,936	5,000	29,028	0	34,028	1,990,438	89,030	2,113,496	54,986	2,485,148
0	31,624	0	31,624	0	13,631	0	13,631	27,659	1,500	42,790	588	75,426
0	0	0	0	0	0	0	0	0	0	0	0	195,015
581,946	1,458,796	0	2,040,742	57,093	164,292	0	221,385	4,722,568	648,058	5,592,011	239,619	8,084,707

Abbreviations
NNP = Net national product
GNP = Gross national product
CG = Consumer goods
PG = Producer goods
IG = Investment goods

Table 37
Input-output table: Seville pole 1971 (Ptas thousands) at 1969 prices

Inputs	Foodstuffs industry	Textile industry	Paper processing industry	Chemicals industry	Building materials industry	Metal processing industry	Miscellaneous	Energy	Line total
Pole industries/sectors									
Foodstuffs industry	0	0	0	0	0	0	0	0	0
Textile industry	0	0	0	0	0	0	0	0	0
Paper processing industry	329	0	0	731	0	1,300	0	0	2,360
Chemicals industry	0	0	0	0	3,214	0	0	0	3,214
Building materials industry	0	0	0	0	10,590	0	0	0	10,590
Metal processing industry	0	0	0	0	0	3,730	5,000	0	8,730
Miscellaneous	1,600	0	0	0	0	0	0	0	1,600
Energy	15,789	9,988	5,694	56,588	131,131	32,108	3,776	0	255,074
Inter-industrial relationship in pole	17,718	9,988	5,694	57,319	141,721	40,352	8,776	0	281,568
Purchases from rest of province	1,052,177	365,018	137,143	517,048	662,731	345,626	17,082	95,114	3,191,938
Imports									
Huelva	378	0	0	43,928	28,003	0	0	0	72,309
Rest of Spain	128,162	35,610	373,279	200,336	474,949	836,453	151,136	0	2,199,925
Foreign countries	525,847	80,000	54,100	56,580	304,182	424,196	17,617	0	1,462,522
Total	654,387	115,610	427,399	300,844	807,134	1,260,649	168,753	0	3,734,756
Wages and salaries	84,211	43,623	45,774	46,754	321,166	503,719	39,752	1,200	1,086,199
Social insurance, companies' share	23,452	13,584	12,039	12,184	88,068	90,358	12,474	300	252,459
Interest	37,111	26,064	20,987	31,364	92,924	119,042	6,060	5,100	338,652
Profits	192,801	36,706	124,071	76,930	471,401	569,458	38,085	114,883	1,624,335
Contribution to NNP at factor cost	337,575	119,977	202,871	167,232	973,559	1,282,577	96,371	121,483	3,301,645
Indirect taxes	27,278	14,830	20,932	14,683	57,758	64,213	5,205	916	205,615
Contribution to NNP at market prices	364,853	134,807	223,803	181,915	1,031,317	1,346,790	101,576	122,199	3,507,260
Depreciation	29,667	41,910	18,647	43,673	184,262	75,255	8,359	37,761	439,534
Contribution to GNP at market prices	394,520	176,717	242,450	225,588	1,215,579	1,422,045	109,935	159,960	3,946,794
Gross output value	2,118,802	667,333	812,665	1,100,799	2,827,165	3,068,672	304,546	255,074	11,155,056

| Sales to the rest of Seville | | | | Huelva | | | | Exports | | | Stock changes semi-finished and finished goods | Gross output value |
CG	PG	IG	Total	CG	PG	IG	Total	Rest of Spain	Foreign countries	Total		
433,022	262,456	0	695,478	59,571	32,000	0	91,571	939,484	392,269	1,423,324	0	2,118,802
35,200	411,437	0	446,637	9,504	1,895	0	11,399	183,726	16,681	211,806	8,890	667,333
200	186,896	0	187,096	0	16,949	0	16,949	494,562	109,500	621,011	2,198	812,665
67,370	84,483	0	151,853	2,000	17,677	0	19,677	771,538	162,835	954,050	-8,318	1,100,799
39,012	860,185	0	899,197	0	123,868	0	123,868	1,636,502	143,478	1,903,848	13,530	2,827,165
16,035	547,650	0	563,685	5,000	43,423	0	48,423	2,199,262	238,211	2,485,896	10,361	3,068,672
7,150	38,876	52,300	98,326	0	13,631	6,000	19,631	172,102	12,760	204,493	127	304,546
0	0	0	0	0	0	0	0	0	0	0	0	255,074
597,989	2,391,983	52,300	3,042,272	76,075	249,443	6,000	331,518	6,397,176	1,075,734	7,804,428	26,788	11,155,056

Abbreviations
NNP = Net national product
GNP = Gross national product
CG = Consumer goods
PG = Producer goods
IG = Investment goods

Table 38
Flows 3 and 4: purchases by the pole industries in Huelva from pole industries in Seville and vice versa*

Seville \ Huelva	Timber processing industry	Chemicals industry	Building materials industry	Miscellaneous	Total
1967					
Foodstuffs industry					
Textile industry					
Paper industry					
Chemicals industry		35,819 ←			35,819
Building materials industry					
Metal industry					
Miscellaneous					
Energy					
Total		35,819			35,819
1969					
Foodstuffs industry				378 ←	378
Textile industry					
Paper industry	142 ↑	1,200 ↑		9,516 ↑	10,858
Chemicals industry		30,857 ←			30,857
Building materials industry		3,670 ←	61,200 ↑		64,870
Metal industry					
Miscellaneous					
Energy					
Total	142	35,727	61,200	9,894	106,963

*The arrow points to the purchasing sector.
Sectors in which there are no transactions are not entered.

Table 39
Flows 5 and 7: purchases by the pole industries in Huelva from the
rest of the province of Huelva and the rest of the province of
Seville, 1967* (Ptas thousands)

Rest of Huelva \ Huelva pole \ Rest of Seville	Timber processing industry	Chemical industry	Building materials industry	Metal industry	Miscella-neous	Energy	Total
Rest of Huelva							
Forestry	64,885	0	0	0	0	0	64,885
Extractive industries	0	64,456	2,400	0	77	0	66,933
Metal industry other than metal processing industry	0	0	0	1,550	0	0	1,550
Metal processing industry	0	0	0	260	0	0	260
Gas and water	0	8,925	0	0	0	0	8,925
Wholesale and retail trade	6,016	5,533	275	304	93	20,386	32,607
State**	0	2,423	0	329	0	222	2,974
Insurance and miscellaneous services	4,834	3,231	0	222	228	0	8,515
Total	75,735	84,568	2,675	2,665	398	28,608	186,649
Rest of Seville							
Forestry	13,751	0	0	0	0	0	13,751
Extractive industries	0	0	1,250	0	0	0	1,250
Chemical industry	880	0	0	0	0	0	880
Metal industry other than metal processing industry	0	0	0	440	0	0	440
Metal processing industry	0	0	0	6,840	0	0	6,840
Wholesale and retail trade	0	0	375	0	0	6,185	6,560
Insurance and miscellaneous services	0	0	0	0	0	0	0
Total	14,631	0	1,625	7,240	0	6,185	29,681

*Sectors in which there are no corresponding transactions are not entered.
**Leases for industrial sites.

211

Table 40
Flows 5 and 7: purchase by pole industries in Huelva from the rest of the province of Huelva and the rest of the province of Seville, 1969 (Ptas thousands)

Rest of Huelva / Huelva pole / Rest of Seville	Foodstuffs industry	Timber processing industry	Chemicals industry	Building material industry	Metal industry	Miscellaneous	Energy	Total
Rest of Huelva								
Forestry	0	93,166	0	0	0	0	0	93,166
Extractive industries	0	0	127,788	13,865	0	78	0	141,731
Metal industry other than metal processing industry	0	0	0	0	4,774	0	0	4,774
Metal processing industry	0	0	0	0	800	0	0	800
Gas and water	229	18	18,692	80	19	49	0	19,087
Wholesale and retail trade	200	9,440	42,225	3,139	1,690	3,023	52,355	112,072
State	257	0	4,864	50	1,221	11	305	6,708
Insurance and miscellaneous services	0	7,010	21,028	137	2,187	3,770	0	34,132
Total	686	109,634	214,597	17,271	10,691	6,931	52,660	412,470
Rest of Seville								
Forestry	0	18,871	0	0	0	0	0	18,871
Extractive industries	0	0	0	1,437	0	0	0	1,437
Chemical industries	0	1,123	16,000	0	0	0	0	17,123
Metal industry other than metal processing industry	0	0	0	0	1,400	0	0	1,400
Metal processing industry	0	0	0	0	924	0	0	924
Wholesale and retail trade	0	25	1,200	670	1,662	0	0	3,557
Insurance and miscellaneous services	0	25	1,800	0	467	0	27,072	29,364
Total	0	20,044	19,000	2,107	4,453	0	27,072	72,676

212

Table 41
Flows 6 and 8: purchases by the pole industries in Seville from the
rest of the province of Seville, and from the rest of the province
of Huelva, 1967 (Ptas thousands)

Rest of Seville / Rest of Huelva / Seville pole	Foodstuffs industry	Textile industry	Paper industry	Chemicals industry	Building materials industry	Metal industry	Miscellaneous	Energy	Total
Rest of Seville									
Agriculture	443,087	256,185	0	199,000	0	0	0	0	898,272
Extractive industries	0	0	0	0	70,107	0	0	0	70,107
Textile industry	0	13,135	0	0	0	0	0	0	13,135
Timber processing industry	0	0	0	0	0	0	0	0	0
Paper industry	0	175	62,550	0	24,969	0	0	0	84,694
Chemicals industry	0	0	0	24,600	0	0	0	0	24,600
Cement industry	0	0	0	0	7,288	0	0	0	7,288
Metal industry other than metal processing industry	0	0	0	0	309	51,636	0	0	51,945
Metal processing industry	0	0	0	0	9,387	7,749	0	0	17,136
Gas and water*	296	0	0	0	0	1,493	0	0	1,789
Wholesale and retail trade	59,064	11,022	1,765	7,076	67,406	25,313	930	0	172,576
Insurance and miscellaneous services	18,660	8,838	6,624	4,229	34,495	18,078	689	25,206	116,819
Total	521,107	289,355	70,929	234,905	210,961	104,269	1,619	25,206	1,458,351
Rest of Huelva									
Agriculture	5,300	0	0	0	0	0	0	0	5,300
Cement industry	0	0	0	0	9,254	0	0	0	9,254
Foundries	0	0	0	0	0	0	0	0	0
Total	5,300	0	0	0	9,254	0	0	0	14,554

*Water partly from own springs.

213

Table 41a
Flows 6 and 8: purchases by the pole industries in Seville from the
rest of the province of Seville and from the rest of the province of
Huelva, 1969 (Ptas thousands)

Rest of Seville / Rest of Huelva	Foodstuffs industry	Textile industry	Paper industry	Chemicals industry	Building materials industry	Metal industry	Miscellaneous	Energy	Total
Rest of Seville									
Agriculture	684,037	319,300	0	409,234	0	0	0	0	1,412,571'
Extractive industries	0	0	0	0	165,133	0	0	0	165,133
Textile industry	0	13,672	0	0	0	0	0	0	13,672
Timber processing industry	0	0	0	0	58	0	0	0	58
Paper industry	0	215	87,040	0	40,492	0	0	0	127,747
Chemicals industry	172	0	0	31,150	0	0	0	0	31,322
Cement industry	0	0	0	0	27,201	0	0	0	27,201
Metal industry other than metal processing industry	0	0	0	0	746	101,324	0	0	102,070
Metal processing industry	211	0	0	0	7,352	14,883	0	0	22,446
Gas and water	573	0	0	27,718	418	1,763	215	0	24,687
Wholesale and retail industry	110,128	20,390	2,780	27,116	99,567	29,113	468	0	289,562
Insurance and miscellaneous services	39,295	11,441	8,279	27,901	69,613	17,379	1,334	72,374	242,616
Total	829,416	365,018	98,099	517,119	410,580	164,462	2,017	72,374	2,459,085
Rest of Huelva									
Agriculture	10,178	0	0	12,061	0	0	0	0	22,239
Cement industry	0	0	0	0	1,380	0	0	0	1,380
Foundries	0	0	0	0	13,356	0	0	0	13,356
Total	10,178	0	0	12,061	14,736	0	0	0	36,975

Bibliography

(*Note:* * *denotes an unpublished work*)

Angelet Cladellas, J. and Clusa Oriach, J., 72: 'Desarallo regional y localización industrial en España' in *Boletín Estudios Económicos,* No. 86, Bilbao 1972, p. 449 et seq.

Archibugi, F., 69: 'La planificación física y económica en el desarrollo nacional' in *Ciudad y Territorio,* 1969, p. 6 et seq.

Aujac, H., 60: 'La hiérarchie des industries dans un tableau des échanges industriels et ses conséquences dans la mise en oeuvre d'un plan national décentralisé' in *Revue Economique,* vol. XL, 1960, p. 169 et seq.

Aydalot, P., 65: 'Etudes sur le processus de polarisation et sur les réactions des industries anciennes à la lumière de l'expérience à Lacq' *Cahiers de l'ISEA,* Series L, March 1965.

Banco de Bilbao, 67: *Renta Nacional de España y su distribución provincial,* year 1964, Bilbao 1967.

Barbancho, A. G., 67: *Las migraciones interiores españolas,* Madrid 1967.

Barbancho, A. G., 68: *Las ciudades medias, discurso de Apertura,* Facultad de Ciencias Políticas Económicas y Comerciales de la Universidad de Granada 1968/69.*

Barlow Report, 40: *Report of the Royal Commission on the Distribution of the Industrial Population,* London 1940.

Bauchet, P., 55: *Les tableaux économiques, analyse de la région Lorraine,* Paris 1955.

Beck, R., 68: 'Regionalisierung und territoriale Neugliederung der Verwaltung in Spanien' in *Administrative Archives,* vol. 59, 1968, p. 17 et seq.

Berry, B. J. L. and Pred, A., 61: *Central place studies: A bibliography of theory and applications,* Philadelphia 1961.

Berry, B. J. L., 61: 'City size distribution and economic development' quoted from *Regional Development and Planning,* J. Friedmann and W. Alonso, Cambridge 1964, p. 138 et seq.

Berry, B. J. L. and Garrison, W. L., 58: 'Recent developments of central place theory', Papers and Proceedings of the Regional Science Association, IV, 1958, p. 107 et seq., here quoted from the reprint in *Urban Economics,* W. H. Leahy, D. L. McKee, D. Dean, New York and London 1970, p. 117 et seq.

Blaug, M., 64: 'A case of emperor's clothes: Perroux' theories of economic domination' in *Kyklos,* vol. 17, 1964, p. 551 et seq.

Boeke, J. H., 53: *Economics and economic policy of dual societies,* Harlem 1953.

Böventer, E. v., 62: 'Die Struktur der Landschaft. Versuch einer Synthese und Weiterentwicklung der Modelle J. H. v. Thünens, W. Christallers and A. Loschs' in *Optimales Wachstum und optimale Standort-verteilung, Schriften des Vereins für Sozialpolitik* N.F. 27, R. Henn, G. Bombach and E.v. Böventer, Berlin 1962, p.77 et seq.

Borts, G. H., 60: 'The equalization of returns and regional economic growth' in *American Economic Review,* vol. 50, 1960, p. 319 et seq.

Borts, G. H. and Stein, J. L., 1964: *Economic growth in a free market,* New York and London 1964.

Boudeville, J. R., 57: *'L'économie régionale espace opérationnel',* Institut de Science Economique Appliquée, Paris 1957.

Boudeville, J. R., 65: 'Frontiers and interrelations of regional planning' in *Problems of economic development,* E. A. G. Robinson, London 1965, p. 456 et seq.

Buttler, F., 69: 'Alternativen der spanischen Regionalplanung' in *Informationen des Institut für Raumordnung,* No. 15/69, Bad Godesberg 1969, p. 427 et seq.

Buttler, F., 70: 'Política regional de redistribución de ingresos y estructuración espacial en el marco de los planes de desarrollo' in *De Economía,* No. 111, Madrid 1970, p. 177 et seq.

Buttler, F., 73: *Entwicklungspole und räumliches Wirtschaftswachstum,* Tübingen 1973.

Buttler, F., 72: 'Análisis de atracción y planificación económica del espacio' in *Boletín de Estudios Económicos,* No. 86, Bilbao 1972, p. 405 et seq.

Buttler, F., Gerlach, K. and Liepemann, P: Funktionsfähige regionale Arbeitsmärkte, Paderborn 1974.

Carrillo-Arronte, R., 70: *An empirical test on interregional planning,* Rotterdam 1970.

Castillo, J. C., 68: *La sociedad de consumo,* Madrid 1968.

Chenery, H. B., 60: 'Patterns of industrial growth' in *American Economic Review,* vol. 50, 1960, p. 624 et seq.

Chenery, H. B., and Watanabe, T., 58: 'International comparisons of the structure of production' in *Econometrica,* vol. 26, 1958, p. 487 et seq.

Chinitz, B., 66: 'Appropriate goals for regional economic policy' quoted from the reprint in McKee, D. L., Dean, R. D. and Leahy, W. H.,

Regional Economics, Theory and Practice, New York, London 1970, p. 221 et seq.

Christaller, W., 33: *Die zentralen Orte in Süddeutschland,* Jena 1933.

Clark, C., 45: 'The economic function of a city in relation to its size' in *Econometrica,* vol. 13, 1945, p. 97 et seq.

Cohen, St., 69: *Modern Capitalist Planning: The French Model,* Cambridge, Mass. 1969.

Comisaría del Plan de Desarrollo, 63: *I Plan de Desarrollo Económico y Social,* Madrid 1963.

Comisaría del Plan de Desarrollo, Ponencia de Desarrollo Regional, 68: *II Plan de Desarrollo Económico y Social,* Madrid 1968.

Comisaría del Plan de Desarrollo/Italconsult, 68: *Estudio para la Determinación y promoción de un conjunto integrado de industrias en Huelva-Sevilla-Cadiz,* Madrid/Rome 1968.

Comisaría del Plan de Desarrollo, 69: *II Plan de Desarrollo Económico y Social,* Madrid 1969.

Comisaría del Plan de Desarrollo, 70: *Proyecto de un modelo econométrico de desarrollo,* Madrid 1970.*

Comisaría del Plan de Desarrollo, 70: *RGR, Contabilidad regional para las provincias de Huelva y Sevilla,* Madrid 1970.*

Comisaría del Plan de Desarrollo, 71: *Especificación de un modelo de desarrollo regional,* Madrid 1971.*

Comisaría del Plan de Desarrollo, 71: *Estimación de la renta provincial de 1971,* Madrid 1971.*

Comisaría del Plan de Desarrollo, Directrices . . . , 71: *III Plan de Desarrollo Económico y Social,* directives on development policy, working document, Madrid 1971.*

Comisaría del Plan, 72: *'Evaluación económica de los polos de desarrollo'* Estudios del Instituto de Desarrollo Económico, vol. 1, Madrid 1972, vol. II 1973.

Comisaría del Plan, 72: *Tercer Plan de Desarrollo,* Madrid 1972.

Comisaría del Plan de Desarrollo, 72: *III Plan de Desarrollo, Desarrollo Regional,* Madrid 1972.

Consejo Económico Sindical Nacional, 67: *Legislación sobre Polos de Promoción y Desarrollo Industrial,* Madrid 1967.

Consejo Económico Sindical Nacional, 69: *Tablas input-output de la economía española,* Madrid 1969.

Dahrendorf, R., 57: *Soziale Klassen und Klassenkonflikt in der industriellen Gesellschaft,* Stuttgart 1967.

Darwent, D. F., 69: 'Growth poles and growth centers in regional planning' – a review in *Environment and Planning,* vol. I, 1969, p. 5 et seq.

Davin, L. E., Degeer, L. and Paelinck, J., 59: *Dynamique économique de la région liègoise,* Paris 1959.

Délégation à l'aménagement du territoire et à l'action régionale, 69: 'schéma général d'aménagement de la France, la façade méditeranéenne', Paris 1969.

Denison, E., 67: *Why growth rates differ,* Washington 1967.

Derwa, L., 57: 'Analyse input-output de la région liègoise?' *Revue de Conseil Economique Wallon,* September-November 1957.

Eckstein, O., 65: *Water resource development, the economics of project evaluation,* Cambridge, Mass. 1965.

Egner, E., 63: 'Der Einfluß der europäischen Wirtschaftsgemeinschaft und der überseeischen Industrialisierung auf die westdeutsche Industrie' in *Forschungs- und Sitzungsberichte der Akademie für Raumforschung und Landesplanung,* vol. 23, Hanover 1963, p. 107 et seq.

Egner, E., 66: 'Art. Dual Economies' in *Entwicklungspolitik, Handbuch und Lexikon,* H. H. Walz, H. Besters and E. E. Bösch, Stuttgart, Berlin, Mainz, 1966, p. 1079 et seq.

Egner, E., 67: *Política regional y desarrollo económico,* Bilbao 1967.

Elkan, P. G., 65: 'How to beat backwash: The case for customs-drawback unions' in *Economic Journal,* vol. LXXV, 1965, p. 44 et seq.

Fernández-Rodríguez, F., 72: 'La política regional de los planes españoles de desarrollo' in *Boletín de Estudios Económicos,* no. 86, Bilbao 1972, p. 431 et seq.

Friedmann, J., 59: 'Regional planning: A problem in spatial integration' in Papers and Proceedings of the Regional Science Association, vol. 5, 1959, p. 167 et seq.

Friedmann, J., 68: 'The strategy of deliberate urbanization' in *The Journal of the American Institute of Planners,* Nov. 1968, p. 364 et seq.

Friedmann, J., 70: *Towards a National Urbanization Policy: Problems, Decisions and Consequences,* Copenhagen 1970.*

Friedmann, J., 72: 'A general theory of polarized development' in *Growth Centers in Regional Economic Development,* N. Hansen, New York and London 1972, p. 82 et seq.

Gerfin, H., 64: 'Gesamtwirtschaftliches Wachstum und regionale Entwicklung' in *Kyklos,* vol. 17, 1964, p. 565 et seq.

Giersch, H., 63: 'Das ökonomische Grundproblem der Regionalpolitik' in *Jahrbuch für Sozialwissenschaft,* 14, 1963, p. 386 et seq.

218

Hägerstrand, T., 66: 'Aspects of the spatial structure of social communication and the diffusion of information', *Papers and Proceedings of the Regional Science Association,* vol. 16, 1966, p. 27 et seq.

Hansen, N. M., 65: 'Unbalanced growth and regional development' *Western Economic Journal,* vol. IV, 1965, p. 3 et seq.

Hansen, N. M., 67: 'Development pole theory in a regional context' in *Kyklos,* vol. 20, 1967, p. 709 et seq.

Hansen, N. M., 68: *French regional planning,* Edinburgh 1968.

Hansen, N. M., 71: *Criteria for a growth center policy,* Geneva, UNRISD, April 1971.*

Hansen, N. M., 71a: *Intermediate Size Cities as Growth Centers,* New York, Washington, London 1971.

Hansen, N. M., 70: *Rural Poverty and the Urban Crisis,* Bloomington 1970.

Hauser, Ph. M., 63: 'The social, economic, and technological problems of rapid urbanisation' in Hoselitz, B. F. and Moore, W. E., *Industrialization and Society,* The Hague 1963.

Hermansen, T., 70: 'Development poles and development centers in national and regional development — elements of a theoretical framework' in *A review of the concepts and theories of growth poles and growth centers,* United Nations Research Institute for Social Development, Geneva 1970, p. 1 et seq.

Hesse, H., 68: Importsubstitution und Entwicklungspolitik, in *Zeitschrift für die gesamte Staatswissenschaft,* vol. 124, 1968, p. 641 et seq.

Hirschman, A. O., 67: *Die Strategie der wirtschaftlichen Entwicklung,* Deutsch, Göttingen 1967.

Hoover, E. M., 48: *The location of economic activity,* New York, London, Toronto 1948.

Hoselitz, B. F., 60: *Sociological aspects of economic growth,* Glencoe 1960.

IBRD, 62: *'Informe del Banco Internacional de Reconstrucción y Formento' El Desarrollo Económico de España,* Madrid 1962.

Instituto Nacional de Estadística, 65: *'Encuesta de presupuestos familiares, resultados provisionales, nacionales y provinciales',* Madrid 1965.

INE, 68: *Migración y estructura regional,* Madrid 1968.

INE, 70: *Boletín mensual estadístico,* Madrid 1970.

INE, 70: Instituto Nacional de Estadística. *'Contabilidad nacional de España'.* Years 1966, 1967, 1968 and estimates for 1969. Madrid 1970.

Isard, W., Schooler, E. W., Vietorisz, Th., 59: *Industrial complex analysis*

and regional development, New York and London 1959.
Isard, W., 60: *Methods of regional analysis,* New York, London 1960.

Jansen, P.G., 68: *Infrastrukturinvestitionen als Mittel der Regionalpolitik,* Gütersloh 1968.
Jochimsen, R., 66: *Theorie der Infrastruktur,* Tübingen 1966.
Jürgensen, H. and Marx, D., 64: *Regionalplanung und wirtschaftliches Wachstum,* Essen 1964.

Kaldor, N., 70: 'The case for Regional Policies' in *Scottish Journal of Political Economy,* Nov. 1970, p. 337 et seq.
Kau, W., 70: *Theorie und Anwendung raumwirtschaftlicher Potential-modelle,* Tübingen 1970.
Klaassen, L. H., 65: *Aménagement économique et social du territoire,* Paris 1965.
Klaassen, L.H., 67: *Methods of selecting industries for depressed areas,* Paris 1967.
Klaassen, L. H. and van Wickeren, A. C., 69: 'Interindustry relations; an attraction model' in Bos, H. C., *Towards Balanced International Growth,* Amsterdam 1969, p. 245 et seq.
Klaassen, L. H., 70: 'Growth poles in economic theory and policy' in *A review of the concepts and theories of growth poles and growth centers,* United Nations Research Institute for Social Development, Geneva 1970, p. 91 et seq.
Körner, H., 67: 'Industrielle Entwicklungspole als Instrument der Regional-politik in Entwicklungsländern' in *Kyklos,* vol. 20, 1967, p. 684 et seq.
Körner, H., 70: 'Sozialökonomischer Dualismus als Herausforderung für die Infrastrukturpolitik' in *Grundfragen der Infrastrukturplanung für wachsenden Wirtschaften, Schriften des Vereins für Socialpolitik* N.F. 58, H. Arndt and D. Swatek, Berlin 1970, p. 201 et seq.
Kuklinsky, A. R., 70: 'Regional development, regional policies and regional planning. Problems and issues' in *Regional Studies,* vol. 4, 1970, p. 269 et seq.
Kuznets, S., 66: *Modern economic growth,* New Haven and London 1966.

Labasse, J. and Laferrère, M., 60: *La région lyonnaise,* Paris 1960.
Lasuen, J. R., Lorca, A., Oria, J., 68: 'Desarrollo económico y dis-tribución de las ciudades por tamaño' in *Arquitectura,* 1968, p. 5 et seq.
Lasuen, J. R., 69: 'On growth poles' in *Urban Studies,* vol. 6, no. 2, 1969, p. 137 et seq.

Lasuen, J. R., 71: *A generalization of the growth pole notion,* Madrid 1971.*

Lösch, A., 44: *Die räumliche Ordnung der Wirtschaft,* Jena 1944.

Marx, D. 66: *Wachstumsorientierte Regionalpolitik,* Göttingen 1966.

Mennes, L. B. M., Tinbergen, J., and Waardenburg, J. G., 69, *The element of space in development planning,* Amsterdam 1969.

de Miguel, A., 68: *Estructura regional del comportamiento económico: renta, ahorro, consumo y nivel de vida,* Madrid 1968.*

Myrdal, G., 67: *Economic theory and underdeveloped regions,* London 1957.

Nederlands Economisch Instituut, 71: *Une analyse d'attraction pour les Asturies,* Rotterdam 1971.*

Neutze, G. M., 65: *Economic policy and the size of cities,* Canberra 1965.

North, D. C., 64: 'Location theory and regional economic growth' in *Regional development and planning,* J. Friedmann and W. Alonso, Cambridge, Mass. 1964, p. 240 et seq.

Nurkse, R., 53: *Problems of capital formation in underdeveloped countries,* Oxford 1953.

Olsen, E., 71: *International trade theory and regional income differences, United States 1880-1950,* Amsterdam 1971.

Paelinck, J., 63: 'La teoría de desarrollo regional polarizado' in *Revista de Economía Latinoamericana,* no. 9, Caracas 1963, p. 1 et seq.

Paelinck, J., 65: 'La Théorie du développment régional polarisé' in *Cahiers de l'ISEA* (Series L, 15) March 1965, p. 5 et seq.

Pedersen, P. O., 69: *Innovation diffusion in urban systems,* Lund 1969.*

Perloff, H. S., Dunn, E. S., Lampard, E. E. and Muth, R. F., 60: *Regions, resources and economic growth,* Baltimore 1960.

Perpiña y Grau, R., 69: 'La constitución económica de España como muestra de comunidades heterogéneas y ante el mercado común europeo' in *Boletín de Estudios Económicos,* vol. 23, 1969.

Perpiña y Grau, R., 71: 'La problemática de delimitación espacial regional' in *Boletín de estudios económicos* vol. 26, 1971, p. 675 et seq.

Perroux, F., 50: 'Economic space, theory and application' *Quarterly Journal of Economics,* vol. 64, 1950.

Perroux, F., 55: 'Note sur la notion de pôle de croissance' in *Economie Appliquée,* 1955, p. 307 et seq.

Perroux, F., 60: 'La firme motrice dans la région et la région motrice' in *Théorie et politique de l'expansion régionale, Actes du colloque international de L'Institut de Science Economique de l'Université de Liège,* 1960.

Plaza Prieto, J., 68: *El desarrollo regional y España,* Madrid 1968.

Piñera Alvarez, P., 72: 'La tabla input-output de la economía asturiana 1968' in *Boletín de Estudios Económicos,* no. 86, Bilbao 1972, p. 537 et seq.

Popescu, O., 64: 'Probleme der wirschaftlichen Entwicklung Lateinamerikas' in *Gestaltungsprobleme der Weltwirtschaft,* publication for A. Predöhl, published by H. Jürgensen, Gottingen 1964, p. 374 et seq.

Pütz, Th., 60: 'Die wirtschaftliche Konzeption' in *Zur Grundlegung wirtschaftspolitischer Konzeptionen,* H. J. Seraphim, Schriften des Vereins für Sozialpolitik, N.F. 18, Berlin 1960, p. 9 et seq.

Richardson, H. W., 69: *Regional economics,* London 1969.

Richardson, H. W., 71: 'Regional development policy in Spain' in *Urban Studies,* 1971, p. 39 et seq.

Richardson, H. W., 72: *Some Aspects of Regional Development Policy in Spain,* OECD report, June 1972.*

Richter, Ch. E., 69: 'The impact of industrial linkages on geographic association' in *Journal of Regional Science,* vol. 9, no. 1, 1969, p. 19 et seq.

Richter, Ch. E., 70: 'Systematic relationships between industrial linkages and the agglomeration of manufacturing industries' in *Review of Regional Studies,* vol. 1, 1970, p. 37 et seq.

Rittenbruch, K., 68: *Zur Anwendbarkeit der Exportbasiskonzepte im Rahmen der Regionalanalyse,* Berlin 1968.

Ritter, U., 66: 'Art. Industrieparks' in *Entwicklungspolitik, Handbuch und Lexikon,* H. H. Walz, H. Besters and E. E. Bösch, Stuttgart, Berlin, Mainz 1966, p. 1253 et seq.

Ritter, U., 71: 'Die siedlungsstrukturellen Grundlagen der Entwicklungsplanung' in *Voraussetzungen einer globalen Entwicklungspolitik und Beitrage zur Kosten- und Nutzenanalyse,* Schriften des Vereins für Socialpolitik, N.F. 59, R. Meimberg, Berlin 1971, p. 163 et seq.

Ritter, U., 72: *Siedlungsstruktur und wirtschaftliche Entwicklung,* Berlin 1972.

Rodwin, L., 61: 'Metropolitan policy for developing areas' in *Regional economic planning,* W. Isard and J. H. Cumberland, Paris 1961, p. 221 et seq.

Rosenfeld, F., 64: *Structure et perspectives économiques de la province de Turin,* Metra III, 4, 1964.

Saigal, J. C., 65: *The Choice of Sectors and Regions,* Rotterdam, University Press 1965.

Salvatore, D., 72: 'The Operation of the Market Mechanism and Regional Inequality' in *Kyklos,* vol. XXV, 1972, p. 518 et seq.

Samuelson, P. A., 48: 'Der Ausgleich der Faktorpreise durch den internationalen Handel' first published in *Economic Journal,* vol. 58, 1948, p. 163 et seq., here quoted from Rose, K., *Theorie der internationalen Wirtschaftsbeziehungen,* Cologne/Berlin 1966, p. 69 et seq.

Sargent-Florence, P., 44: 'The selection of industries suitable for dispersion into rural areas' in *Royal Statistical Journal,* vol. 107, 1944, p. 93 et seq.

Schumpeter, J., 12: *Theorie der wirtschaftlichen Entwicklung,* Leipzig 1912.

Scitovsky, T., 54: 'Two concepts of external economies' in *Journal of Political Economy,* 1954, p. 143 et seq.

SEMA, 61: *Effets des industries du gaz natural de Lacq sur l'économie du département des Basses-Pyrénées,* Paris 1961.

Siebert, H., 67: *Zur Theorie des regionalen Wirtschaftswachstums,* Tübingen 1967.

Siebert, H., 69: 'Regionalwirtschaftslehre in den USA: ein Überblick' in *Jahrbuch für Sozialwissenschaft,* vol. 20, 1969, p. 51 et seq.

Siebert, H., 70: *Regionales Wirtschaftswachstum und interregionale Mobilität,* Tübingen 1970.

Stanford Research Institute and School of Planning and Architecture of New Delhi and Small Industry Extension Training Institute of Hyderabad, 68: *Costs of urban infrastructure for industry as related to city size in developing countries,* Standord 1968.

Streit, M. R., 69: 'Spatial associations and economic linkages between industries' in *Journal of Regional Science,* vol. 9, 1969, p. 177 et seq.

Streit, M. R., 71: 'Probleme regionalpolitischer Diagnose und Projection' in *Schmollers Jahrbuch,* vol. 91, 1971, p. 669 et seq.

Streit, M. R., 71a: 'Regionalpolitische Aspekte des Wachstumspolkonzepts' in *Jahrbuch für Sozialwissenschaft,* vol. 22, 1971, p. 221 et seq.

Szamanski, S., 71: 'Some empirical evidence of the strengths of linkages between groups of related industries in urban-regional complexes' in *Papers and Proceedings of the Regional Science Association,* vol. 27, 1971, p. 137 et seq.

Tamames, R., 68: *Los centros de gravedad de la economía española,* Madrid 1968.

Tamames, R., 68a: *España ante el segundo plan de desarrollo,* Barcelona 1968.

Thumm, U., 68: *Die Regionalpolitik als Instrument der französischen Wirtschaftspolitik,* Berlin 1968.

Tiebout, C. M., 56: 'Exports and regional economic growth' in *Journal of Political Economy,* 64, 1956, quoted from *Regional development and planning,* J. Friedmann and W. Alonso, Cambridge, Mass. 1964, p. 256 et seq.

Tiebout, C. M., 60: 'Community income multipliers: a population growth model' in *Journal of Regional Science,* vol. 2, 1960, p. 75 et seq.

UN 63: *A study of industrial growth,* UN Department of Economic and Social Affairs, New York 1963.

Utría, R. D., 71: *Social Variables in Regional Development,* UNRISD/71/C. 11, Geneva, August 1971, hectographed.

van Wickeren, A. C., 71: *Inter industry relations: some attraction models,* Enschede 1971.

van Wickeren, A. C., 72: 'Un análisis de atracción para la economía asturiana' in *Boletín de Estudios Económicos,* no. 86, Bilbao 1972, p. 507 et seq.

van Wickeren, A. C. and Smit, H., 71 'The dynamic attraction model' in *Regional and Urban Economics,* vol. 1, no. 1, Amsterdam 1971, p. 89 et seq.

Williamson, J. G., 65: 'Regional inequality and the process of national development' in *Economic Development and Cultural Change,* vol. XIII, no. 4, part 2, 1965, p. 3 et seq.

Index

Paelinck: *63* 63, 64; *63,10* 65; *63,32* 62; *65* 30, 63, 64; *65,12* 25; *65,44* 43

Pedersen *69* 38

Per capita incomes by provinces 54, 65, 68, 113, 186

Perloff, Dunn, Lampard and Muth, (1960) 43

Perroux 29: *50* 91; *50,89* 30; *55* 27; *55,311* 29; *55,317* 30; *60,203* 27

Planning Commission: first development plan *63,150* 61; report of regional development *68,7* 56; Project '69 *69,62* 80; Project '70 *70* 6; Specification '71 *71* 6; third plan: *72,217* 75, *72,223* 76, *72,243/4* 77, *72,247/8* 79, *72,251* 77, 83, *72,252* 79, *72,323* 54, *72,324* 56, *72,327* 62, *72,331* 76, *72,337/8* 62, *72,338* 66

Plaza Prieto *68,254* 69

Polarisation, and regional growth theory 17–48: principle of circular causation 17–24; sectoral polarisation 24–32; sectoral-regional polarisation 32–5; attraction problem 32–5; regional polarisation, not necessarily sectoral as well 36–40; spatially polarised economic growth, two approaches to 40–4; résumé 44–8; should identification of metropolitan, urban and rural zones be starting point for general? 75–8

Pole: activities, importance of, vis-à-vis regional and national accounts 112–20; -hinterland relationships 141–6, 180, 182; industries, sales and purchases and 140, 144, 180; programme, incorporation of, in national urbanisation strategy (third plan), *see under* Urbanisation etc.; promotion, methods and instruments of 67–73; *see also* Deglomeration poles; Development poles; Growth pole; Polarisation; Wages pole

Population statistics 113

Port installations 100–1

Production data of this study 99–112

Production phase, overall effects of 153–72: income effects, direct and indirect 153–9; regional consumer expenditure multiplier 159–72

Productivity, average labour 109

Promotion districts, map of Spanish 73

Public credit 130, 175

Purchases and sales in pole industries 140, 144

Pütz *60,11* xii

Regional accounts and pole activities 112–20

Regional and sectoral planning, model of, discussed, *see* Sectoral and regional planning

Regional growth theory and polarisation, *see* Polarisation and regional growth theory

Regional-sectoral polarisation 32–5, 36–40

RGR: *24* 162; *27* 161, 164; *41* 162

Research, field programme of 91–8: definition 91–3, of pole 91–2, of hinterland 92–3, of choice of years 93; methods and instruments 93–5; overall system of investigation 96–7; objections to 98

Richardson: *69,247* 172; *69,365* 57; *69,366* xii; *69,415* xi; *71,50* 191; *72,2* 13, 15; *72,4* 7; *72,8* 16; *72,39/40* 80

Richter: *69,19* 32; *69,24* 78; *69,24* 33; *70,37* 32

Rittenbruch: *68,54* 172; *68,55* 160; *68,56* 172

Ritter: *66,1254* 190; *70,163* 21, 22; *72,57* 40; *72,79* 55; *72,106* 40

Road building 100–1

Rodwin *61* 37

Rural zones, identification of, as possible starting points for general polarisation? 75–8

Saigal *65* 14

Sales and purchases in pole industries 140, 144

Sales tax 153

Schumpeter 29; *12* 4; *12,463* 27; *12,485, 489, 490* 27

Scitovsky *154,143* 29

Sectoral polarisation 24–32

Sectoral and regional planning, model of, discussed 5–16; setting the problem 5–7; two versions for a regional pattern 7–12; critique of the pattern 12–16

Sectoral production structure and economy 114

Sectoral-regional polarisation 32–5, 36–40

SEMA (Société d'Économique et de Mathématique Appliquée) 62, 63, 66, 95, 195

Seville, industrial growth pole at 67–70, 92–6, 178–87: detailed data in general survey 99–120 *passim*; structure of investments and finance 121–35 *passim*; input-output linkages 137–52 *passim*;

227

production phase, overall effects of 153–72 *passim*; fixed capital investment and newly created jobs, comparative table of 173; infrastructure investments, comparative table of 173; subsidies and public credits, comparative table of 175
Sewage 100–1
Siebert: *67* 43; *67,1* 17
Spain: development tendencies 53–9, diagnosis 53–5, objects of regional policy 55–9; planning commission, *see* Planning commission; programme of development poles 61–73, theoretical basis 62–5, prospects 65–7, methods and instruments of pole promotion 67–73; promotion districts, map of 73; regional policy, objectives of, diagnosis 53–5, objects 55–9
Spatially polarised economic growth 40–4
Stanford Research Institute *68* 37
Streit: *69,177* 32, 77; *69,182* 33, 78; *71,674* 77, 80; *71a,227* 82; *71a,228* 188; *71a,230* 189; *71a,231* 189
Study, general survey of this 99–120: investment, production and employment 99–112; pole activities in regional and national accounts 112–20
Subsidies 175

Tamames: *68,50/1* 55; *68,120* 72; *68,124* 69
Thumm *88,162/3* 175
Tiebout *60,76* 162
Toledo, deglomeration pole at 61
Trade balances vis-à-vis national and foreign economy 147–52

Urbanisation, incorporation of pole programme in strategy of national (third plan) 75–88: metropolitan, urban and rural zonal identification – is this the starting point for general polarisation? 75–8; decentralisation 79–87, principles 79–83, adaptation of traditional growth pole concept 83–7
Urban zones, identification of, as possible starting point for general polarisation 75–8
Utría *71* 82

Valladolid, development pole at 61, 67–70, 77, 178–87; results of development pole at 173–5
Value creation, gross 104–5, 118, 120

van Wickeren: *71* 32; *71,3* xi; *71,88* 34
van Wickeren and Smit, *71,89* 34–5
Vigo, development pole at 61, 67–70, 178–87; results of development pole at 173–5
Villagarcia de Arosa, development pole at 61

Wage pole 117
Water supply 100–1

Zaragoza, development pole at 61, 68–70, 178–87; results of development pole at 173–5